SECOND EDITION

Type Rules!

the designer's guide to professional typography

Ilene Strizver

John Wiley & Sons, Inc.

This book is printed on acid-free paper. ♾

Published by John Wiley & Sons, Inc., Hoboken, New Jersey
Published simultaneously in Canada

For general information on our other products and services or for technical support, please contact our Customer Care Department within the United States at (800) 762-2974, outside the United States at (317) 572-3993 or fax (317) 572-4002.

Wiley also publishes its books in a variety of electronic formats. Some content that appears in print may not be available in electronic books. For more information about Wiley products, visit our web site at www.wiley.com.

Library of Congress Cataloging-in-Publication Data:

Strizver, Ilene, 1953-
Type rules! : the designer's guide to professional typography
/ by Ilene Strizver. – 2nd ed.
p. cm.
ISBN-10: 0-471-72114-x (paper)
ISBN-13: 978-0-471-72114-7
1. Type and type-founding. 2. Graphic design (Typography)
I. Title. II. Title: Designer's guide to professional typography.
Z250.S92 2006
686.2'21–dc22

2005022230

Printed in the United States of America

10 9 8 7 6 5 4

TABLE OF CONTENTS

DEDICATION

This book is dedicated to my father, Leonard Strizver, who taught me to believe in myself and that the sky was the limit to what I could accomplish. Unfortunately he did not live long enough to see his words take shape in my life.

I hope I have made you proud, dad.

PREFACE

This second edition of *Type Rules!* is new and improved in many ways. The content not only has been revised, expanded, and updated to reflect current standards in type, design, and technology but three new components have been added: TECHTIPS, TYPETIPS, and Exercises.

- TECHTIPS are instructional sidebars on how to achieve some of the typographic principles and techniques mentioned within, using the two most popular and widely used design applications: Adobe InDesign CS2 and QuarkXPress 7.0.
- TYPETIPS are sidebars containing helpful hints and tasty tidbits explaining some of the information in more detail.
- And, last but definitely not least, the Exercises are tasks and assignments intended to assist in learning and understanding the typographic principles contained within, as well as applying them in actual design projects. The supplements, which follow each chapter, are intended for educators and students, but can be used by anyone wanting to reinforce and apply the material within (and possibly winding up with some great portfolio pieces as well!).

* * * * *

This edition of *Type Rules!* has been written from the perspective of a Mac user using OS 10.3. Why? Although the PC still holds the lion's share of the personal computer market, most serious graphic designers (excluding web designers) use a Mac. In addition, I wanted to maintain the integrity of the information presented here, and since I use a Mac, I write from that point of view.

It is also important to mention the occasional confusion in reference to fonts in the new OpenType format. This font format, which is explained in depth in chapter 2, has some very different characteristics and properties from both Type 1 and TrueType, but not all software supports these features. I have made every effort to explain any possibly confusing information, but I urge you to read chapter 2 for a clearer understanding of these issues before skipping around the rest of the books.

NOTE: During the writing of this edition, QuarkXPress 7.0 was in testing stages only and not a released product. For that reason, I was not able to include screen shots of the user interface as illustrations for the TECHTIPS. In addition, every attempt has been made to keep the information accurate, but I am not responsible for changes that have been made to the software subsequent to the production of this book.

ACKNOWLEDGMENTS

As someone whose academic beginnings focused on music and fine art, I was extremely lucky to have crossed paths with some of the most open-hearted and talented individuals in the world of typography and graphic design, almost in spite of myself. Aaron Burns, Ed Benguiat, Herb Lubalin, Bob Farber, and Allan Haley permanently altered my life's path, and I will be forever indebted to them. Their creative brilliance coupled with their incredible generosity of spirit ignited within me a passion for type that will never be satiated.

Through the years, there have been countless graphic designers, type designers, typographers, and other creative professionals who have unselfishly shared their knowledge and passion for type and design with me. To all of them I offer my deepest thanks, for without them, this book never would have come to be.

I want to extend a heartfelt thanks to my typographic "partners in crime," James Montalbano, Mark Jamra, Ken Barber, Otmar Hoefer, Thomas Phinney, and David Lemon, who have generously and willingly shared their expertise and resources.

A very warm thanks to my special friends Maxim Zhukov, Fred Brady, Christopher Slye, and Nat Brockman who so very generously offered their time and professional assistance to help make this a better book.

I would like to extend my deepest gratitude to all the instructors who willingly shared their teaching methods and assignments with me and, as well, to their students who allowed the use of their assignment solutions for publication.

I could never express enough appreciation to all my students and workshop attendees who continue to keep me on my toes, push me to learn newer and better methods, technique, and software, challenge me to offer a better explanation, and whose talent, enthusiasm, and passion for learning inspire me to be the best I can be.

And last but not least, a very special thanks my editor, Margaret Cummins, whose belief in me and in this book, combined with her own vision of what it could be, inspired me to new heights.

Type is all around us, in everything we read, from product packaging in the grocery store to television commercials, from greeting cards, books, and magazines to storefront signs. Learning to read and write the alphabet is one of the first things we are taught in school, and that process often begins before nursery school with television shows and videos intended for the hungry and curious minds of two- and three-year-olds.

Type and printed matter communicate not only information to us but also influence decisions we make on a daily basis. Whether we realize it or not, type and the way it appears affects which CD and book cover catches our eye, which detergent might make the whites whiter, and which movie might be the scariest or most romantic. Much of this process goes on unconsciously, which is why the art and craft of typography is so invisible to the average person. But its unseen nature by no means diminishes the importance and influence type has on the quality and substance of our daily lives.

Type Rules! is intended for anyone interested in typography, be they a novice computer user or a professional graphic designer. There is something here for everyone, whether you know a little or a lot about type. This book does not have to be read front to back; you may thumb through the chapters and stop wherever something sparks your interest or read it chapter to chapter. This book will stimulate and satisfy the neophyte's interest in type as well as offer advanced information and techniques to professional graphic designers who want to improve their work.

Typography is not taught in many design schools. When it is, the focus is usually on typographic design in its broadest sense, not the nuts and bolts of how to set type tastefully and effectively; addressing this void is my primary objective. This book is intended to help you learn how to communicate effectively and professionally with type, using features available in most page-layout programs. It is not meant to teach you how to use software; there are user manuals and numerous books, tapes, and CDs that can help you with that.

* * * * *

I can trace my interest in type and letterforms back to the posters I drew for my junior high school elections. I can remember spending hours on the lettering, measuring out the strokes of each character, the spaces between each letter, as well as the spaces between the lines. Those posters would appear extremely crude by professional standards, but my interest in the geometry of letters and the relationships between their positive and negative spaces was evident even then.

After studying music and then fine art in college, I was lucky enough to have landed a seat in Ed Benguiat's lettering class at the School of Visual Arts in New York City; my life was never to be the same again. Ed instilled in me the passion for type that I have today, and that with which I will attempt to infect you. The bad news is if I succeed, there is really no cure for it; the good news is "catching it" will open your eyes to so many exciting things you have never seen before, and it allows you to enjoy and appreciate the world around you in a completely new way.

"The story of type doesn't actually be-gin with type per se, but with the beginning of man-kind and civiliza-tion. Type ha

CHAPTER ONE

A BRIEF HISTORY OF TYPE

The story of type doesn't actually begin with type per se, but with the beginning of mankind and civilization. Type has only existed for about 550 years, but its beginnings are rooted in the life of the caveman himself, as it was his developing needs and habits that led civilization on a path toward the evolution of the alphabet and subsequently the invention of type and printing. It is certainly possible to learn to use type effectively and even tastefully without knowing about its roots; but to fully understand and appreciate type today, it is important to know something of the past.

Milestones in the history of type are highlighted throughout this chapter. Some of the dates, chronology, and details vary from source to source, but the spirit of the events remains the same; these events have taken mankind on a glorious ride from the crudest forms of cave drawings to the bits and bytes of type in the digital age.

SOUNDS TO SYMBOLS

For many years, early man communicated purely with sound. Verbal language, which is heard and not seen as opposed to visual language (or visible language, as it is often called), has many limitations: it is gone the instant it is spoken and heard, and it is therefore temporary. Stories, history, and other information could not be passed on from generation to generation in a permanent way, only by direct word of mouth.

The earliest attempts to record stories and ideas were through cave drawings; the first known is dated around 25,000 BC. These drawings, or pictographs, were very simple representations of people, places, and things, and for this reason, they were relatively easy to learn and understand. Although this was a very simple form of written commu-

This aboriginal rock painting, located in a cave in Queensland, Australia, c. 13,000 BC, is a distinctive example of the earliest form of written communication. Photograph courtesy of Axel Poignant Archive.

nication, it was certainly more permanent than sound, and much of it has survived the ravages of time and still exists today.

Around 3000 BC, the Sumerians developed cuneiforms, a writing system that consisted of wedge-shaped forms carved into clay tablets and other hard surfaces. Cuneiforms evolved from the pictographs that the Sumerians had adapted earlier and were one of the first writing systems to read left to right. Its wedge-shaped forms were the result of the increasing use of a stylus, a writing tool whose straight edges and triangular corners produced these geometric forms.

As time passed, there was a need for more symbols to represent ideas and other concepts in addition to just "things." This led to the development of ideograms, or symbols, representing ideas and actions. This new, expanded system was more difficult for the masses to understand, as it was not purely representational but more symbolic in nature. This separated society into two groups: those who could understand this system, and those who could not. The spoken and written language had become very different from each other, requiring the learning of two unrelated systems of communication.

As society became more complex, the existing system did not meet its increasing needs and was no longer satisfactory; something more was needed. This need subsequently led to the development of letter symbols that, when put together, represented words.

The Phoenicians, a society of traders and skilled craftsmen on the eastern coast of the

PHOENICIAN	NAME	PHONETIC NAME	EARLY GREEK	CLASSICAL GREEK	NAME	GREEK	ENGLISH
𐤀	aleph		A	A	alpha	Α α	*a*
𐤁	beth	*b*	8	B	beta	Β β	*b*
𐤂	gimel	*g*	1	Γ	gamma	Γ γ	*g*
𐤃	daleth	*d*	Δ	Δ	delta	Δ δ	*d*
𐤄	he	*h*	Ǝ	E	epsilon	Ε ε	*e*
𐤅	waw	*w*	Ϝ		digamma		
𐤆	zayin	*z*	I	Z	zeta	Ζ ζ	*z*
𐤇	ḥeth	*ḥ*	日	H	eta	Η η	*ê*
𐤈	teth	*ṭ*	⊗	Θ	theta	Θ θ	*th*
𐤉	yod	*y*	≷	I	iota	Ι ι	*i*
𐤊	kaph	*k*	ꓘ	K	kappa	Κ κ	*k*
𐤋	lamed	*l*	1	Λ	lambda	Λ λ	*l*
𐤌	mem	*m*	M	M	mu	Μ μ	*m*
𐤍	nun	*n*	И	N	nu	Ν ν	*n*
𐤎	samekh	*s*			xi	Ξ ξ	*x*
𐤏	ayin		O	O	omicron	Ο ο	*o*
𐤐	pe	*p*	˥	Π	pi	Π π	*p*
𐤑	sade	*s*	M		san		
𐤒	qoph	*q*	Ϙ		qoppa		
𐤓	reš	*r*	ᑫ	P	rho	Ρ ρ	*r*
𐤔	šin	*sh/s*	ϟ	Σ	sigma	Σ σς	*s*
𐤕	taw	*t*	X		tau	Τ τ	*t*
				Y	upsilon	Υ υ	*u, y*
					phi	Φ φ	*ph*
				X	chi	Χ χ	*kh*
					psi	Ψ ψ	*ps*
				Ω	omega	Ω ω	*ô*

This chart shows the evolution of the Greek alphabet, originally adapted from the twenty-two-character, all-consonant Phoenician alphabet. The Greeks added several new characters as well as vowels.

Mediterranean, took written language a giant step ahead from the pictograms and ideograms.

Around 1000 BC, the Phoenicians developed twenty-two symbols that corresponded to the twenty-two key sounds of their language. Their idea was to connect the twenty-two symbols representing written sounds to imitate the spoken words, eliminating the memorization of hundreds of unrelated symbols. This unique concept was the first attempt to connect the written language with the spoken word; we now call this phonetics.

Around 800 BC, the Greeks embraced the Phoenician invention and took it one step further by adding vowels and naming the symbols. They also employed boustrophedon (meaning "as the ox plows"), a system in which one reads from left to right on one line and right to left on the next.

The Greek writing system employed boustrophedon (meaning "as the ox plows"), a system in which one reads alternately from left to right on one line and right to left on the next. Notice how the letters are reversed from one line to another.

Much later, the Romans, a highly developed society, made further changes by adding more letters, bringing this writing system even closer to our modern-day alphabet. They made other advances as well. The Roman scribes, in their attempt to write more quickly and efficiently, began joining and slanting the letters in harmony with the natural motion of the hand. They also added ascenders and descenders, as well as condensed forms of the alphabet to conserve space.

Upper: The lettering at the base of the Trajan column, dated 114 AD. Lower: Close-up of the inscription on the base of the Trajan column, considered to be one of the most beautiful and best-known examples of Roman letterforms. Photographs courtesy of Bill Thayer & Graphion.

One of the most important contributions to early writing by the Romans was Trajan's column, dated 114 AD. It showcases one of the most beautiful and best-known examples of Roman letterforms. The lettering, which is incised at the base of the column, is a classical, elegant, and exquisitely balanced combination of form, proportion, and simplicity. It has been, and continues to be, a powerful inspiration to type designers throughout the world.

Special mention should be made here of the tremendous contributions to the art of writing by the Chinese and by other Asian cultures. Although their writing systems are not alphabetic, but rather consist of thousands of symbols, their extreme artistry, subtlety of form, and mastery of the art of calligraphy have been a continuous source of beauty, poetic elegance, and inspiration to all who come in contact with them.

Engraved portrait of Johannes Gutenberg from Andre Thevet's Les Vrais Portraits et Vie des Hommes, *Paris, 1584. Courtesy of Huntington Library.*

GUTENBERG AND MOVABLE TYPE

Until the fifteenth century, all books were hand-copied by scribes, as exemplified by the many breathtakingly beautiful and exquisitely written and illustrated manuscripts that were created for religious purposes in monasteries.

In 1448 that all changed with the birth of printing, after which the world would never be quite the same. Johannes Gutenberg, a goldsmith from Mainz, Germany, is credited with the invention of movable type. (There is some controversy about that, as some credit Laurens Coster of Haarlem in the Netherlands with its invention; others credit Pi Sheng of China with inventing movable type in 1045, more than 400 years earlier.) Gutenberg accomplished this by carving the characters of the alphabet in relief onto metal punches, which were then driven into other pieces of metal called matrices. Molten metal was then poured into these matrices, making the actual type, which was identical to the original relief punches. The type was then fit into printing presses that were capable of printing multiple images in a very short time. This was called letterpress printing, and its distinct characteristic is that each character makes a slight impression on the paper, giving it a rich, tactile quality.

Early type design imitated the pen-drawn styles of the scribes. Gutenberg's first typeface was in the style of the heavy blackletter popular in Germany at that time, and it contained over three hundred characters, including ligatures and abbreviations. As the popularity of printing became more widespread, a variety of different typestyles emerged based on popular handwriting styles of that time, including those favored by Italian humanist scholars. Nicolas Jenson and Aldus Manutius were two printers of the time who designed typestyles that were influential and inspirational, even to this day.

Gutenberg then went on to print the Bible, the first book printed from movable type. This invention truly changed the world, as it was no longer necessary for scribes to spend months and years

Close-up of the blackletter typeface used to set the Gutenberg Bible.

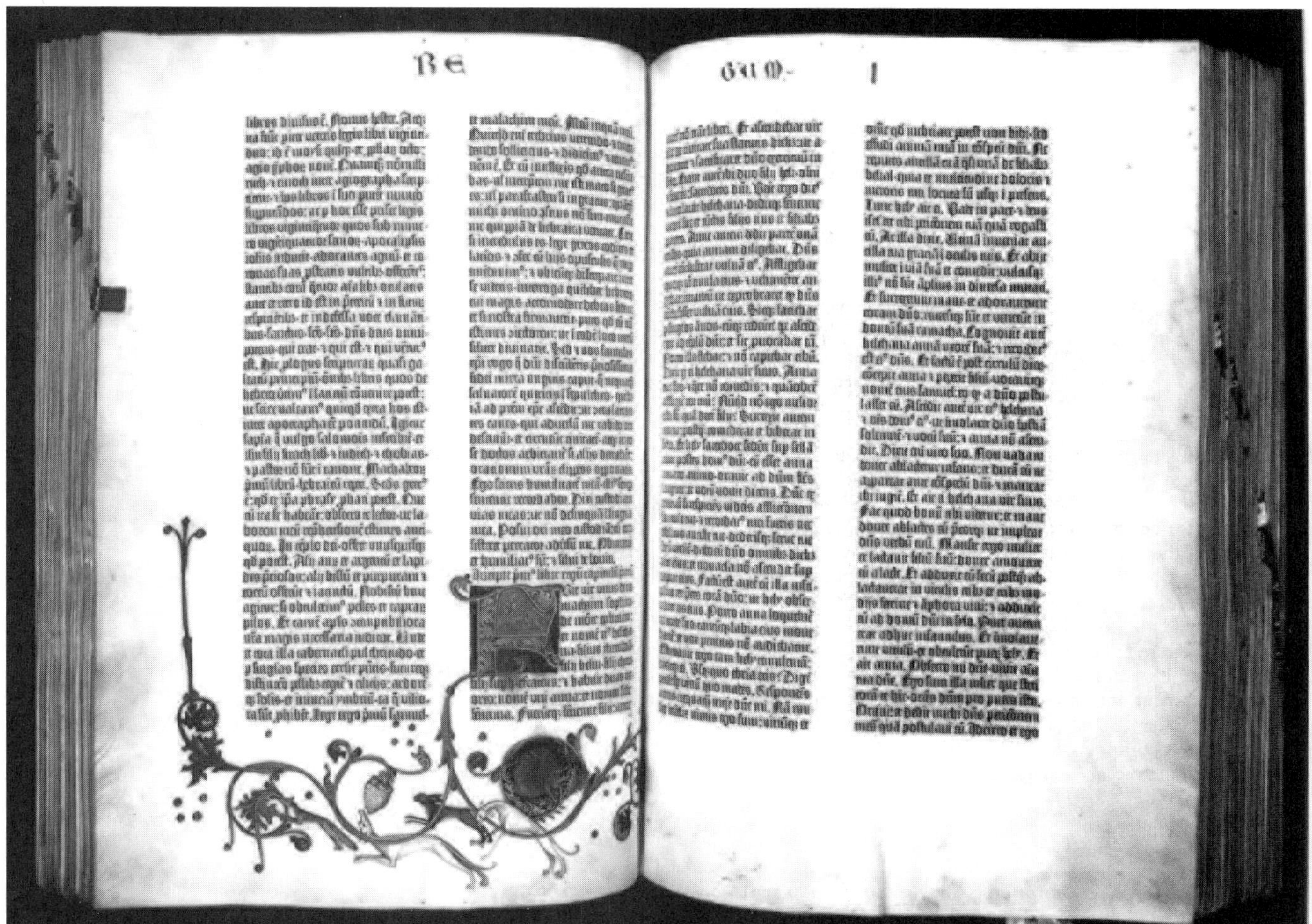

A spread from the Gutenberg Bible, the first book printed from movable type. Beginning of the Book of 1 Kings, Mainz, Germany, 1450–5. Courtesy of Huntington Library.

(and lifetimes, actually) hand-copying books.

This historical milestone, which now enabled history, news, religious writings, and other kinds of information to be circulated more easily and freely, brought forth many other changes, such as improvements in printing presses, papers, and inks. It also inspired many others to design typefaces to make use of this transformational invention.

Type designers were extremely influential in shaping the printed word over the centuries. The sixteenth century brought us the beautiful proportions of the work of Claude Garamond and Robert Granjon. In the next hundred years, the balanced designs and readable typestyles of William Caslon emerged. Giambattista Bodoni and Firmin Didot were tremendously influential in the eighteenth century with their elegant and graceful designs. The nineteenth century gave way to the oldstyle characteristics of William Morris's work, and the twentieth century brought us many designs inspired by the geometric Bauhaus style. Many thousands of typeface styles available to us today are in large part due to the originality, artistry, and craftsmanship of five centuries of talented printers and designers, only a handful of which are highlighted here.

At this point in history, it is important to note the influence that the technology had on the look of type. The new printing technology with all its

De diſſectione partium corporis humani, Liber ſecundus.

Procemium.

Væ partes in humano corpore ſolidiores & exteriores erant, quæ'q; ipſam machinam potiſſimum conſtituebant, ſatis iam explicatæ nobis videntur libro ſuperiore. Sequitur, vt internas percurramus quæ maximè pertinent ad vitam, & ad earum facultatum quibus incolumes viuimus conſeruationem. In quo (quemadmodũ inſtituimus) ſubſtantia, ſitus, forma, numerus, cõnexio, earum partium de quibus ſermo futurus eſt, breuiter exponenda. Ad quod munus ſtatim aggrediemur, ſi pauca prius de inſtituto ac de iudicio noſtro ſubiunxerimus. Quanq̃ enim hic noſter in ſcribendo ac diſſecando labor, complures non modo in anatomes cognitione, ſed etiam in Galeni ſententiæ interpretatione iuuare poterit: tamen interdũ veremur, ne quibuſdam nomen hoc anatomicum ſit inuiſum : mirentúrq; in ea diſſectione tantum nos operæ & temporis ponere: cum alioqui ab ijs qui nummorum potius quàm artis aucupio dant operam facile negligatur. Atq; ita nobis occurritur, dum quærunt: ſatiſne conſtanter facere videamur, qui cum corporis humani partiũ longiori indagationi ſtudemus, quæ magis ſunt vtilia, imprimiſq; neceſſaria prætermittimus: ſatius eſſe affirmantes, eius rei cognitionem ſicco (vt aiũt) pede percurrere, in qua alia certa, alia incerta eſſe di-

Quid dictum libro ſuperiore.

Quid ſecundo libro dicetur.

Purgatio aduerſus eos, qui longiorem anatomes indagationem minus probãt

Roman type by Claude Garamond, from the print shop of Simon de Colines, Paris, 1545.

DIT
ILES
GARES

Sample of Firmin Didot types cut around 1800.

Actual Bodoni "type." Carved punches were driven into other pieces of metal called matrices. Molten metal was then poured into these matrices, making the actual type. Courtesy of Sumner Stone.

Quouſque
tandem a-
butêre, Ca-
tilina, pa-
tientiâ no-

The grace and elegance of the type of Giambattista Bodoni is evident in this page from the Manuale Tipografica (1818), which is considered to be one of the greatest type specimen books ever printed.

exciting advances, as well as the many beautiful and functional typefaces that were inspired by it, had its limitations, particularly when we look back from where we are now. Because each character was on a separate piece of metal, the space between the particular characters could not be adjusted to create a more even type color (known as "kerning") unless the letter combination was designed as a ligature or was combined on one piece of type. Additionally, line spacing could not be reduced beyond "setting solid," which allowed space for the ascenders and descenders. This meant that an all-cap setting had to have a lot of line spacing even if there were no ascenders and descenders. This created a very open, "letter-spaced" look that was characteristic of that time and that is still desired by some for its historical accuracy and its readability.

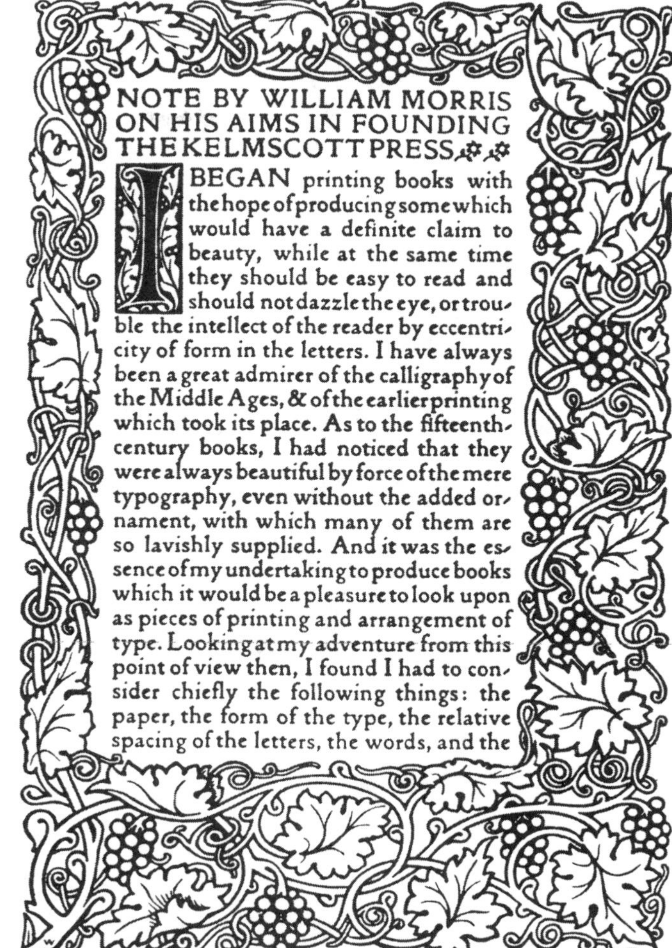

NOTE BY WILLIAM MORRIS ON HIS AIMS IN FOUNDING THE KELMSCOTT PRESS.

I BEGAN printing books with the hope of producing some which would have a definite claim to beauty, while at the same time they should be easy to read and should not dazzle the eye, or trouble the intellect of the reader by eccentricity of form in the letters. I have always been a great admirer of the calligraphy of the Middle Ages, & of the earlier printing which took its place. As to the fifteenth-century books, I had noticed that they were always beautiful by force of the mere typography, even without the added ornament, with which many of them are so lavishly supplied. And it was the essence of my undertaking to produce books which it would be a pleasure to look upon as pieces of printing and arrangement of type. Looking at my adventure from this point of view then, I found I had to consider chiefly the following things: the paper, the form of the type, the relative spacing of the letters, the words, and the

Golden Type and page border by William Morris. From a note by William Morris on his aims in founding the Kelmscott Press. Source: Kelmscott Press, 1898.

This cover design by Herbert Bayer illustrates the influence of the Bauhaus, c. 1923. (Original: red and blue letters on a black background.)

Typeface design by Herbert Bayer, 1925. This Bauhaus design is a minimalist, sans serif "unicase" typeface.

PHOTOTYPE

The development of new and improved presses continued through the centuries, but it wasn't until the late nineteenth and early twentieth centuries that groundbreaking improvements in typesetting equipment were achieved.

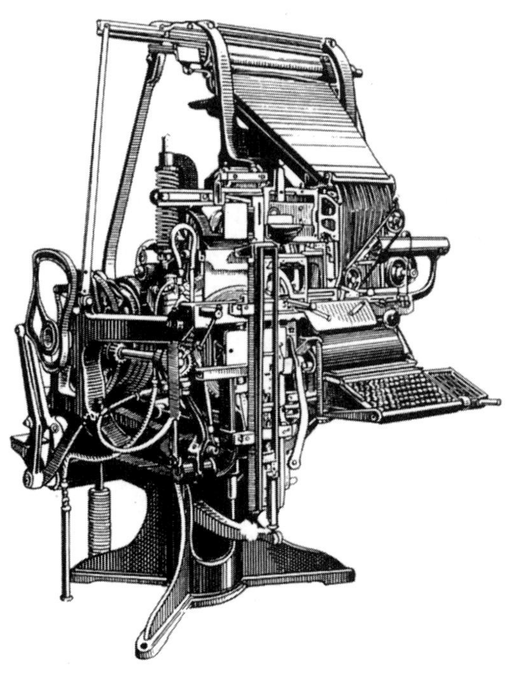

Linotype machine invented by Ottmar Mergenthaler.

In addition to its lack of speed and reliability, one of the primary limitations of metal-type composition, as it is referred to, was the inability to justify type automatically, that is, without the manual insertion of metal spaces between the letters. The Linotype machine, invented by Ottmar Mergenthaler in the 1880s, as well as other typesetters that followed, including one from Monotype, sped up the printing process immensely (including justification) and finally eliminated the need to set type by hand one letter at a time. The greatly increased speed that resulted from the replacement of hand composition by machine composition had a major effect on newspapers by allowing them to extend their deadlines to print late-breaking news. This typesetting change went hand-in-hand with advancements in the printing industry, such as offset lithography, a photographic process that gradually replaced letterpress printing,

Technology took a huge leap ahead in the mid-1950s with the development of phototypesetting. Several companies, the most prominent being Mergenthaler and Intertype, developed and improved a photographic process of setting type whereby typefaces were made into negatives through which light was focused onto photosensitive paper, producing an image of the type. The improvements over hot, metal typesetting were qualitative as well as quantitative. Typesetting could now be done electronically rather than mechanically, setting over five hundred characters per second compared to perhaps five or six previously, and the equipment took up much less space. Images became sharp and crisp, corrections could be made electronically, and most importantly, there was now complete flexibility with regard to intermixing styles, weights, and sizes; letter spacing and kerning; line spacing and word spacing; hyphenation and justification; overlapping; and other photographic special effects as well. The elimination of so many restrictions in the typesetting process had a major effect on typography and typographic design.

HERB LUBALIN

One of the most prominent figures in typography and typographic design in the sixties and seventies was Herb Lubalin, a hot, innovative, and fearless New York designer. His groundbreaking and adventurous use of type, particularly in the publication *U&lc* (designed and edited by Lubalin and published by International Typeface Corporation) influenced designers around the globe. His work incorporated tight letter and line spacing, extreme kerning with acute attention to every typographic detail, and the overall use of type and innovative new typefaces in ways never before seen. In addition, he handled type in a illustrative way seldom done before, either by employing typographic forms as graphic elements of the design or by creating typographic puns.

Why did he do this? Because he could, as these were capabilities never before possible with type. The typographic trends initiated by Herb Lubalin and imitated by

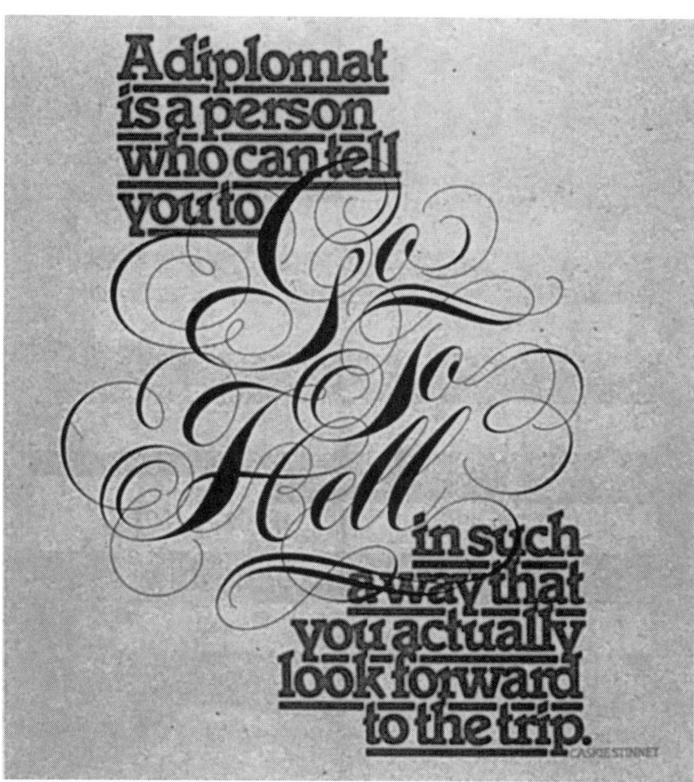

The work of Herb Lubalin broke with tradition in every possible way. He created the following three pieces for U&lc, *the typographic journal published by International Typeface Corporation. As the editor and designer of* U&lc, *he was able to present his innovative typographic ideas in the perfect vehicle. Courtesy of International Typeface Corporation.*

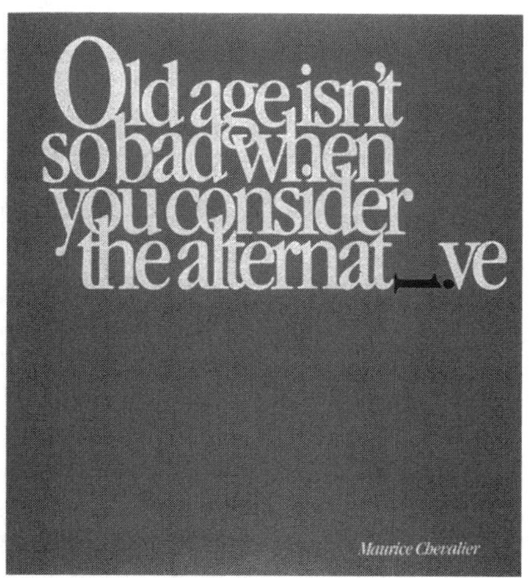

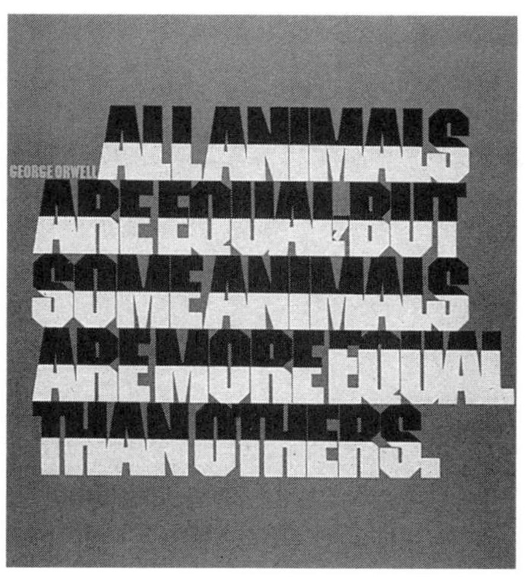

Above: This piece combines a bold typeface set with tight letter and line spacing with a very elegant hand-lettered script to illustrate a point typographically.
Top right: The overlapping ascenders and descenders of this piece take a back seat to the dramatic effect of the "i" lying on its side. The message is visual as well as editorial.
Bottom right: The message expressed here with the use of very tightly set caps is made even stronger by the placement of black-and-white color breaks, especially the world "equal."

countless others, particularly the emphasis on tight type at the occasional expense of readability, were a reaction to the restrictions of the hot, metal typesetting that preceded them. This style has its critics (as well as its admirers) today, but it is important to understand how and why it came about to appreciate its tremendous importance and influence on the evolution of type and typographic design.

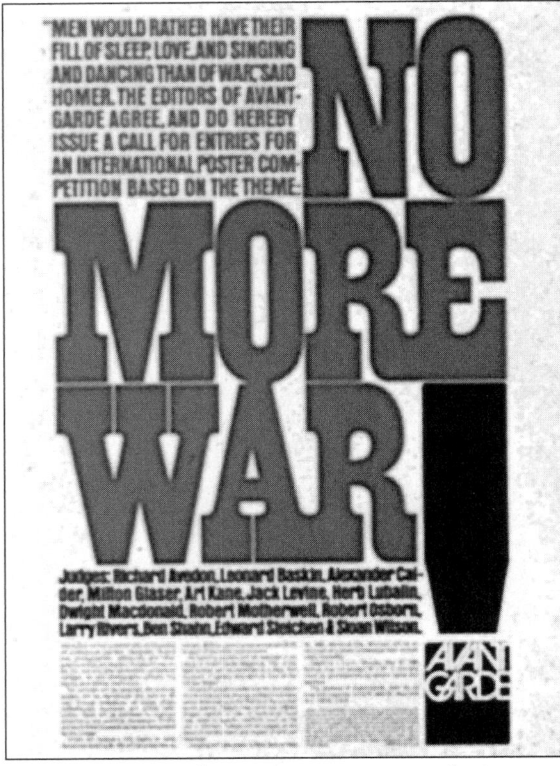

An announcement of an antiwar poster contest by Avant Garde magazine. Herb Lubalin's use of color, tight type, and very deliberate type alignment (including hung punctuation) create a jigsaw puzzle effect in this powerful piece. Courtesy of Rhoda S. Lubalin (estate of Herb Lubalin).

INTO THE DIGITAL AGE

The twentieth century continued to bring advances in typesetting technology at breakneck speed. Phototypesetting had been in use little more than two decades when digital typesetting methods took hold in the 1980s. Because it was so expensive and new, only professional typographers in type shops adapted this electronic technology. The new digital typesetters were capable of composing type and integrating photos and artwork and layout at one workstation. Digital color separation and retouching, stripping, and platemaking were to follow shortly. At this point, typesetting was still in the capable hands of professionals who spent many years learning the craft and trade of typography. This was all to change in the next few years.

In 1985, the world was irreversibly altered with the introduction of the Macintosh (Mac) computer, the first affordable "desktop computer" developed by Apple under the leadership of Steve Jobs. Other manufacturers, led by IBM, were developing versions of their own, which came to be known as personal computers or PCs. These PCs had different operating systems than Macs but the same affordability and focus. Now it was possible for virtually anyone to set type on the computer as desktop publishing blazed the path toward desktop typography.

This award-winning logo designed for a never-published magazine not only states the name but illustrates it as well. Herb Lubalin considered the suggestion of a fetus inside the logo one of his finest typographic designs. Courtesy of Rhoda S. Lubalin (estate of Herb Lubalin).

This new, exciting, and increasingly more affordable technology was improving at every turn. At the same time, page-layout applications, such as PageMaker and QuarkXPress, as well as the more illustration-oriented programs, such as Adobe Illustrator and Aldus Freehand, were being developed. As the memory and speed of desktop computers increased, so did the features and capabilities of these programs, eventually including the ability to set and fine-tune type. Simultaneously, companies and foundries, such as International Typeface Corporation (ITC), Adobe, Linotype, Compugraphics, and Berthold, shifted their focus to developing digital versions of their existing typeface libraries, as well as releasing new and different designs. Smaller, more specialized foundries, such as FontBureau, Emigre, T-22, and FontShop, began to emerge and introduced some very innovative and cutting-edge type designs. The introduction of type design programs, such as Letraset FontStudio, Macromedia Fontographer, and Ikarus-M, gave anyone the tools to create fonts. These developments led to the democratization of type design and contributed to the many thousands of fonts commercially available today. The quality of these typefaces ranged from very high end to extremely poor, leaving the daunting task of deciphering "which was which" to the end user.

Graphic design production methods were changing in dramatic ways as well. Paste-ups and mechanicals (the manual creation of camera-ready artwork, using paper proofs and wax or rubber cement) were being replaced by digital page makeup, which was cheaper, faster, and much more flexible. Type no longer needed to be sent out to expensive type shops, and instead it was set by graphic designers and production artists, as well as administrative assistants.

The problem with this new way of setting type is why a book like this exists. Setting good typography is an art and craft that in the past took many years to master and required highly skilled professionals who devoted their careers to developing such mastery. Today, however, most of those working with typography have little education in type, including, with few exceptions, most designers (although some of the better design schools are beginning to address this important subject). The unfortunate result of this situation has been the proliferation of poor typography.

Another contributing factor to this problem was that the earliest versions of page-layout programs did not have the capability to fine-tune type. Thankfully today's updated software programs are much more sophisticated and robust and are quite capable of creating excellent typography; but it still requires a skilled and knowledgeable person to achieve this. The computer is just a tool; it is a means to an end, not an end in itself. Many designers and production artists are not versed in the factors that contribute to the creation of fine typography, and they are not aware of and familiar with the features in their page-layout programs that can achieve this. With practice, however, you will acquire the eye necessary to see type as a professional does, as well as the ability and motivation to create it.

EXERCISE

Design Guidelines

Nancy Sharon Collins, Assistant Professor, 2004–5, Nicholls State University, Thibodaux, Louisiana

1. Think first.
2. Sketch everything you think. Get it out of your brain onto the page, any page, where your client and audience can read it.
3. Define your objective(s). Make a priority list. Start with the most important information at the top. List all other elements in sequence beneath it. Let this be your master, map, and guide.
4. Try not to bring preconceived notions to any project. Stay open-minded and open to change. Don't get too attached to any one idea. At any point, your client or the project itself can do a 360-degree turn on you, and you will have to alter your design accordingly.
5. Do all your research before you start on the computer.
    - **a.** Keystroke all original text into a word processing program to edit for content, spelling, and typographically correct punctuation. (Do not do this in a design program–you will get too wrapped-up in the design and lose sight of editing the text.)
    - **b.** Check all art for compatibility with the design program(s) you are planning to use.
    - **c.** Pin or tape your priority list within easy view.
    - **d.** Make your own type specimen book (see chapter 3).
    - **e.** Keep a scrapbook of "orphan type" (typographic ideas found on one-off media, such as old signs, old magazines, old packaging; look at junk mail, pulp fiction, club flyers, cereal boxes, etc.).
    - **f.** For major elements (headlines, etc.), make rough type studies of at least 3 to 5 styles. Utilize typography from nondigital media (hand-drawn, collage, or orphan type).
    - **g.** Make low-resolution (for position only) scans of all of your art, and store them in one folder so you can access easily and edit later.
    - **h.** Create 5 to 10 primary and secondary type studies. Pin them on the wall. Stand back and look at them. Choose or make more.

6. Compose a few (5 to 10) sample designs with all components in quick, rough form.

  a. Pin or tape them on the wall and critique them.

  b. Edit out the weaker ones.

  c. Create Style Sheets or use old-fashioned typographic specifications, written by-hand.

  d. The design(s) you choose to execute should be the easiest to defend. Ask yourself: How quickly does the design address the original problem? Does the design really reflect the target audience? Are all key components readable according to the appropriate hierarchy? This sounds terrible and boring, but a successful design not only must look nice but it must function to succeed!

7. Print out your design often. Pin or tape designs to wall. Critique as you go, replacing weak elements with stronger solutions.

8. Make sure your final design "reads" according to your original priority list.

9. Have someone else proofread your work, even if you use a spell-checker.

10. Keep all phases of your work. If you have to backtrack, you will have everything.

11. Organization is key. If you have to find a particular phase or element, you should know exactly where to find it.

12. Make sure your final printout appears exactly as you intend. If not, go back, figure out why not, fix it, and print again.

EXERCISE

Historical Design

Ilene Strizver, Faculty, School of Visual Arts, New York, New York

Objective

To research and explore influential periods and styles in history as it applies to typography and (typo)graphic design.

Assignment

Step 1: Write a 500 to 700 word summary on the typography and design of three of the topics listed below. Include at least three illustrations with captions.

Futurism
Russian Constructivist
Swiss Grid
Suprematism
Bauhaus
Art Nouveau
Art Deco
William Morris and the Kelmscott Press
Bauhaus
Herb Lubalin and the New York Style

Step 2: Select one of the three topics you have written about, and design a piece in that style. The format is 10 x 10 inches square. It can be all type or primarily type and image. It can be black and white or color.

EXERCISE

Typographic Timeline

Ilene Strizver, Faculty, School of Visual Arts, New York, New York

Objective

• To become familiar with the sequential history of type and typography.
• To develop an understanding of what led to the transition from one period to another.

Assignment

Research and create a typographic timeline from the invention of movable type through the present time. Include the following:

• Typeface classifications from chapter 3 (additional classifications may be added).
• Influential type designers and pioneers.
• Milestone typeface designs.
• Influential stylistic periods.
• Important type foundries.

Use charts, graphics, color, and appropriate typography as necessary to visually express the information in a clear, accurate, and visually attractive and effective way.

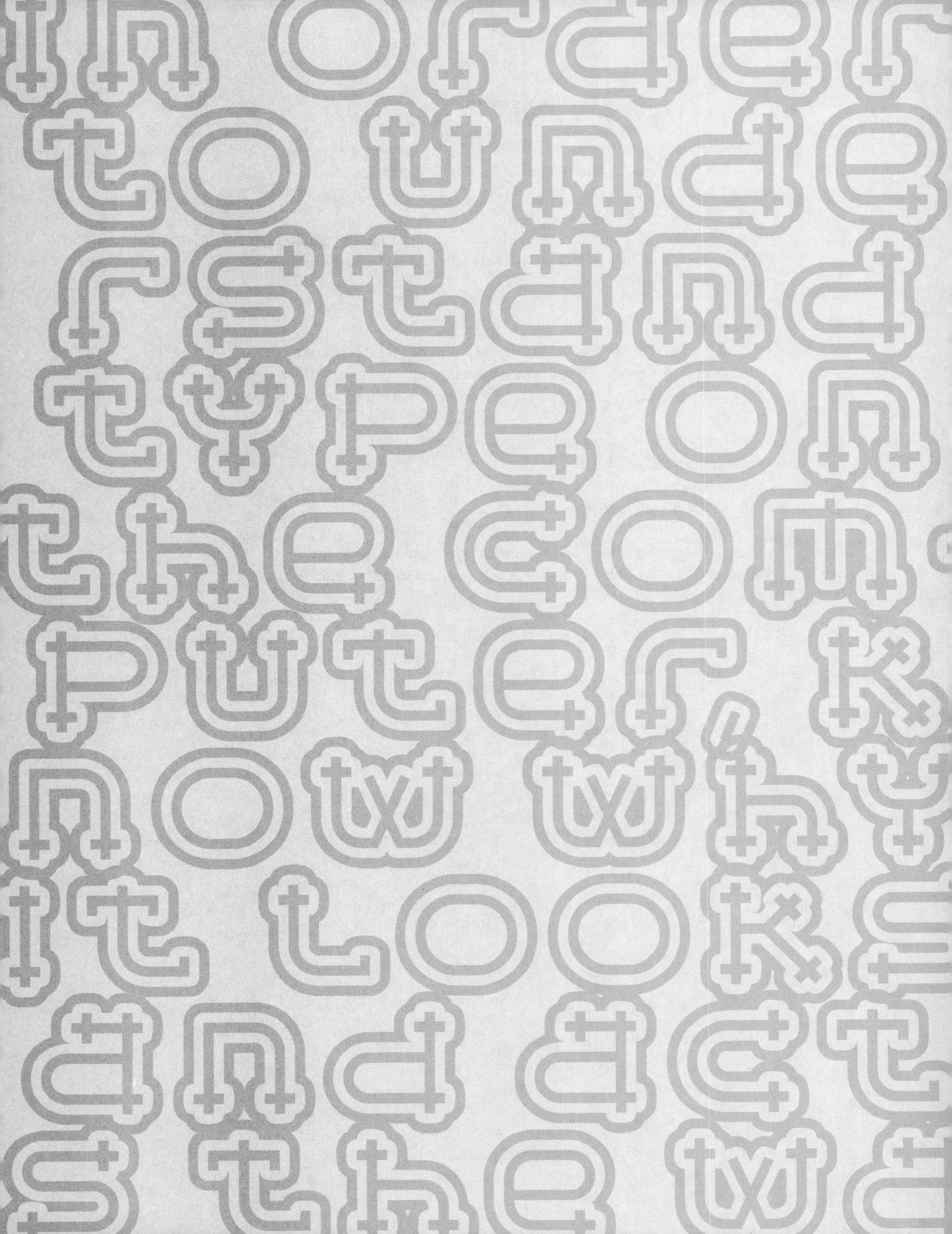
in order
to unde
rstand
type on
the com
puter, k
now why
it looks
and act
s the w

CHAPTER TWO

FROM METAL TO MAC:
UNDERSTANDING FONT TECHNOLOGY

Say the word "technology" to a lot of folks and they instantly break out in a cold sweat. But to understand type on the computer, why it looks and acts the way it does, and how to make the most of it, it is essential to comprehend a few things.

The following are just a few of the most commonly used (and perhaps abused) terms that will begin to give you an understanding of the basic principles of type and fonts on the computer.

WHAT IS A FONT?

What exactly is a font? The term has changed dramatically since computers have come into being. In traditional typography, specifically in days of metal type (or hot type), a font was a collection of metal characters representing the complete character set of a particular design (all the characters, numerals, signs, symbols, etc.), all of the same weight, style, and size. Ten point, twelve point, and any other size of the same design were all separate fonts.

Today, a font refers to the complete character set of a particular type design or typeface in digital form. Although it refers to only one weight and style, it is not size specific as in the days of hot metal. Digital fonts are scalable, that is, size independent; any point size type can be set from one font.

FONT FORMATS

Currently, there are three font formats to choose from: Type 1, TrueType, and the newest format, OpenType. If you are a graphic designer, chances are you have been primarily using PostScript Type 1 fonts, which have been the publishing standard since the late 1980s. On the other hand, if you do web design or work with Microsoft Windows software, you most likely use your share of TrueType fonts; this format has also been used by Apple and Microsoft for system fonts. The availability of OpenType fonts has added a third format to the mix, and one definitely worth exploring.

ITC Legacy Serif

abcdefghijklmnopqrstuvwxyz
ABCDEFGHIJKLMNOPQRSTUVWXYZ
0123456789ÆŒØæœøßfiflªº
!¡?¿'"*$¢£ƒ%‰°&§¥†‡<+=>_
[](){}#@¶|/\/˜^®©™
,.:;“”‘’‹›«»·•‚„…-–—1´¨`ˆ˜¯˘˙˚¸˛˝ˇ
áàâäãåÁÀÂÄÃÅçÇéèêëÉÈÊËíìîïÍÌÎÏ
ñÑóòôöõÓÒÔÖÕúùûüÚÙÛÜÿŸ

In the digital world, a font refers to the complete character set of a particular type design or typeface in digital form. This showing of ITC Legacy Serif is a good example, and it displays all the glyphs included in the font.

To understand the differences between Type 1, TrueType, and OpenType fonts, it is necessary to get a bit technical. But don't worry: you don't have to commit this to memory to set good type. Just try to remember the basic principles.

Type 1 (or PostScript) Fonts

Type 1 (also known as PostScript Type 1) was developed by Adobe Systems in the mid-1980s. This format is based on a computer language called PostScript, which describes type and graphics in a way that allows for precise, sharp printing at any size.

Type 1 consists of two components: bitmapped or screen font and a printer or outline font. Both are required to view and to print a font. Type 1 is the preferred format in the graphic arts and publishing industry, accounting for 75 percent of professional-quality font purchases. This is primarily because imagesetters–a device that service bureaus and printers use to output type and graphics at high resolution–use PostScript technology. Because of this shared technology, Type 1 tends to be more reliable, with fewer font conflicts when printing.

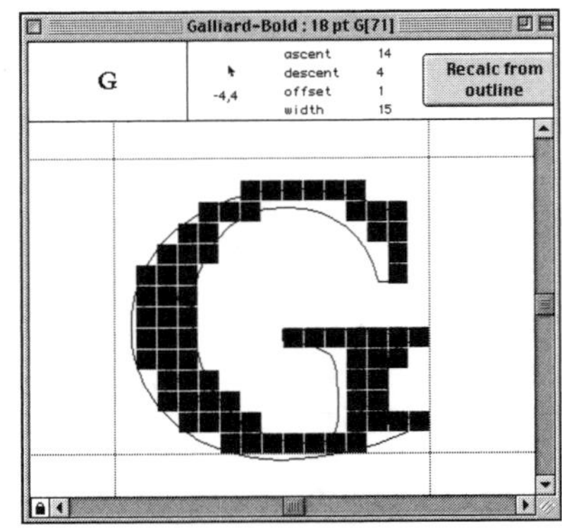

In a bitmapped font all the characters are represented as pixels so it can be viewed on your screen. This illustration shows the arrangement of pixels for a character at a particular point size superimposed over the outline.

Bitmapped or screen fonts. The bitmapped font is responsible for representing the font on your screen. Your screen represents all images, both graphics and type, with small dots or, more accurately, pixels. The typical screen has 72 dots per inch, commonly abbreviated as 72 dpi. In a bitmapped font, all the characters are represented as pixels, or bitmaps, so it can be viewed on your screen, thus the term screen font. The relatively low number of dots per inch on your screen (also referred to as screen resolution) compared to your printer makes smaller point sizes increasingly more difficult to display sharply and clearly, giving them the appearance of having more "jaggies" (jagged edges). This is why text can often be difficult to read on your computer screen.

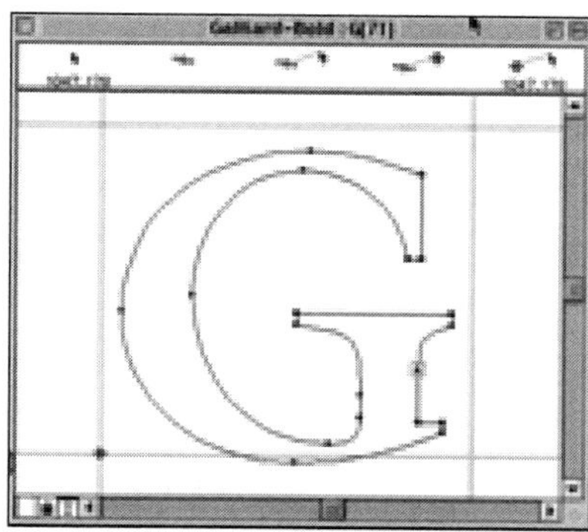

The image above is a digital representation of an outline. A printer font is scalable, which means it can be enlarged or reduced to any size, rendering as crisp and sharp an image as your printer or output device is capable of printing.

Printer or outline fonts. This is the part of the font that is necessary to print your job. It is essentially the outline of each character stored as a mathematical description, thus the name outline font. The printer font is scalable, which means it can be enlarged or reduced to just about any size, rendering as crisp and sharp an image as your printer or output device is capable of. Your PostScript printer acts as the brain that makes this interpretation. (This is quite the opposite of the screen font, which is fixed and needs to be generated for each size.)

TrueType Fonts

Several years after the development of Type 1 fonts, Apple Computer and Microsoft joined forces to develop TrueType. This format consists of a single file that contains both screen and printer font data. It is most commonly used by Windows users and the nondesign community, with the exception of "core" TrueType fonts, which generally come standard on computer operating systems.

TrueType differs from its predecessor mainly, and most importantly, in its expanded "hinting" capability. Hints are digital instructions built into a font to improve its on-screen and printed appearance, predominantly at small sizes. It is extremely time-consuming and costly to produce a font that features this enhanced clarity, so while some TrueType fonts have it (core fonts, for example); others do not.

TrueType might sound good to you, but keep in mind that the graphic design community favors Type 1 fonts, which are preferred for the quality of their output and their reliability. This is particularly so if you intend to output your work at a service bureau (or at your offset printer if it will be making the film), as they usually gripe at jobs using TrueType fonts. If you are using TrueType fonts, it is a good idea to discuss this in advance with your service bureau to see what their policy is and if they have any special instructions. TrueType fonts are fine for word processing jobs that have no printing considerations.

OpenType Fonts

OpenType is a kind of superset of Type 1 and TrueType font formats with added enhancements. The new features that benefit designers the most provide multiplatform support, expanded character sets, and glyph substitution.

Multiplatform support. A font with multiplatform support means that the same OpenType font will run on both a Mac and a Windows machine, as opposed to Type 1 and TrueType fonts, which need to be purchased for either a Mac or a PC. This is a real convenience when your office uses both platforms, or you use a PC at work and a Mac at home (or vice versa).

This also means that with consistent character encoding inherent in multiplatform support, many problems associated with the transferring of documents from Mac to PC (or vice versa) will go away. The most annoying problem is when characters in the original file automatically change to different ones, such as apostrophes and f-ligatures becoming question marks and accented cap Os. No more "search and replace" to correct this irritating problem!

From the simple to the sublime! Adobe Bickham Script Pro (an OpenType font) comes with a huge selection of swash and alternate characters, enabling a "plain vanilla" setting to be easily transformed into an elegant, highly embellished showing, previously attainable only from the skillful hands of a calligrapher. (More subtle effects can also be achieved.)

Expanded character sets. OpenType fonts allow type designers and foundries to include many more characters than the 256 we are used to with Type 1 and TrueType fonts. This means it can (but doesn't necessarily) include true-drawn small caps, oldstyle figures, extended ligature sets, swash and alternate characters (see page 123 in chapter 6 for more on contextual alternates), fractions, ordinals, proportional and tabular figures, dingbats and symbols, as well as extensive foreign language support, to say the least, all in one font. This advance will make it a lot less complicated to access these useful typographic features that used to require extended, alternate, or expert set fonts.

It is important to be aware that although an OpenType font is backwards-compatible in its most basic form with the most recent operating systems, the expanded character set is only accessible by software that supports it.

Glyph substitution. This capability goes hand-in-hand with an expanded character set. OpenType fonts have a brain and know when to insert certain ligatures, swashes or special characters. For instance, some swash characters are intended for the beginning or the end of a word to avoid crashing into other letters. When this feature is turned on in a supporting application, the correct swash will be automatically inserted. If the copy is changed, it will change the swash character as necessary.

It can get a bit more complicated when lots of alternates are available in a font; make sure that the characters automatically inserted are the ones you want. You might have to "manually" insert the others, although it is very easy to do once you become familiar with the process.

Availability. More and more fonts are available in OpenType format. Some are new releases, while others are existing fonts that have been remanufactured, sometimes with additional characters such as alternates, swashes, small caps, and oldstyle figures. Do your research carefully to find out ahead of time which additional characters are available with each font if that is important to you.

ANIMATION
A
AN
ANI
ANIM
ANIMA
ANIMAT
ANIMATI
ANIMATIO
ANIMATION
ANIMATION

House Industries designed Ed Interlock (an OpenType font) with a built-in intelligence to control the use of its hundreds of ligatures in such a way that it "thinks like a designer" and selects the appropriate ligature to maintain balance, particularly in the horizontal strokes. The top showing is set with "contextual alternates" turned off. When this feature is turned on (below), look how characters and ligatures change depending on what is next to it.

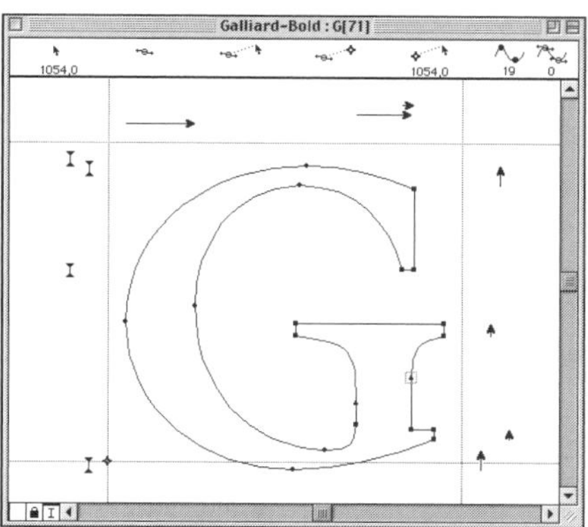

The markings around this character illustrate the hints, or instructions, that have been incorporated into a font to make type look good on screen as well as when printed.

HINTING

Hints are instructions that have been incorporated into a font to make your type look good on the screen as well as when printed. Remember that your printer converts all images into dots? Well, the hints tell your printer which dots to turn on and which to turn off when converting the scalable outline into the screen and printed version. This function is particularly necessary to improve the quality of type on the screen as well as low-resolution printers, 300-dpi printers in particular. This is less of a problem for printers that are 600 dpi and up.

FONT MANAGEMENT UTILITIES

A good font management utility is a necessity for those who have lots of fonts (as most designers do!). It is a way of managing and organizing your fonts and accessing just the ones you need for a particular job without having to move them in and out of your Fonts folder. This way they don't take up valuable space on your random access memory (RAM), and you don't have ridiculously long font listings on the font menu of your application.

Many of these helpful utilities can identify and resolve font ID conflicts, identify and remove duplicate fonts, as well as repair corrupt fonts. Some of the more popular ones are Extensis Suitcase, Master Juggler Pro, Font Reserve, and Font Agent. Some even come bundled with software that enables you to view and print font samples.

TECHTIP

Font Icons

If you use Mac OS 10, you will notice that the font icons have changed from OS 9 (and earlier versions). Although some foundries use customized icons, these are the generic versions that are commonly used by most foundries:

LWFN–Outline, or printer font.
FFIL–Font suitcase containing bitmap (or screen font) and font metrics (including kerning, etc.). More than one weight of a type family can be contained in a suitcase.
OTF–OpenType font; everything contained in one file.
NOTE: A Type 1 font consists of both an LWFN and a FFIL file, a TrueType font has all components contained in the FFIL file, and an OpenType font is an all-in-one OTF file.

TYPETIP

Style-Linked Fonts

Most major font foundries (as well as some of the smaller ones) style-link font families. This means that a true-drawn bold weight (as opposed to a "fake" computer embolded version) can be accessed via the bold style button, a companion "true-drawn" italic (as opposed to a "fake" computer slanting) can be accessed via the italic style button, and often an actual bold italic weight can be accessed with both buttons.

Style bar shortcuts for style-linked font families can be a real time saver when switching from one "style-linked" family to another, as the italic and bold weights change automatically without having to manually highlight and select the weight for each one. But make sure the family is style-linked beforehand to take advantage of this handy feature.

You can check with the foundry or manufacturer of a font to find out if it is style-linked, but the simplest way is often to find out yourself. Create a test document, listing the font family and weights twice. In the first listing, access the italic and bold weights from the font menu; in the second, use the style bar or keyboard command. If they are not style-linked, QuarkXPress will use fake styling (this is a very nasty no-no!), while Adobe InDesign will not change them at all. If they look exactly the same (you might need to print out to be sure), they are style-linked.

InDesign and QuarkXPress Keyboard Commands:

italic	shift / com / i
bold	shift / com / b

Maiandra Regular
Maiandra Italic
Maiandra Demi Bold
Maiandra Demi Bold Italic

Maiandra Regular
Maiandra Italic
Maiandra Demi Bold
Maiandra Demi Bold Italic

In this simple test, the upper showing of Maiandra was styled with the style bar in QuarkXPress, resulting in fake styling, while the font menu was used for the lower setting. The results indicate that Maiandra is not a style-linked typeface.

EXERCISE

Keyboard Layout Charts

Ilene Strizver, Faculty, School of Visual Arts, New York, New York

Objective

- To become familiar with the keyboard locations of commonly used but hidden signs, symbols, punctuation, and dingbats.
- To create a user-friendly reference for these glyphs.

Assignment

The common English qwerty computer keyboard has only 47 active character keys, but the standard Type 1 or TrueType font can contain almost four times that amount (depending on which platform you use: Mac or PC). These hidden characters can be accessed via specific keyboard combinations.

Step 1: Create a keyboard layout chart (either Mac or PC) for the complete character set of a standard Type 1 or TrueType text font. Select a legible font from a reputable foundry. Do not use a display font, as they don't always have complete character sets. The format is 8 ½ x 11 inches. Label columns clearly and concisely. Make the chart usable, practical, readable, and attractive. Convert the final chart into a PDF (Adobe portable document format) file. Make a template from your native file for future use.

Step 2: Using the template from Step 1, create a keyboard layout chart for ITC Zapf Dingbats.

Step 3: Using the template from Step 1, create a keyboard layout chart for an OpenType font with an expanded character set.

Many type
faces will
look simila
to the uns
killed eye a
first glance
but in time
you will no
only be abl
to see how

CHAPTER THREE

WHAT MAKES A TYPEFACE LOOK THE WAY IT DOES?

Why are there so many typefaces? Why do we need new ones? And what are the differences between them all? These are some of the most commonly asked questions about type, and understandably so. With over forty thousand typefaces in existence and new ones being designed as we speak, both the novice and the professional can easily become lost in a sea of typoconfusion.

Type design is similar to other kinds of product design in that it combines personal expression and interpretation with the needs and trends of the times. As technology changes, so does society as a whole, and changing personal tastes and styles are often a reflection of this, as is the desire to stand out from the crowd. Automobiles, furniture, watches, clothing, and even household items, such as telephones, toasters, and teacups, are all essential, functional items that are constantly changing and being redesigned and subsequently purchased anew or replaced by consumers. We never seem to have enough choices. The same is true for typefaces, with one major difference–the appropriate choice of a typeface is essential to the success and effectiveness of your message.

Some typefaces, such as text faces, are chosen for their functionality, while others are chosen to be new and different and eye-catching, as are most display designs. Before we can understand the differences between typefaces, it is important to be able to see the differences. This is an acquired skill that can be learned by anyone who is interested, akin to using a muscle you've never used before in a sport or acquiring a taste for different kinds of apples or beer. Many typefaces will look similar to the unskilled eye at first glance, but in time you will not only be able to see how they differ but also understand how those differences are important to the effectiveness and appeal of your job.

PARTS OF A CHARACTER

Typefaces, or alphabets, consist of many different characters. Each character is made up of different parts, all of which have a name. Knowing the terminology in the following list not only makes it easier to communicate about typefaces and their characteristics but educates your eye to see and to recognize the underlying structure of various designs and subsequently the differences between them.

Arm–A horizontal stroke that is attached on one end and free on the other.
Arm or leg–The upper or lower (horizontal or diagonal) stroke that is attached on one end and free on the other.
Ascender–The part of a lowercase character (b, d, f, h, k, l, t) that extends above the height of the lowercase x.
Bar–The horizontal stroke in characters such as A, H, R, e, or f.
Baseline–The invisible line on which most characters sit.
Bowl–A curved stroke that creates an enclosed space within a character (which is then called a counter).
Cap height–The height of capital letters from the baseline to the top of caps, most accurately measured on a character with a flat bottom (E, H, I, etc.).
Counter–The partially or fully enclosed space within a character.
Descender–The part of a character (g, j, p, q, y, and sometimes J) that descends below the baseline.
Ear–The small stroke that projects from the top of the lowercase g.
Hairline–A very thin stroke most often common to serif typefaces.
Link–The stroke that connects the top and bottom part (bowl and link) of a two-storey lowercase g.
Loop–The lower portion of the lowercase g.
Serif–The projections extending off the main strokes of the characters of serif typefaces. (See "Serif" under Type Categories below.) Serifs come in two styles: bracketed and unbracketed. Brackets are the supportive curves that connect the serif to the stroke, creating a somewhat softer look. Unbracketed serifs are attached sharply and usually at 90-degree angles.
Shoulder–The curved stroke of the h, m, or n.
Spine–The main curved stroke of the S.
Spur–A small projection off a main stroke, found on many capital Gs.
Stem–A straight vertical stroke or main straight diagonal stroke in a letter that has no verticals.
Stress–The direction of thickening in a curved stroke.
Stroke–A straight or curved line.
Swash–A fancy flourish replacing a terminal or serif.
Tail–The descender of a Q or short diagonal stroke of an R.
Terminal–The end of a stroke not terminated with a serif.
x-height–The height of lowercase letters is usually based on the lowercase x, not including ascenders and descenders.

arm
ascender
bowl
ear
bar
counter
descender
cap height
shoulder
link
loop
serifs
spine
stem
stress
swash
stroke
spur
x-height
tail
terminal

TYPE CATEGORIES

Many attempts have been made to divide type styles into historic classifications, oftentimes resulting in a dry and somewhat cumbersome read. The following section will attempt to simplify and demystify the type classification system to give you a basic understanding of where the many hundreds of types came from, how they differ, and why.

Although it is not necessary to commit these categories to memory, there is value in understanding the origins of type and what makes one typeface different from another. Not only will you be building a good foundation for your growing typographic knowledge, but by reading about the differences between the typefaces, you will get a clearer picture of the anatomy of a character and how it varies from one typeface to another. It is an excellent way to fine-tune your ability to see type and know what you are looking at.

SERIF

This is a large category of typefaces with one common denominator: all have serifs. Simply put, serifs can be described as extensions, protrusions, or, more elegantly put, finishing strokes extending from the ends of a character. Although they are decorative and stylistic in nature, they are said to enhance readability by guiding the eye from one character to the next. They also serve to distinguish typefaces with similar shapes from each other.

Many categories of typeface fall under this heading, with the primary ones described below:

Oldstyle

This category of typefaces originated between the late fifteenth and the mid-eighteenth century. It is characterized by curved strokes with the axis inclined to the left, little contrast between thick-and-thin strokes, headserifs that are usually angled, and bracketed serifs.

abcdefghijklmnopqrstuvwxyz
ABCDEFGHIJKLMNOPQRSTU

Adobe Caslon

Transitional

Typefaces within this category represent the eighteenth century as a time of transition between oldstyle and modern design. They have the following characteristics: the axis of the curved strokes is barely inclined or more vertical than diagonal, there is more contrast between thick and thin strokes than in oldstyle, and serifs are thinner, flat, and bracketed.

abcdefghijklmnopqrstuvwxyz
ABCDEFGHIJKLMNOPQRSTU

ITC New Baskerville

Modern

This refined and more delicate style is characterized by high or dramatic contrast between the thick and thin strokes, curved strokes on a vertical axis, and serifs that are horizontal with little or no bracketing.

abcdefghijklmnopqrstuvwxyz
ABCDEFGHIJKLMNOPQRSTUV

ITC Bodoni

Clarendon

This style made popular in the 1850s has a strong vertical weight stress, heavy, bracketed serifs that are usually square, and slight stroke contrast.

abcdefghijklmnopqrstuvwxy
ABCDEFGHIJKLMNOPQRST

Clarendon

Slab or Square Serif

An early nineteenth-century style, these typefaces have very heavy square serifs, little or no bracketing, and hardly any stroke contrast, appearing monostroke. They are often geometric or square in style.

abcdefghijklmnopqrstuvwxyz
ABCDEFGHIJKLMNOPQRSTUV

ITC Lubalin Graph

Glyphic

Glyphic type styles are lapidary (carved or engraved) rather than pen-drawn in nature. They have a vertical axis, minimum stroke contrast, and often have triangular or flaring serifs.

ABCDEFGHIJKLMNOPQRSTUVWXYZ
ABCDEFGHIJKLMNOPQRSTUVW

Copperplate

SANS SERIF

From the French word for "without," sans serif typefaces are without serifs. These were some of the first styles to be cut in stone, and they have had periodic returns to popularity due to their simplicity, as well as their somewhat industrial look. These are some of the most common categories of sans:

19th Century Grotesque

This style was the first popular sans. Its distinguishing features are contrast in stroke weight, a squared look to some curves, a "spurred" G, and a double-bowl (also referred to as a two-storey) g.

abcdefghijklmnopqrstuvwxyz
ABCDEFGHIJKLMNOPQRSTUVWXYZ

News Gothic

20th Century Grotesque

This neo-grotesque style has less pronounced stroke contrast and is more refined in form than its predecessor. It has lost the squared curve and has a single-bowl g.

abcdefghijklmnopqrstuvwxyz
ABCDEFGHIJKLMNOPQRSTUVW

Univers

Geometric

These typefaces have strong geometric shapes, such as the perfect circle o, etc. They usually have monotone strokes.

abcdefghijklmnopqrstuvwxyz
ABCDEFGHIJKLMNOPQRSTUVW

ITC Avant Garde Gothic

Humanistic

Humanistic type styles were an attempt to improve the readability of sans serifs by applying a sans serif structure to the classical Roman form; more simply, they are based on the proportions of Roman capitals and oldstyle lowercase, with an apparent stroke contrast.

abcdefghijklmnopqrstuvwxyz
ABCDEFGHIJKLMNOPQRSTUVW

Optima

SCRIPTS

These designs represent a large category of typefaces derived from or imitative of handwriting or calligraphy. They include a wide variety of styles and characteristics, and they are much more fluid than more traditional type styles.

Formal

These very elegant typestyles are characterized by flowing loops and flourishes with graceful, rhythmic strokes. These designs are most often connecting scripts and imitate the cursive penmanship of the nineteenth century.

abcdefghijklmnopqrstuvwxyz
ABCDEFGHIJKLMNOPQRST

Bickham Script Pro

abcdefghijklmnopqrstuvwxyz
ABCDEFGHIJKLMNOPQR

Redonda

Casual and Brush Scripts

These scripts are designed to look informal, as though quickly drawn with a pen, brush, or similar writing instrument. Their strokes can be connected or not, and they tend to be warm, friendly, and relaxed.

abcdefghijklmnopqrstuvwxyz
ABCDEFGHIJKLMNOPQRSTUVWXYZ

Mistral

Calligraphic

This broad category of typestyles strives to imitate the writing or lettering of the calligrapher whose work is hand-drawn and customized for each job (custom made). Calligraphic typestyles often look as if they were drawn with flat-tipped pens or brushes, and they occasionally include the drips, spots, blotches, and irregularities inherent in the process.

abcdefghijklmnopqrstuvwxyz
ABCDEFGHIJKLMNOPQRSTU

Ballerino

HANDWRITING

Handwriting fonts are typographic interpretations of actual handwriting or hand printing. The stylistic range is extremely diverse and can be anything from a connected scrawl to a quirky, bouncy, irregular hand printing.

abcdefghijklmnopqrstuvwxyz
ABCDEFGHIJKLMNOPQRSTUVWXYZ

Deelirious

abcdefghijklmnopqrstuvwxyz
ABCDEFGHIJKLMNOPQRSTU

Dartangnon

BLACKLETTER

Blackletter type styles evolved from the early handwritten forms of liturgical writings and illuminated manuscripts. This style went from writing to type when it was used to set the Gutenberg Bible, the first book printed with movable type.

Blackletter typefaces are characterized by a dense, black texture, and highly decorated caps. The lowercase consists of narrow, angular forms with dramatic thick to thin strokes and serifs.

abcdefghijklmnopqrstuvwxyz
ABCDEFGHIJKLMNOPQRS

Fette Fracktur

abcdefghijklmnopqrstuvwxyz
ABCDEFGHIJKLMNOPQRSTUVW

Old English

TITLING FONTS

These are type designs that have been specifically designed for headline or display settings. Titling fonts differ from their text counterparts in that their scale, proportion, and design details have been altered to look best at larger sizes. This commonly includes a more extreme weight contrast and often more condensed proportions. While usually all cap, single weight variants of larger text families, titling fonts can also be stand-alone designs.

ABCDEFGHIJKLMNOPQRSTUV

ITC Golden Cockerel Titling

ABCDEFGHIJKLMNOPQRSTU

Bembo Titling

DECORATIVE AND DISPLAY

This very broad category encompasses many hundreds of type styles that do not fit into any of the preceding categories, as they are designed primarily for headlines and meant to be distinctive, original, and eye-catching. They adhere to few or no rules and constraints and defy pigeonholing of any kind.

ABCDEFGHIJKLMNOPQRSTUVW
ABCDEFGHIJKLMNOPQRSTU

ITC Abaton

abcdefghijklmnopqrstuvwxyz
ABCDEFGHIJKLMNOPQRSTU

ITC Farmhaus

abcdefghijklmnopqrstuvwxyz
ABCDEFGHIJKLMNOPQRSTUV

ITC Curlz

ABCDEFGHIJKLMNOPQRSTUVWXYZ

ITC Rennie Mackintosh

ABCDEFGHIJKLMNOPQRSTUV

ITC Beesknees

abcdefghijklmnopqrstuvwxyz
ABCDEFGHIJKLMNOPQRSTUVWXYZ

ITC Pious Henry

abcdefghijklmnopqrstuvwxyz
ABCDEFGHIJKLMNOPQRSTUVWXYZ

Teknik

abcdefghijklmnop
ABCDEFGHIJKLMNOPQ

ITC Freddo

abcdefghijklmnopqrstuvwxyz
ABCDEFGHIJKLMNOPQR

Coquette

TYPETIP

One- and Two-storey "a"s and "g"s

The lowercase "a" and "g" come in two styles: one-storey (also called single bowl) and two-storey (also called double bowl). The one-storey versions are simpler in form and are what we learn to read from. Two-storey versions have their tradition in historical typefaces of the serif variety, but they have been adapted in numerous other type designs, including sans serif designs and many other contemporary type styles.

Although two-storey versions are not usually used for true italics (as opposed to obliques, which tend to mirror the styles used in their Roman counterparts), they can appear anywhere a type designer chooses to use them, and they do not necessarily come in pairs either!

Aa Gg
Aa Gg

Plantin (upper) and Plantin Schoolbook (lower) illustrate the different designs of the two-storey and one-storey a and g.

EXERCISE

Think Like a Type Designer

Ilene Strizver, Faculty, School of Visual Arts, New York, New York

Objective

- To fine-tune sensitivity to the shape, structure, proportions, and design characteristics of a typeface.
- To improve the powers of observation and attention to detail.
- To understand the factors that contribute to making a consistent typeface design.

Instructor Preparation

Step 1: Set the complete lowercase of three very different typefaces (I use a traditional serif, a condensed sans, and a contemporary serif, such as Bodoni, Impact, and Bodega Serif) on an 8 ½ x 11 inch, horizontal format. Set the characters centered in three lines so there is plenty of space between the letters and lines. Place the typeface name on the top for identification. This is the master character showing. Print out one set.

Step 2: Create a second version of the above masters in the following way: remove the title, as well as five of the following characters: a, e, g, k, r, s, t, and x. Leave the spaces empty. These are the missing character templates. Print out enough for one per student. (I print out extras for those who want to do more than one.)

Assignment

- Distribute one each of the three missing character showings from Step 2 above, along with the tracing paper and markers. Instruct students to draw the five missing characters; they should be filled in roughly, if they have time. Emphasis should be placed on the concept and intention, not the execution. They MUST complete all five characters.
- The final tracing should have the missing characters drawn in position along the baseline, so it can be placed on top of the template and both taped to the wall. Give them about 20 minutes. **NOTE:** Do not let them use pencils or other fine-tipped tools, or they will spend too much time on perfecting the outline and less on the design concept.

Critique

Place one master on the wall at a time, starting with a sans serif if possible. Have students place all tracings and templates of that typeface alone on the wall at the same time. Review one character at a time, comparing their drawings to the true solution. Discuss how they made their decisions, if they fit the overall design (even if they are different), and why the true solution makes sense. Discuss factors such as design consistency, width, ascender and descender length, overall proportions, stress, location of weight contrast, etc.

Supplies

- 9 x 12 inch tracing pad, at least 2 sheets per student.
- Fine, black marker (Sharpie or any kind that is not too thin).

EXERCISE

Personal Type Specimen Book *(Individual Project)*
Ilene Strizver, Faculty, School of Visual Arts, New York, New York

Objective
• To create a functional, practical, and expandable personal specimen book of all fonts available on one's computer.
• To become familiar with the history, appearance, usability, and functionality of each font.

Assignment
Step 1: Collect six different type-specimen showings–three text and three display. They should be actual specimen showings from font catalogs or from PDF specimen showings supplied by many font web sites.

Step 2: Examine and analyze each of them carefully, considering appropriateness, practicality, and ease of use. Consider factors including overall layout; character layouts; size and style of text showing, including point size and leading; labeling; and any other factors. Make a list of pros and cons for each of the six showings.

Step 3: Design two different 8 ½ x 11 inch specimen-showing templates: one for text and one for display. Allow room on left margin for a three-hole punch. Include complete typeface name, foundry, designer, date, and a listing and sample character of all the weights and versions in the type family. Include its category, which can be serif (text), sans (text), display, ornament, or image fonts. Make your templates the best possible tools for font selection, taking into consideration your list of pros and cons.

Step 4: Set your entire font library in one of these templates.

Step 5: Proof carefully. Then print out and put in binder, creating dividers for serif, sans, display, ornaments, and images.

EXERCISE

TYPE SPECIMEN BOOK AND TYPEFACE ANALYSIS *(Group Project)*

Audrey G. Bennett, Associate Professor, Rensselaer Polytechnic Institute, Troy, New York

Objective

- To research a type designer and typeface.
- To create one specimen page for a class Type Specimen Book.
- To acquire an in-depth understanding of every aspect of a typeface, including readability, legibility, as well as historical factors contributing to its design.

Assignment

Part 1: Type Specimen Book

You will create an 8 ½ x 11 inch specimen page to be part of a class Type Specimen Book.

Specifications

Format: 8 ½ x 11 inches.

Margins: For front page, ½ inch on top, right side, and bottom; 1 inch on left (to allow for binding or hole punching). Reverse for back page.

Front Page

- Research a type designer of your choice and buy one of his or her text fonts.
- Set header as follows: first line, name of typeface in 18 point (pt) bold; second line, designer and year of design; and third line, name of foundry. Set second and third lines in 14 pt book or regular.
- Use the font to set the following character in 48 pt, centered caps, lowercase, numerals, punctuation, and other symbols, as shown in example.
- Set the paragraph shown below at 9/12, 10/13, and 12/15, left justified. Adjust the tracking if necessary to make the text the most readable.

Back Page

- Identify 6 to 8 distinguishing characteristics of the font.
- Create a grid of 3 ½ x 3 ½ inch boxes with .5 pt rules.
- Within each box, show one or more of these characteristics, using both image (enlarged character or part of a character) and descriptive text.

Part 2: Typeface Analysis

Write and design in an essay of 1,500 words on standard, letter-sized paper about the type designer and his or her font that you chose in Part I. Use the font to typeset your essay.

Analyze the readability of the three type specimens you prepared in Part I. Describe the font in detail. Discuss its distinctive features and letters. Show an example of the font in use in a professional context. Which social and technological issues influenced its design? You may use image-based graphics in your paper.

Futura
Paul Renner
Adobe Type Library

48 POINT FUTURA

ABCDEFGHIJKLMNOP
QRSTUVWXYZabcdef
ghijklmnopqrstvwxyz1
234567890$.,'"-:;!?&

FUTURA 9/12
The text you are reading is dummy text. It gives you on idea of Futura's readability. All of the text in this paragraph has been typeset in Futura at nine points on twelve points of leading. You should kern and track text typeset with these specifications to achieve maximum readability. Leading, kerning, tracking, x–height, and line–length are some of the factors that influence the readability of text.

FUTURA 10/13
The text you are reading is dummy text. It gives you an idea of Futura's readability. All of the text in this paragraph has been typeset in Futura at ten points on thirteen points of leading. You should kern and track text typeset with these specifications to achieve maximum readability. Leading, kerning, tracking, x–height, and line–length are some of the factors that influence the readability of text.

FUTURA 12/15
The text you are reading is dummy text. It gives you an idea of Futura's readability. All of the text in this paragraph has been typeset in Futura at twelve points on fifteen points of leading. You should kern and track text typeset with these specifications to achieve maximum readability. Leading, kerning, tracking, x–height, and line–length are some of the factors that influence the readability of text.

Futura
Paul Renner
Adobe Type Library

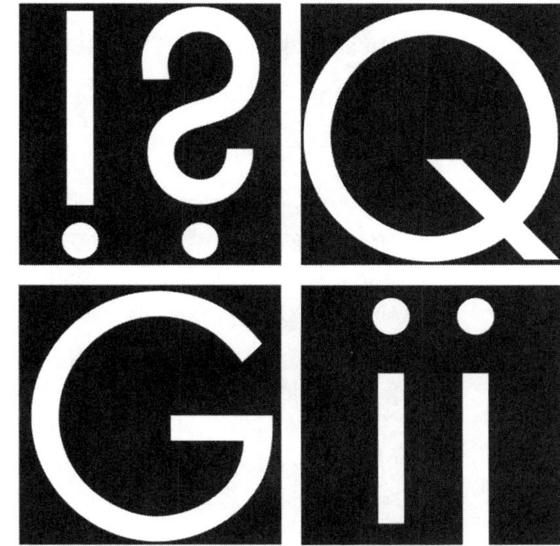

Futura embodies Bauhaus ideology. It features strict geometric shapes and lacks any embellishments, creating a stark minimalist appearance. Distinguishing characteristics of Futura include constant line strokes, straight lines, and arcs that are very circular. Futura's geometric and contemporary look is evident in the characters j, i, question mark, and exclamation point due to their straight lines and compass-like curves.

Specimen pages designed by Hunter Dougless. Courtesy of Hunter Dougless.

EXERCISE

On Beyond Zebra: The 27th Letter Assignment

Virginia Rougon Chavis, Assistant Professor, The University of Mississippi, University, Mississippi

Objective

The purpose of this assignment is to develop a more acute understanding of and appreciation for the intricacies of the letterforms that make up a typeface.

Assignment

Create an upper- and lowercase 27th letter of the western alphabet. Create a name for the letter, a place in the alphabet, and a new sound (one that is not already taken in the English language). You will focus on the stress, stroke, and serif of each individual letter, all of which contribute to the overall look, personality, and readability of the typeface.

Process

Step 1: Choose a text typeface from one of the following categories: oldstyle, transitional, modern, Egyptian, or contemporary. Create 15 to 20 preliminary sketches using that particular typeface during class to create a 27th letter. **HINT:** Try to use no more than 4 strokes, as if you were to write the letter in your own handwriting.

Step 2: Pick 3 to 5 of the best forms and re-create digitally at a point size of 300.

Step 3: You will choose the best of these three designs with help from the class during an in-progress review.

Step 4: Find a place in the alphabet where your letterform (upper- and lowercase) fits best, and reproduce the alphabet including its 27th letter. This should be done at 60 point. Position the entire alphabet next to your letter.

Step 5: Come up with a short paragraph, using the new 27th letter at least five times. Place this paragraph on the bottom of the page.

Specifications

- One 8 ½ x 11 inch black and white print.
- Portrait or vertical format.

Evaluation

- Adherence to specifications.
- Craftsmanship.
- Creativity.
- Attention to letterforms.
- Attention to placement in the alphabet.

ABCDEFGH
IJKLMNOPQRS
TUVWXƆYZ

abcdefghijklm
nopqrstuvwxɔyz

Amber Brewer's solution to the 27th Letter Assignment is based on Adobe Garamond. Courtesy of Amber Brewer.

Type has the power
to make or break a
job. Every typeface
has a different pers
onality, and the ab
ity to convey differe
nt feelings and mo
ds, some more than
others. Display typ

CHAPTER FOUR

SELECTING THE RIGHT TYPE FOR THE JOB

Type has the power to make or break a job. Every typeface has a different personality and the ability to convey different feelings and moods, more than others. Display typefaces, also known as headline typefaces, tend to be stronger in personality, sometimes trading legibility at smaller sizes for a more powerful feeling. They can evoke strength, elegance, agitation, silliness, friendliness, scariness, and other moods. Text designs, often used for blocks of copy, are more subtle in mood and emphasize legibility. Their personalities tend to be whispered rather than shouted.

Although typeface selection is a very personal, subjective decision, there are some guidelines and unofficial rules that will help you narrow your search and ultimately help you make the right choice.

Arriba arriba
RETRO BOLD
ITC Clover
ITC Jambalaya
ITC Schizoid
Fette Fraktur
Jazz
ITC Vintage
ITC Ziggy

Every typeface has its own personality and ability to convey different moods and feelings, some more than others. Display typefaces tend to be stronger in personality, sometimes trading legibility at smaller sizes for a more powerful feeling.

DESIGN GOALS

The first and foremost step in selecting a typeface is knowing your goals. As a designer, your primary responsibility is to serve the client using your design and problem-solving skills. It is not to make their job into your own personal award-winning design statement. Personal self-expression to the exclusion of the needs of the project are what fine art is all about, but this is not the goal of graphic design.

Every job requires a different approach. An annual report might call for a typeface with a high degree of legibility that also captures the

These portfolio pieces by Jim Spiece combine expressive typography with illustration to convey childlike whimsy (above) and a very inviting French culinary experience (right). Courtesy of Jim Spiece.

The typeface used on this book cover designed by Richard Fahey screams out excitement, danger, and intrigue in conjunction with the illustration. Book covers need to capture one's attention quickly amidst a sea of other books, and this one makes its point in a strong way. Courtesy of Richard Fahey.

spirit of the company, but a book cover might need a face that catches the eye and tells a story in a split second, amidst a sea of other books. A travel brochure might need to evoke the excitement and flavor of a foreign country, while a textbook or novel might call for a pleasing, readable text face that doesn't tire the eyes after long lengths of copy.

To focus your design goals and subsequently the most appropriate typefaces to use, start by identifying the age, attention span, and demographics of your audience. Different typefaces attract a different audience, both subliminally and overtly. Children are drawn to easy-to-read, childlike fonts: seniors to larger settings that have more clarity and legibility; teens to more edgy, expressive designs. After you consider your audience, ask yourself how much reading you are asking them to do and what information you are expecting them to walk away with. Once you identify your design objective, your typeface choices will narrow considerably.

Gill Sans
Optima
News Gothic
Minion
Expo Sans
ITC Legacy
Syntax
Avenir
Schneidler
Giacomo
Laurentian
ITC Century
Silica

Counters, x-height, character shapes, stroke contrast, etc., all contribute to the legibility of a typeface. These text faces are extremely legible due to their clean, consistent, and uncomplicated design features, which make it easy to distinguish one letter from another.

LEGIBILITY AND READABILITY

One often hears type described as being legible and/or readable. Although they both relate to the ease and clarity with which one reads type, they actually refer to two different things: legibility refers to the actual design of the typeface, while readability refers to how the typeface is set.

The legibility of a typeface is related to the characteristics inherent in its design, including the size of its counters, x-height, character shapes, stroke contrast, serifs or lack thereof, and weight, all of which relate to the ability to distinguish one letter from another. Not all typefaces are designed to be legible. This is more of a consideration for text designs where the degree of legibility relates directly to holding the reader's attention for the duration of the copy. Display designs are generally used for a few words in larger settings where the objective is to be instantly noticeable and to convey a mood or a feeling, so legibility might not be as important.

These display designs forgo a high degree of legibility for a stronger personality, elaborate and more expressive shapes, and a more distinctive look. When the objective is to be instantly noticeable and to convey a certain mood or feeling, extreme legibility might not be a priority.

This logo for Greenhood + Company, created by Vrontikis Design Office, trades slickness and readability for an intentional low-tech look, which is in direct opposition to what you would expect from a company specializing in new media and technology. Typographic irony can be a powerful tool. Courtesy of Vrontikis Design Office.

Of all delectable islands the Neverland is the snuggest and most compact, not large and sprawly, you know, with tedious distances between one adventure and another, but nicely crammed. When you play at it by day with the chairs and table—cloth, it is not in the least alarming, but in the two minutes before you go to sleep it becomes very real.

Of all delectable islands the Neverland is the snuggest and most compact, not large and sprawly, you know, with tedious distances between one adventure and another, but nicely crammed. When you play at it by day with the chairs and table—cloth, it is not in the least alarming, but in the two minutes before you go to sleep it becomes very real.

Readability is related to how you arrange the type and is affected by size, leading, line length, alignment, and letter and word spacing. Even a legible typeface, like ITC Flora, can lose readability when set 14/15. But its readability improves dramatically when set 12/18.

Readability is related to how you arrange the type. Factors affecting type's readability include size, leading, line length, alignment, letterspacing, and word spacing. So it follows that a legible typeface can be made unreadable by how it is set, while a typeface with poor legibility can be made more readable with these same considerations.

WHAT MAKES A GOOD TYPEFACE?

Every designer wants to select the best typeface for the job, but many are puzzled by what actually makes a good design. Appearances can be deceptive, especially to the untrained eye! So then how can you tell a good typeface from a poorly designed one? What are the characteristics that make a well-designed typeface? Although developing a good "typographic" eye takes time and patience, here are some basic points to consider when making this determination:

Consistent Design Characteristic

A good typeface will have consistent design characteristics throughout. This includes heights (including the overhangs of curved characters), character width, stroke width, ascenders, descenders, serif details if a serif typestyle, as well as the individual nuances and idiosyncrasies of the design. Related characters will be similar in spirit, if not in actual design. Even a grungy, nonconforming display face can be consistent in its inconsistencies.

Consistency

Consistency

Consistency

Alfon's consistent design traits (top) are evident in its character widths, thick and thin strokes, serif treatment, as well as the stroke endings of the s and c. Extreme Sans (middle) displays consistent character shapes, stroke thickness, rounded stem endings, and rounded geometric shapes. Even a rather inconsistent-looking display design, such as ITC Bodoni Brush (bottom), can be consistent in its inconsistencies, as seen in its baseline and x-heights, thick and thin strokes (yes, even the chunky thicks are consistent!), and overall character widths.

Legibility

As mentioned earlier, this refers to the ease with which the characters, words and design as a whole can be read. It is of primary importance in text typefaces that are meant to be used at smaller sizes and for longer text. Legibility is an important factor in display faces as well, unless the designer has other objectives in mind.

Spacing

A typeface that is well-spaced is neither too tight nor too open, and most importantly has even spacing between characters throughout the design. Unfortunately many type designers don't pay as much attention to proper and consistent spacing, which dramatically affects the look of a design, as they do to the design of the actual letterform. This is usually due to lack of training, as most type designers are self-taught.

A typeface that is well-spaced is neither too tight nor too open, and has even spacing between characters.

A typeface that is well-spaced is neither too tight nor too open, and has even spacing between characters.

Poor and inconsistent spacing between characters and words can make a well-designed face, such as ITC Juice, look spotty and uneven (left). When evenly spaced (as is the original, on the right) it is a rhythmic design with even-texture and color.

Kerning

Even a typeface that is spaced properly has character combinations that are too open or too tight (although a well-spaced design will have fewer). These character pairs should be adjusted by the type designer with the creation of kern pairs. Once again, this is often neglected by designers, often due to unfamiliarity with this aspect of type design. *(See chapter 8 for more on kerning.)*

Even kerning
Even kerning

Uneven kerning, as displayed in the upper setting of ITC Conduit, is evident in the tight ve, er, and ng combos, as well as the too open ke, rn, and ni combos. The bottom showing (as it appears in the original font) is much more even and consistent.

Even Color and Texture

This is actually one of the most important aspects that makes up a good design, which relies on a combination of all of the above to achieve. Another important but somewhat unnoticed factor in even color and texture is proper word spacing. The right amount allows a typestyle to be read easily without the words either running together or separated by oversized white spaces that interrupt the color and overall readability of the design.

So, you see, there is more to type design than the actual shapes of the characters. As you begin to notice these characteristics, your eye will get sharper and you will more easily differentiate a well-designed typeface from the rest of the pack.

Typographic excellence [is]
nothing more than attitude.
Contemporary advertising,

Typographic excellence [is]
nothing more than attitude.
Contemporary advertising,

A preliminary version of Oldrichium (upper), while true to its historical source, has uneven stroke thickness and weight contrasts, inconsistent letterspacing, and too much word spacing. The final version (lower) was adjusted to improve the overall color and texture while maintaining the idiosyncrasies of the design, resulting in a more balanced, even-textured, yet still authentic, typeface.

TEXT VS. DISPLAY

There are two main categories of type: text and display. Simply put, text type is designed to be legible and readable at small sizes. This usually implies fairly clean, consistent, uncomplicated design features, more open spacing than a display face, and thin strokes that hold up at smaller sizes. Display type, on the other hand, can forgo the extreme legibility and readability needed for long blocks of text at small sizes for a stronger personality, elaborate and more expressive shapes, and a more stylish look.

Many typefaces do not adhere to these descriptions, however, and can be used for both text and display. Some even look their best at midrange sizes. So when you are choosing a font, try to see a word grouping set at a size close to what you will be using. It is very difficult to visualize what 14-point text will look like from a 60-point "a to z" showing.

TYPOGRAPHIC ILLUSTRATION

Sometimes a design cries out for a solution that blends type with illustration to get a concept across in a strong, nonverbal way. This could mean incorporating type within an illustration, making typographic glyphs illustrative, or even making the type part of (or related to) the illustration. The use of typographic illustration and visual puns can be a clever, powerful, and useful tool for effective design.

This freeform, quirky, and dynamic lettering was designed to mimic the qualities of the artist's music. The lettering was created with a sponge brush by the designer Kayla Silber.

This logo practically designed itself, according to Bob Aufuldish of Aufuldish & Warinner. "It was primarily a matter of finding the best question mark that could be flipped so it would read as an S. It turned out that the Caslon Italic question mark was perfect–we just rotated it so it was upright." Courtesy of Aufuldish & Warinner.

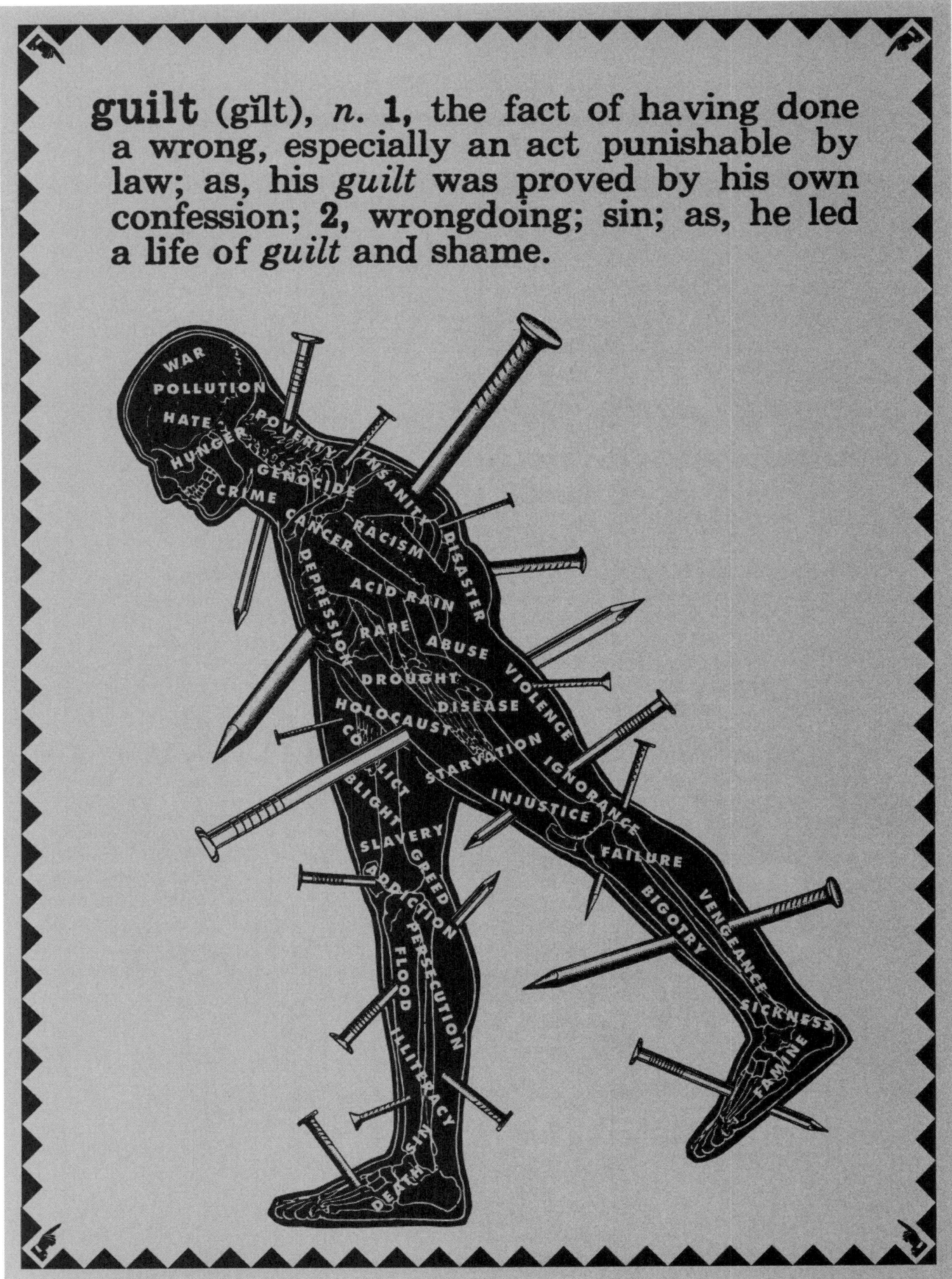

This poster by Scorsone/Drueding powerfully illustrates the concept of guilt by embedding the plight of humankind (set in Futura Bold caps) within a dark, stylized illustration of a man pierced with nails. This is an extremely effective use of typographic illustration. Courtesy of Scorsone/Drueding.

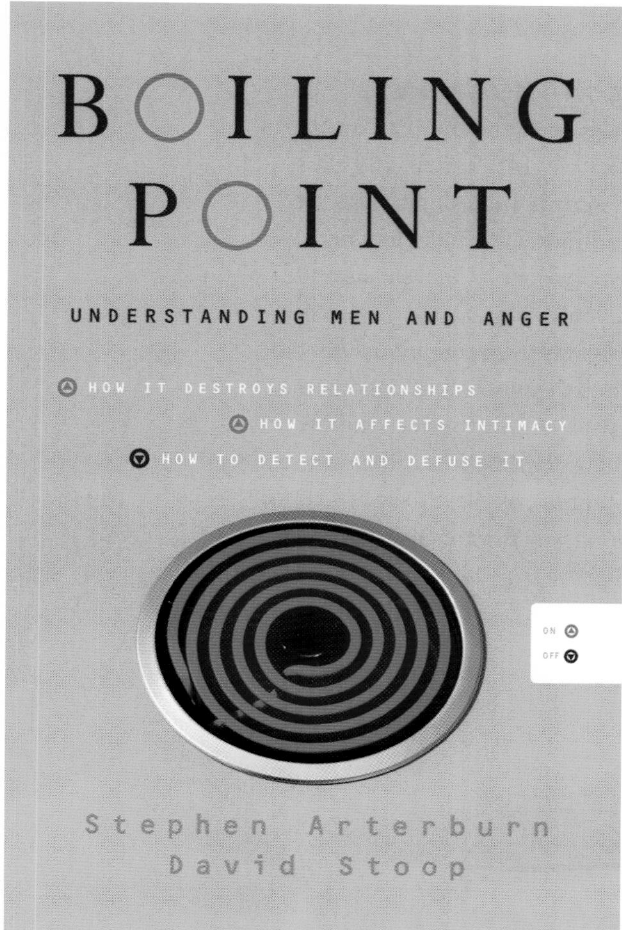

This seemingly simple yet well-thought-out book cover is made even stronger by replacing both Os in the title with oversized degree symbols set in a fiery red to reinforce the title as well as the concept of anger. These Os create a visual tie-in with the circular pattern of the red-hot burners. Designed by Red Canoe. Courtesy of Red Canoe.

Once again the letter O has a double meaning as it becomes a continuation of coins shaken out of a taxpayer's pocket in another book cover by Red Canoe. The primitive illustration blends with the book title set in News Gothic, while the rest of the type is set in Trixie, a distressed typewriter font, suggesting grassroots posters and fliers announcing rebellions of an earlier era. Courtesy of Red Canoe.

This book's title suggests its type treatment in this highly stylized, dramatic book cover by Daniel Pelavin. He created geometrically constructed characters that overlap and are separated by gradated color in the style of A. M. Cassandre. Courtesy of Daniel Pelavin.

This logo for a lightbulb intertwines type with image as the u has been modified to become a lightbulb. Its bright yellow color, signifying light, strengthens the image. Designed by Mansi Desai. Courtesy of Portfolio Center.

SCRIPT, CALLIGRAPHIC, AND HANDWRITING FONTS

Script and calligraphic fonts are in a class of their own, and they can overlap both text and display categories. They can be very elegant, formal, and classy or very humanistic, quirky, and individualistic. Scripts and calligraphics are often used for invitations, announcements, headlines, and initial letters; handwriting fonts are great for informal correspondence as well as ads and brochures requiring a more personal, informal look.

The number of fonts in these categories has swelled tremendously in the last several years due to their popularity with both designers and neophytes. Before making your selection, look the fonts over carefully for the legibility of both the caps and lowercase, as well as their appropriateness for your job. These fonts are fun to use, but use them with caution, as they make a very strong graphic statement that can either go a long way toward communicating your message or stop your audience cold.

Kuenstler Script
Linoscript
Bickley Script
San Remo Casual
ITC Kendo
Scruff
ITC Kick
Coquette
ITC Deelirious
Emmascript

These script, calligraphic, and handwriting-inspired typefaces can be very elegant, formal, and classy, or be humanistic, quirky, and quite individualistic. They are fun to use, but use them with caution as they make a very strong–sometimes too strong–graphic statement.

Sick
OF THE SAME OLD PAPER?

Combining Rougfhouse, a "sick" looking display typeface, with Scala Sans makes the message come alive in this promo piece by SVP Partners. It appeared on airline-style air-sickness bags as well as T-shirts. Courtesy of SVP Partners.

An elegant type treatment for a Mohawk Paper promo by VSA Partners, Inc. A clean, tasteful design results from contrasting script with slab-serif typeface, large with small, cap with lowercase, and black with color. Courtesy of VSA Partners, Inc.

WHEN THE BEST FONT FOR THE JOB ISN'T A FONT

Some jobs require the kind of typographic treatment and interpretation that cannot be achieved with an existing font. No matter how many typefaces you look at, none of them seem to do what you want them to do. Don't panic—at times like these, the unique talents and skills of a hand-letterer or a calligrapher should be seriously considered. The work they do is very specialized and unique and is custom designed to your exact needs. They can create a one-word logo or an entire alphabet for an ad campaign. In a world containing thousands of typefaces, the work and artistry of hand-letterers and calligraphers is invaluable, and it will continue to be an important resource for the design community.

the CORNERSTONE language program lets my teacher give me my own personal assignments. I work at my own speed and I don't have to waste time on things I already know. Nobody else has my same warm-up exercises, reviews, quizzes or learning games. Because nobody else, even my best friend Jennifer, is exactly like me ☺.

These three pieces by hand-letterer Jill Bell could never have been done on a computer with fonts—their warmth and individuality require the design sensibilities, skill, and talent of a human being. Courtesy of Jill Bell.

alabama

Peter Bain, the designer of this logo set in Architype Bayer-Type addresses the repetition of the four as in the seven letter word by customizing the first a. Bain blends the bottom of the existing one-storey a with the imaginary top of a two-storey a. The crossbar that divides the two parts creates the only horizontal axis in the word, creating a dynamic and experimental letterform to lead into the rest of the word. Courtesy of Peter Bain.

Henderson Bromstead Art once again integrates typography with image as a way to downplay the dense copy. "Treating the type as image forces us to consider it as integral to the concept. Rather than something separate and descriptive of the visual, it often IS the visual." Courtesy of Henderson Bromstead Art.

This poster designed by Henderson Bromstead Art for an AIDS organization fundraiser brilliantly blends the red-ribbon symbol of AIDS awareness with clinking champagne glasses to create the perfect image in which to embed the hand-rendered type. Courtesy of Henderson Bromstead Art.

These hand-lettered logos by Gerard Huerta are further examples of results that can only be achieved with the handcrafting of a talented letterer. Courtesy of Gerard Huerta.

This hand-lettered logo for Monsoon Café, drawn by Christina Hsaio for Vrontikis Design Office, captures the essence of the "lands of the monsoon." Every character was drawn to work with those around it; each of the three os are a different design, which would have been almost impossible with a typeface. Courtesy of Christina Hsaio and Vrontikis Design Office.

These three colorful letters say it all in this very simple yet eye-catching invitation by SVP Partners. Courtesy of SVP Partners.

Illustrator and hand-letterer Daniel Pelavin combines oversized, dimensional caps flowing around an outlined, shadow script to create depth, movement, and flow to this colorful, eye-popping book cover. The large caps double as windows to the illustrations within them. Courtesy of Daniel Pelavin.

No typeface would have worked as well as this hand-lettered type by Kevin Pope, who also did the illustration for this Yupo promo piece by SVP Partners; the hand-lettered type and the illustration work together as one. Courtesy of SVP Partners.

The hand-drawn type on the tractor blends in perfectly with the stylized yet primitive style of the illustration. Illustration and design by Bud Snead. Courtesy of Bud Snead.

Robynne Raye of Modern Dog used hand-drawn typography to create these two posters for local plays. Hand-drawing the type in Betty the Yeti allowed the letterforms to be customized to fit the contour of the Yeti, which was drawn by the designer when she was six years old (far left).

The poster on the near left also incorporated hand lettering; if it was set in an actual font, all seven of the Es and five of the Ls would look exactly the same, giving it a static feel. Hand-drawing the type allowed it to remain more random and organic. Both posters courtesy of Modern Dog Design Co.

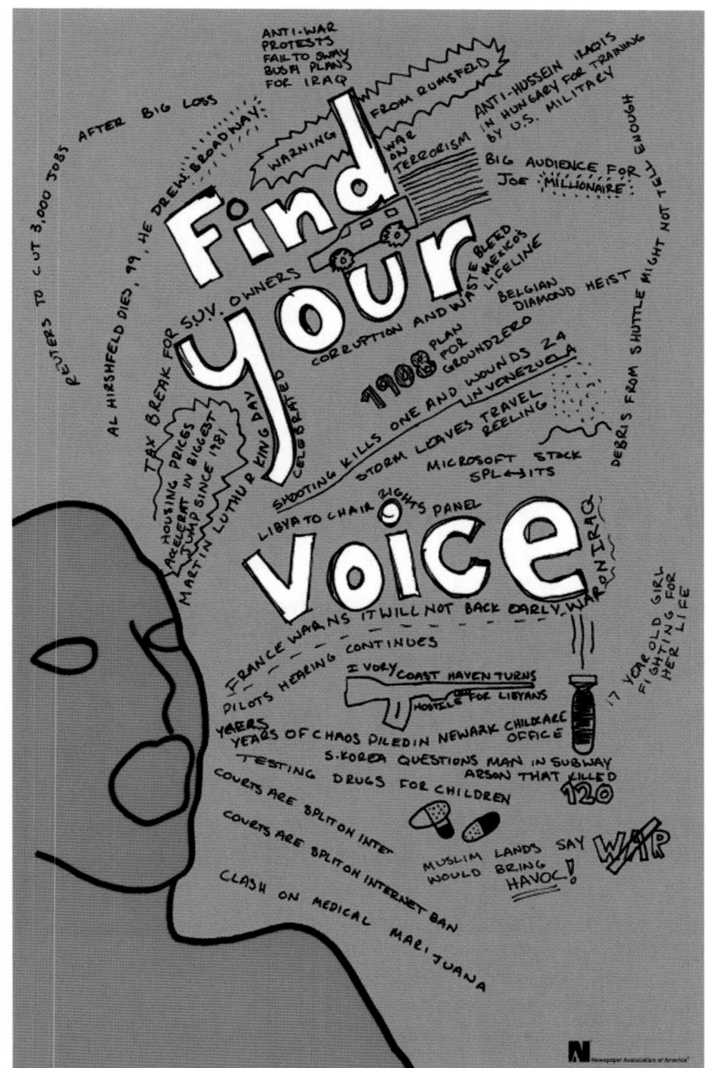

Original handwriting and a simple line drawing was all that was needed to make the point to Find Your Voice and read the newspaper. Handwriting is a natural choice to express one's voice, as both are unique, individual, and personal. Designed by Ben Ginnel. Courtesy of Ben Ginnel.

A very different example of a situation in which the best typeface for the job might not be a typeface at all. This piece for Mohawk Paper Mills, designed by Rigsby Design, addresses the question of "identity" by using a rather crude, inconsistent yet surprisingly rhythmic handwriting throughout the piece, sending a very low-tech, personal message. It works great with the illustrations. Courtesy of Rigsby Design.

Art Chantry once again uses very low-tech methods to achieve the look of an old show card from the 1950s for this rockabilly concert. The vintage feel was created from a combination of cut-and-pasted old fax lettering and images that were assembled, printed, crumpled up, photocopied, enlarged, and touched up. Courtesy of Art Chantry Design Co.

REDLINE, MILLENIUM 3000 and KCMU 90.3 Present

AT POMADE, Wed 12/3 9pm

LIVE

In Person

13 CATS

featuring members of THE STRAY CATS, THE POLECATS, AND THE ROCKATS

with LOS GATOS LOCOS

CD RELEASE PARTY

Showbox

1426 First Ave., Downtown

628-3151

SPECIAL UPDATE: We now have swing lessons every Wednesday at 9pm

This raw, tension-filled logo for a performance troupe designed by Art Chantry reflects the troupe's view of themselves as "straining against convention, ready to explode." The type was created with thrift store ceramic lettering, which was pressed and squeezed onto a copier to achieve the compressed, crowded feel. Courtesy of Art Chantry Design Co.

Vilijam SAROJAN

LOKOMOTIVA 38,
ODŽIBVEJ

deseta od trinaest priča iz knjige »Zovem se Aram«

Vilijam SAROJAN

TRKA
NA PEDESET
METARA

peta od trinaest priča iz knjige »Zovem se Aram«

The primitive yet purposeful headline typography on these Serbian book covers, designed by Jana Nikolic, intentionally forgo modern digital techniques in place of old transfer type with its inherent cracks and other imperfections. The text is set in Aram, a typeface designed specifically for this project at the Faculty of Applied Arts in Belgrade. Courtesy of Jana Nikolic.

TYPE FAMILIES

Special consideration should be given to using type families. These are usually text or text/display families with corresponding Sans, Serif, and sometimes Informal or Script versions. They usually have the same basic structure but with different finishing details, enabling them to work well together.

This is a very safe yet effective way to mix typefaces while keeping your job clean and not overdesigned. Type families have even more mileage if they are available with small capitals (small caps), which give you another option to create emphasis without jarring the reader and disturbing the flow too much.

Compatil Text
Regular & *Italic*
Bold & *Bold Italic*

Compatil Letter
Regular & *Italic*
Bold & *Bold Italic*

Compatil Fact
Regular & *Italic*
Bold & *Bold Italic*

Compatil Exquisite
Regular & *Italic*
Bold & *Bold Italic*

Compatil is an innovative, modular type system consisting of four stylistically related type families with the same proportions and identical character spacing. All styles have been built on a common skeletal structure and consist of Exquisit, a Venetian serif; Text, a transitional serif; Letter, a slab serif; and Fact, a humanist sans serif.

Triplex
Light
Bold
Extra Bold

Triplex Serif
Light
Bold
Extra Bold

Triplex Condensed
Regular
Black

Triplex Condensed Serif
Regular
Black

Emigre Triplex is a stylish type family consisting of Sans and Serif Roman (upright) designs as well as condensed versions. They should be treated as separate designs and used together very carefully; although they have the same roots, their width differences make them more challenging to use together effectively.

ITC Humana Serif
Light & *Light Italic*
Medium & *Medium Italic*
Bold & *Bold Italic*

ITC Humana Sans
Light & *Light Italic*
Medium & *Medium Italic*
Bold & *Bold Italic*

ITC Humana Script
Light
Medium
Bold

ITC Humana is unusual in that it is a calligraphic-based type family having both text and display applications. The Serif and Sans versions are warm, lively, and humanistic, as the name suggests, as well as being quite legible at small sizes. The Script version is a very strong, dramatic, condensed calligraphic design that can be used at larger sizes in conjunction with the Serif and Sans.

ITC Bodoni Six

Book w/ Oldstyle & Small Caps
Book Italic w/ Oldstyle
Bold w/ Oldstyle
Bold Italic w/ Oldstyle

ITC Bodoni Twelve

Book w/ Oldstyle & Small Caps
Book Italic w/ Oldstyle
Bold w/ Oldstyle
Bold Italic w/ Oldstyle

ITC Bodoni Seventy-Two

Book w/ Oldstyle & Small Caps
Book Italic w/Oldstyle & Swash
Bold w/ Oldstyle
Bold Italic w/ Oldstyle & Swash

ITC Bodoni Ornaments

ITC Bodoni Six, Twelve, and Seventy-Two are authentic revivals of Giambattista Bodoni's original designs. These classic yet practical size-sensitive designs are an unusual concept in digital fonts. There are Swashes for the Seventy-Two Italics and several Bodoni ornaments in each font, as well as many more in a font of their own, making this a very versatile family.

ITC Stone Serif

Medium & *Medium Italic*
Semibold & ***Semibold Italic***
Bold & ***Bold Italic***

ITC Stone Sans

Medium & *Medium Italic*
Semibold & ***Semibold Italic***
Bold & ***Bold Italic***

ITC Stone Informal

Medium & *Medium Italic*
Semibold & ***Semibold Italic***
Bold & ***Bold Italic***

ITC Stone Humanist

Medium
Semibold
Bold

The ITC Stone type family consists of Serif, Sans, Informal, and Humanist versions in three weights with Italics. It is an extremely legible, practical, and versatile text family with lots of mixing possibilities.

DOS AND DON'TS

Here are some suggestions and points to consider when choosing and using a typeface:

■ **Do** start with a few basic typefaces and type families, and learn how to use them well. Consider them the backbone of your typographic wardrobe–then you can add to them to fit more specific occasions. Many excellent designers use the same menu of typefaces for most of their jobs, and used appropriately they always manage to look fresh and do the job well.

■ **Do** leave white space. That old adage "less is more" often applies to type and design. No need to fill up every square inch of space–in fact, white space can create drama and emphasize the type.

■ **Do** consider production issues when selecting text type. For instance, when going very small, watch out for disappearing thin strokes, especially when printed.

■ **Do** consider how your type will look at the size you are planning to use it. For instance, when using a thick/thin script (or any typeface with a high weight contrast) for a headline, make sure it doesn't look too clunky at large sizes. What looks great at 18 point might look too heavy and lose its elegance at 96 point.

This typeface should not be set too small or the thins might break up when printed.

This typeface should not be set too small or the thins might break up when printed.

Caslon Openface with its delicate thin strokes is a perfect example of a typeface that looks great at 20 point but becomes more difficult to read at 12 point. It also becomes a challenge to print without the thins breaking up in the process.

■ **Don't** go too big when setting text; smaller with more leading is often more readable than a larger setting with tight leading.

■ **Don't** set to fit. Decide on a point size that looks and reads the best, and adjust leading and line width (or the length of your copy if possible) accordingly.

■ **Don't** tint type with delicate thins. It might break up when printed.

■ **Don't** distort your type with the features available in your page-layout program. Type that has been electronically expanded, slanted, emboldened, and condensed looks very amateurish and is annoying to the eye.

■ **Don't** let the way a typeface looks on a laser proof be the deciding factor in your selection, as it can look much heavier than the actual printed piece. There has been many an unhappy client when the type on a very expensive invitation is too light or has broken up on the printed piece.

MIXING IT UP

A common query when designing with type is: "How can I mix typefaces?" Or, more specifically, "How can I mix typefaces effectively?" When choosing a typeface outside the primary family you are using, there are three things to remember: *contrast, contrast,* and *contrast.* A common mistake is to use two or more faces that are too close in style, making the change not noticeable enough to serve the purpose at hand yet creating a subtle disturbance that detracts from the cohesiveness of your design. Combine typefaces when you want to emphasize or separate a thought, phrase, or text visually. The eye needs to see distinct differences for this to be achieved effectively. These basic principles should keep you on the right track:

Three typefaces: A slab serif, a sans, and a serif work together beautifully in this small but simple and cleanly designed self-promotion piece by Stephen Banham of The Letterbox.

Type combines with hand-drawn lettering to create a logo that mirrors the warmth, nostalgia, and romance that characterizes the restaurant. The script face was hand drawn from an old type specimen book. Designed by Public. Courtesy of Public.

Serif vs. Sans

A good rule of thumb when combining type is to mix a serif and a sans. There are usually strong design differences between them (unless they are part of a type family) that can achieve the contrast you are looking for.

Light vs. Heavy

Using a heavier (or lighter) weight typeface creates a strong visual contrast. This technique is often used for subheads; using a heavy sans, perhaps all caps, within a body of serif text does the trick very well. **NOTE:** Make sure you go heavy enough, because using the next weight up (e.g., book to medium) often results in a weak visual transition.

FOR STARTERS

There are few papers that can withstand the rigors of an exuberant lunch and live to do it again. Yupo can. A synthetic paper formulated to deal with reality — and whatever else you can throw at it. Water-proof, stain-resistant, and insanely durable, Yupo is ideal for menus, posters, banners, tent cards, maps, pamphlets, labels, and point-of-sale materials.

This text treatment, as part of a promotional piece designed by SVP Partners, uses two different sans serif typefaces, but they are different enough to work well together. Suburban, the quirky typeface used for the text, maintains its readability in spite of its small point size and reverse treatment. Courtesy of SVP Partners.

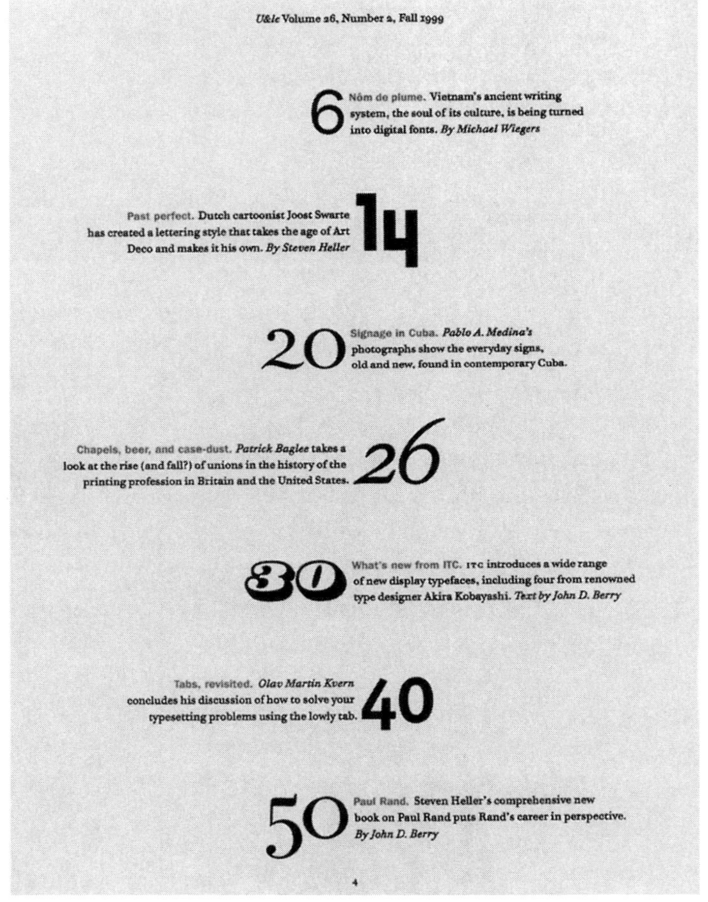

U&lc Volume 26, Number 2, Fall 1999

6 Nôm de plume. Vietnam's ancient writing system, the soul of its culture, is being turned into digital fonts. *By Michael Wiegers*

14 Past perfect. Dutch cartoonist Joost Swarte has created a lettering style that takes the age of Art Deco and makes it his own. *By Steven Heller*

20 Signage in Cuba. *Pablo A. Medina's* photographs show the everyday signs, old and new, found in contemporary Cuba.

26 Chapels, beer, and case-dust. *Patrick Baglee* takes a look at the rise (and fall?) of unions in the history of the printing profession in Britain and the United States.

30 What's new from ITC. ITC introduces a wide range of new display typefaces, including four from renowned type designer Akira Kobayashi. *Text by John D. Berry*

40 Tabs, revisited. *Olav Martin Kvern* concludes his discussion of how to solve your typesetting problems using the lowly tab.

50 Paul Rand. Steven Heller's comprehensive new book on Paul Rand puts Rand's career in perspective. *By John D. Berry*

4

Combine nine different typefaces on one page and get away with it? Mark van Bronkhorst does it and very successfully in this U&lc *table of contents. The different typestyles add visual excitement and interest to an otherwise simple page. Courtesy of Mark van Bronkhorst.*

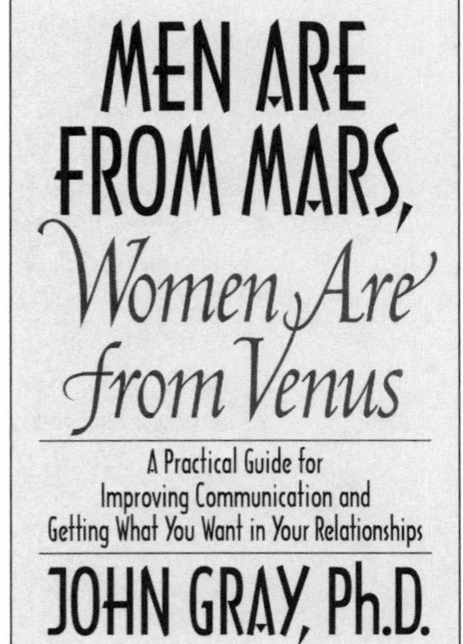

This book cover designed by Andrew M. Newman mixes typefaces in a way that suggests the "gender" differences referred to in their respective titles. Book covers need to get the message across through their look as well as their words. "Men..." is set in Arquitectura and "Women..." is set in Centaur (modified). Courtesy of Andrew M. Newman.

An effective use of width contrast in the two sans typefaces used for this book cover designed by Marty Blake. Setting the wider face, Eagle Bold, in all caps distinguished it even more from its condensed companion, Binner Gothic. Courtesy of Marty Blake.

Marty Blake combines ITC Bodoni Seventy-Two, a historic serif typeface, with Engravers Gothic, as well as using size and case contrast (upper- and lowercase vs. capitals) on this book cover to stimulate a renewed interest in a historical document. Courtesy of Marty Blake.

The dramatic type treatment of the word "HATE" might look hand-lettered, but it actually is a typeface called Carnival. It acts as a kind of typographic illustration in that its powerful appearance evokes the feeling of what it says. Designed by Andrew Newman. Courtesy of Andrew Newman.

Large vs. Small

A good place to change fonts is when type changes size, such as from headline to subhead or text. The distinction will be emphasized that much more.

Wide vs. Narrow (or Regular vs. Condensed)

An expanded headline font above an average-width body text, or a logo split in two using this technique, can create a very powerful contrast.

Cap vs. Lowercase

Another way to get more mileage out of changing fonts is to use all caps for one of the settings, particularly if it is short; but stay away from setting lengthy text in all caps, as it dramatically reduces readability. We read words by their shapes, not by individual letters, and all cap settings eliminate the information (ascenders and descenders) our brains need to read most easily.

The skillful layering of elegant text (Scala Sans and Bickham Script) set upon an oversized logo, both sitting atop gently draped fabric, achieved the upscale feel for this gentleman's fine clothing store. The sophisticated look is meant to play off the sarcastic humor. Designed by Henderson Bromstead Art. Courtesy of Henderson Bromstead Art.

TYPETIP

Type Specimens

One of the challenges of selecting the right typeface is knowing in advance how it will look in its intended use, as well as in print. Printed specimen materials are extremely useful for choosing type, especially those showing a wide range of sizes. They are not as readily available as they used to be—you might have to dig a bit to find them—but they are still invaluable for selecting the right typeface.

Here are some tips to help you make the right choice:

■ Collect as many specimen books, catalogs, brochures, and posters from as many sources as possible. Research web sites, and contact them to ask for sample materials. Many are free but others with large typeface collections are worth purchasing. Don't wait until you need a typeface to start looking for printed samples.

■ Many font foundry web sites offer downloadable PDF specimen showings as a way to save printing costs. Collect as many of these as you can and keep them together. Print them all out and make your own specimen catalog, making a convenient reference that can be easily updated. Separate by text and display and any other categories you find useful.

■ When specimen materials aren't available, or time is of the essence, explore some of the font try-out utilities available on many font web sites. These powerful tools are most useful for viewing larger type sizes. (Text sizes cannot be represented accurately on-screen due to the low resolution of computer monitors.) Many of them enable you to set the text of your choice in any size and type style on-screen. Some even allow you to compare two type styles at a time.

■ Sign up for e-newsletters and other mailings to keep abreast of new releases and pricing specials.

TYPETIP

A Bodoni by Any Other Name...

Bodoni is Bodoni is Bodoni, right? Not necessarily. If there were only one version of Bodoni, perhaps. But, in fact, there is more than one Bodoni, just as there are multiple versions of many other designs. In some cases, one version might have different design details than another; in other instances, only the spacing and proportions might vary. It is critical to be aware of the differences when selecting, specifying, and identifying a font in this category.

Same Name, Different Design

Multiple versions most often occur in revivals of historical typeface designs, such as Garamond, Bodoni, or Caslon. That's because the original designs have been revived by many different type designers and foundries over the years. Each revival offers its own interpretation of the original, which makes them, ultimately, different designs.

A major cause for confusion is that all these different designs may have very similar names. Often, the designer or foundry creating the revival will merely add a prefix or suffix to the name of the original design to distinguish it from its competitors (and, remember, two fonts with exactly the same name installed on your system will cause font conflicts).

Some of the currently available Bodoni versions are ITC Bodoni, Poster Bodoni, E+F Bauer Bodoni, URW Bodoni Antiqua, Monotype Bodoni, Berthold Bodoni Antiqua, and WTC Our Bodoni. These are just a few of the Bodonis now on the market, and they are all different from one another!

Same Design, Different Metrics

A less frequent occurrence (but one with a more complicated explanation) is when two fonts have exactly the same name but space differently or have slightly different proportions.

Here's why: years ago, finished typeface designs were created in analog format–that is, black images on white paper. When the faces were licensed to other foundries, the artwork was provided as photographic prints.

Armed with these prints, each foundry would then "produce" the design for its own equipment. The result could be different spacing, proportions, and even varying designs for the same character. Depending on which foundry produced it, the font might run copy shorter, longer, tighter, more open, or with a varying height for the same point size than another licensed version of the same design.

For the reasons above, you should always note the complete name and manufacturer when purchasing or specifying a typeface. Paying attention to the true identity of your fonts will help you to avoid font-confusion.

Bodoni

Bodoni

Bodoni

Bodoni

Bodoni

Five different Bodonis! From top to bottom: E+F Bauer Bodoni, WTC Our Bodoni, URW Bodoni Antigua, ITC Bodoni Six, and ITC Bodoni Seventy-Two. Despite their similar foundations, each is a distinctive interpretation of an original Bodoni design.

EXERCISE

A Garamond is a Garamond is a Garamond...or is It?

Ilene Strizver, Faculty, School of Visual Arts, New York, New York

Objective

• To become aware of the existence of different versions of a same-named typeface.
• To become aware of the range and scope of these difference.
• To understand the importance of using the complete name of a typeface for identification and specifying purposes.

Background

Historical typefaces, such as Bodoni, Caslon, and Garamond, often have more than one version–sometimes as many as six or more. For instance, some of the available digital versions of Bodoni are ITC Bodoni, Poster Bodoni, EF Bauer Bodoni, URW Bodoni Antiqua, Monotype Bodoni, Berthold Bodoni Antiqua, and WTC Our Bodoni. Different versions of a typeface can very greatly or subtly.

Assignment

Step 1: Research and select three versions of either Garamond, Caslon, or Bodoni.

Step 2: For each version, set a complete character showing, as well as text and display showings at several sizes. Do not alter tracking or kerning.

Step 3: Compare, analyze, and evaluate each of the three versions. Write a 300 to 500 word summary on these differences. Include factors such as the history of each design, its designer and foundry, design philosophy and intentions. Discuss the design traits, proportions, spacing, etc. How are they similar and how do they vary? Include 2 to 3 illustrations with captions.

EXERCISE

Why Are All the Scary Typefaces Pointy?

Christopher Andreola, Adjunct Instructor, Sullivan County Community College, Loch Sheldrake, New York

Objective

Choosing the right typeface for a job can be an overwhelming task. To begin the selection process, it is critical to ask two important questions: what do I want my audience to take away from the design, and what visual means can I use to help do this? Every typeface has a different personality–some shout and others whisper. The challenge is to recognize their personality and make appropriate use of it in your design.

Assignment

Select a typeface whose visual stylistic qualities best demonstrate your rational or emotional understanding of each of the following words:

Patriotic	Sophisticated	Cartoon	Tired
Frightened	Athletic	Foreign	Heroic
Angry	Calm	Friendly	Villain
Shy	Quickly	Technical	Feminine
Joyous	Financial	Weird	Masculine

Process

Step 1: Choose one typeface for each word and set the word in that typeface. You can only use one typeface or type family; no two words can be in the same typeface.

Step 2: For typefaces you have access to on your computer, set the word in caps, lowercase, or mixed case, whichever most effectively captures the chosen word.

Step 3: Set them in a vertical, centered column, between 36 and 48 point, making them all optically the same size (the actual point size might vary).

EXERCISE

Legibility and Readability Study

Peter Bain, Adjunct Faculty, Parsons School of Design, New York, New York
Ilene Strizver, Faculty, School of Visual Arts, New York, New York

Objective

To introduce the effects of point size, leading, and typeface selection in text composition.

Assignment

Select, investigate, and analyze two text settings from actual publications. Replicate the settings in serif and sans serif text typefaces; create alternate versions of those settings by altering the leading and point sizes. Compare the legibility of the different typefaces, and analyze the effects of point size and leading on readability.

Process

Text Selection

Select two publications with at least four pages of continuous text (magazine, book, annual report, etc.). From each of these, identified as A and B below, select one section of text. Using a pica ruler or type gauge, determine the measure or column width of the text type in both. Next, determine the leading or line spacing in both, measuring from baseline to baseline. Indicate the column width and leading in picas and points for both A and B. These two widths will remain the same for the entire assignment.

Typeface Selection

Select either two serif or two sans serif faces. All should be suitable for text. For each typeface, research the year it was released or completed, the typeface designer or punchcutter of that version, and which type foundry or firm issued the type. Make your final choices from what will be available on the computer you will be using.

Text Comparisons

Step 1: You will create text settings with the four typefaces to match formats A and B. Select one paragraph of continuous text of about eight lines. Set the paragraph in all four of the selected typefaces, flush left, rag right alignment; optically match the point sizes in publication samples A and B. Different typefaces appear differently at the same point size, so each typeface might need to be set at a different point size, including half or .5 sizes. Use the column widths and leading that you measured previously. Use fixed values; DO NOT use auto leading. Check your printouts against A and B, examining column widths and line spacing. Place your settings directly on top of the originals, and fold away the white paper margins, to verify that the apparent sizes match. For each variation, indicate the typeface, point size, and leading above the text block.

Step 2: Duplicate these four text blocks five times directly underneath, with some added space, so you have six down. This can be set up on 11 x 17 inch horizontal pages or divided among 8 ½ x 11 inch vertical pages.

Keeping the same column widths from A and B, set each as follows based on the original settings:

Row 1: Text settings from Step 1.
Row 2: Decrease the leading by one point, keeping the point size.
Row 3: Increase the leading by one point, keeping the point size.
Row 4: Increase the leading by two points, keeping the point size.
Row 5: Decrease the point size by one point, keeping the same leading.
Row 6: Increase the point size by one point, keeping the same leading.

You will have created a total of twenty-four settings. What effect does varying the typeface have on legibility? What effects do the changes in leading have on readability? What point sizes look best in the A and B widths? Which typeface in which point size and leading is the most readable? Which is the worst combination of all three and why? Write up your observations.

Tools

Pica ruler or type gauge.

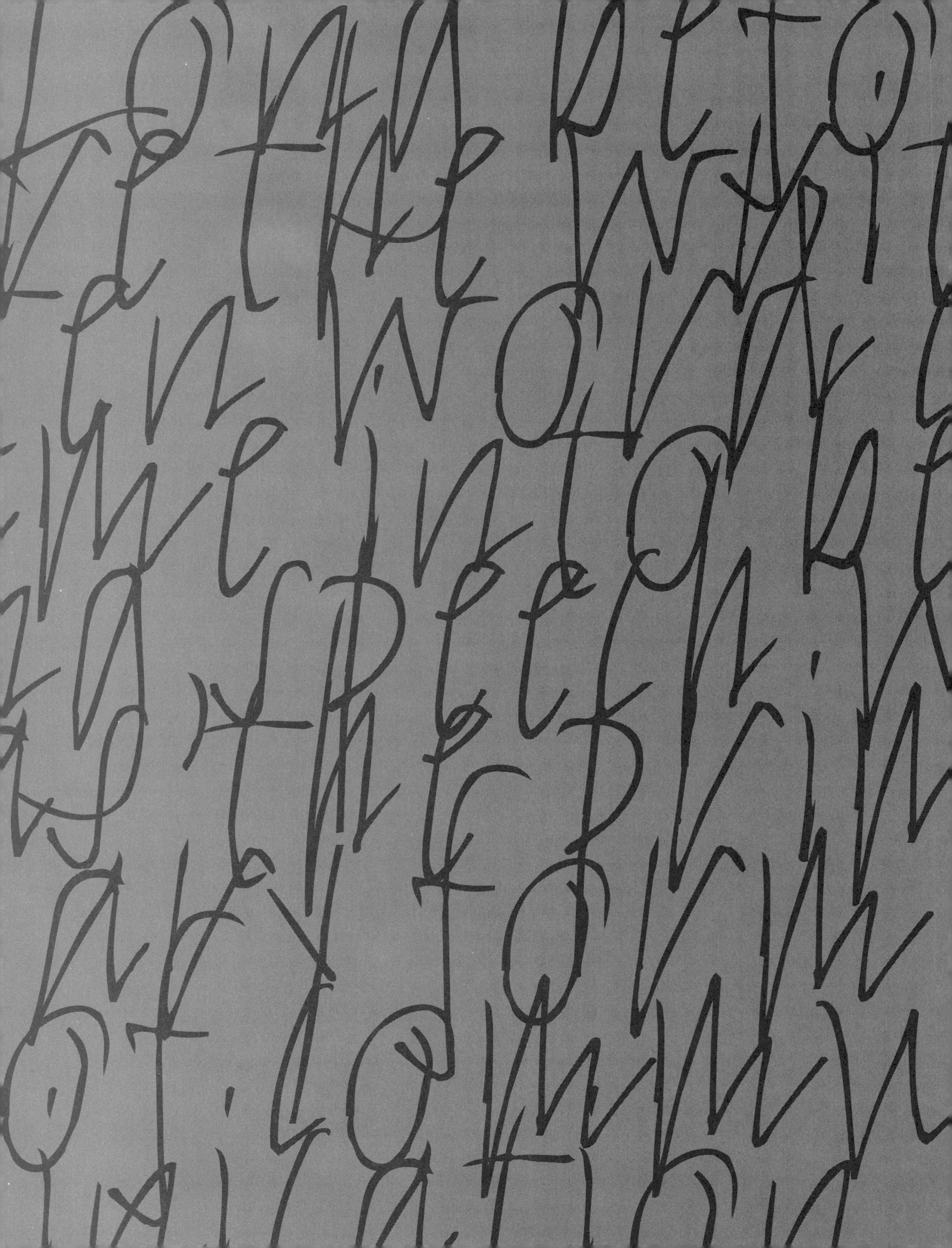

CHAPTER FIVE

BASIC TECHNIQUES FOR EMPHASIS

Before the written word came into being, speech was the primary form of communication. Over the centuries it has evolved into many languages, each with its own individual ability to express hundreds of thoughts and feelings through a unique vocabulary, as well as many nuances of sounds and pronunciation.

When we speak, we communicate our message both verbally and nonverbally. Some of the verbal techniques we use include the tone and inflection of our voice, the volume of our speech in general or of particular words and phrases, the speed at which we speak and say certain words, and as well pauses. Nonverbal communication consists of facial expressions, including movement of the eyes and surrounding muscles, the mouth and lips; the tilt of the head and neck; hand, arm, and shoulder movements; and body posture and total body movement. We often do not realize how much of what we communicate and what we hear and perceive from others is relayed nonverbally.

When communication takes the form of the printed word, none of the above techniques can be directly applied to conveying a message to your audience. In their place, however, there are many typographic techniques that can be used to make up for these missing elements and communicate your message in the most effective way possible. The written word expressed typographically is a rich and wonderful world all its own.

Many of these typographic techniques have evolved over the years, and vary from designer to designer and sometimes from country to country. If you are not familiar with them, use them selectively and sparingly at first until you become more comfortable with them. If you place too many emphasizing techniques in too many places, it will defeat the purpose of making certain elements stand out from the rest and dilute the overall effectiveness of your message, making for a visually busy piece.

ITALICS

The use of italics is probably the most common form of typographic emphasis and is used in both text and display settings. True-drawn italics are an angled typeface most commonly designed as a companion to a roman (straight up and down) design. They are usually a unique and separate design from their roman companion, with differing design features and character widths and often appearing somewhat calligraphic in nature. Obliques are slanted versions of their roman companion with few or no design changes. They are used in much the same way as italics, although they create much less contrast. Some italics designs will stand out more than others from their roman companions, so keep this in mind when choosing a typeface for a job needing a highly contrasting italic.

The millennium is now!
The millennium is now!

True-drawn italics are usually a unique and separate design from their roman companion, with differing design features and character widths and often appearing somewhat calligraphic in nature. ITC Galliard Roman and Italic are a perfect example of this.

The millennium is now!
The millennium is now!

ITC Avant Garde Gothic Medium Oblique is a slanted version of its roman companion with few or no design changes. Obliques are used in much the same way as italics, although they create less contrast.

Italics are most effectively used for soft emphasis of words or phrases within a headline or text–that is, they draw the reader's attention without a significant change in the color of the text. Italics are also used instead of quotations for book and magazine titles and the like. Be sure to use the same weight italic as the roman you are using and not the next weight up; if a double emphasis is desired, you might want to jump two weights to create a more noticeable effect.

Obliques and italics (as well as other font variations) should be accessed from your font menu if possible–and not from your style bar. Some manu-

Avoid italicizing and embolding from your style menu.
Avoid italicizing and embolding from your style menu.
Avoid italicizing and embolding from your style menu.

Avoid italicizing and embolding from your style menu.
Avoid italicizing and embolding from your style menu.
Avoid italicizing and embolding from your style menu.

Italic and bold versions of a typeface should not be accessed through the style bar, only through true-drawn versions of the actual typeface. Computer-generated versions are extremely inferior and should be avoided at all costs. This showing of ITC Stone Serif demonstrates how the computer-generated versions on the top are inferior in design, width, and spacing to the true-drawn originals on the bottom.

facturers link true-drawn italics to their Roman counterparts via the style bar function, but others do not. *(See "Style-Linked Fonts" in chapter 2.)* In these instances, and where italics aren't available, computer-generated italics are created on the fly. These should be avoided at all costs, as this process distorts character shapes in a way that degrades the design and metrics of the typeface and annoys the eye. As mentioned above, true-drawn italics are usually a completely different design, and true-drawn obliques are adjusted for any distortion. Use of computer-generated variants is a sign of an amateur.

BOLDFACE (OR WEIGHT CONTRAST)

The use of boldface, or a bold version of a lighter weight, is a good way to achieve emphasis by way of weight contrast. It is best used for subheads, captions, and stand-alone words and phrases. The use of boldface should be used sparingly within text, and only in particular instances where a strong emphasis is desired, because it creates a somewhat harsh visual interruption in the color. When using a boldface from a family of several weights, it is usually best to jump at least two weights to create a strong enough contrast; a too-small weight contrast at the same point size is at best ineffective and at worst amateurish typography.

Once again, avoid using computer-generated, or "fake," bolding, as it is a poor imitation of a true-drawn version and results in bad weight contrasts and metrics.

Art is worthy of respect
Art is worthy of respect

Art is worthy of respect
Art is worthy of respect

Jump at least two weights to create a strong contrast when using a boldface from a family of several weights. A too-small weight contrast at the same point size is at best ineffective and at worst amateurish typography.

UNDERSCORES

Underscores are a poor typographic method to achieve emphasis and should seldom be used. They are a holdover from typewriter days, when this was the only way to highlight text. Most underscores created in word processing programs (as well as automatic underscores in design programs) cannot be adjusted for weight and position and usually crash through the descenders. If you must use them, create them in design programs with the drawing, pencil, or pen tool so that you can adjust the thickness and the position, remembering to keep them consistent throughout your piece.

There are exceptions to these rules as there are to any rules. Some designers will use underscores as a deliberate design element. In fact, sometimes the underscore

TECHTIP

Underlines in QuarkXPress

QuarkXPress allows you to create custom underline styles with respect to size, color and offset from the text. You can create several underline styles, and even import and export styles. Here is how:
To create custom underline styles or change the default style, go to
• Edit > Underline Styles
To apply custom underline styles, highlight copy and go to
• Styles > Underline Styles
You can import or export styles via the Underline Styles dialog box.

is exaggerated and is extended underneath lines of copy or actually runs through it to achieve a particular look. If this is the effect you are going for, of course go ahead and experiment; but it then becomes part of the style and personality of your design and not a tool for emphasis within text. **NOTE:** The use of an underscore on the Web has an entirely different function, as it usually implies a hyperlink.

POINT SIZE

Varying the point size of your type for emphasis is a technique that should be used very sparingly, particularly within text. It is best reserved for subheads and other stand-alone phrases, and it should not be used within text unless an extreme emphasis is desired as it disturbs the color, texture, and flow of the type.

His knee was
shot. And no one
expected him to play.
Yet when he hobbled onto the court,
the only ones
feeling pain
were the Lakers.

This ad by SVP Partners uses a multitude of type sizes to "help" the reader with the headline and, more importantly, to make a very powerful typographic statement. Courtesy of SVP Partners.

I wish I hadn't cried so much!' said Alice, as she swam about, trying to find her way out. 'I shall be punished for it now, I suppose, by being drowned in my own tears! That **will** be a queer thing, to be sure! However, everything is queer today.'

Changing the point size of words or phrases in text for emphasis is a poor choice; the use of italics or some of the other methods mentioned are usually preferable. (Alice in Wonderland)

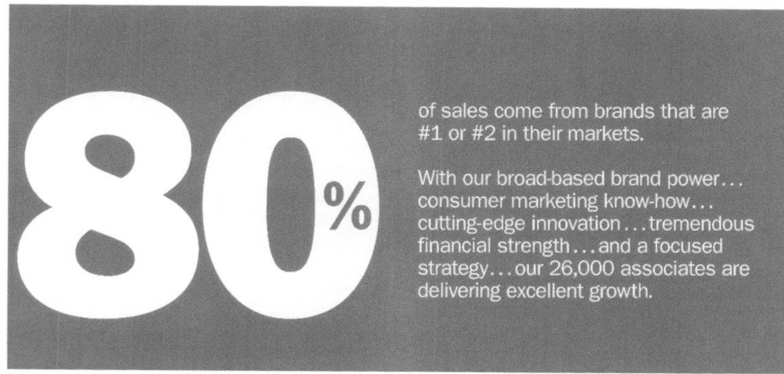

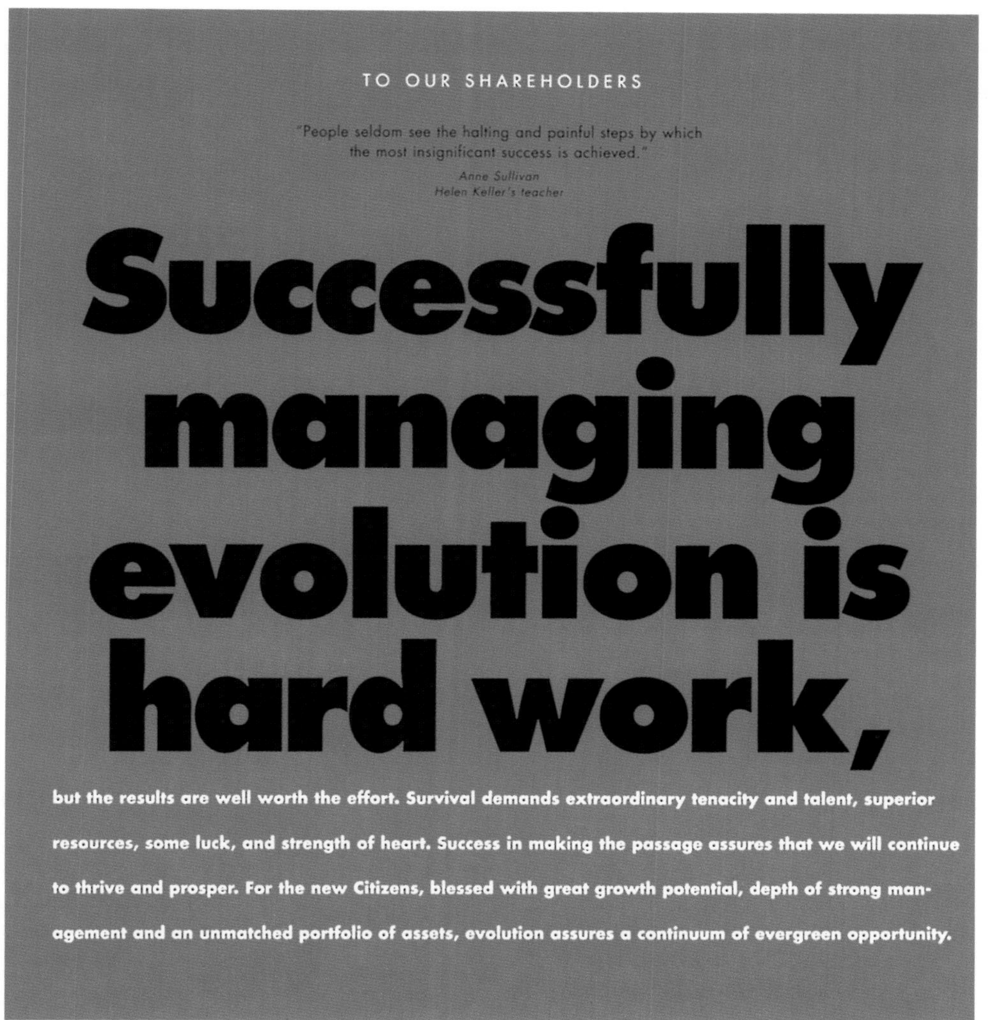

These two pieces, also by SVP Partners, use scale and color to create exciting and effective graphics in a purely typographic environment. The first blows up an important numerical element, balancing the copy to its right. The second makes a headline out of the lead-in to the first sentence, drawing the reader in. Courtesy of SVP Partners.

This poster by Alexander Isley, Inc., effectively organizes and emphasizes many levels of hierarchical information with the use of scale, color, and alignment. Art director: Tara Benyei.

Type within type is how Alexander Isley chose to promote a lecture he was giving. The text is set within hand-drawn letterforms, and certain words and phrases are emphasized through a change in scale. Director, writer, and art director: Alexander Isley. Courtesy of Alexander Isley.

Only two typefaces–Futura Book and Extra Bold–were used to create this energetic, dynamic poster designed by Polite Design. Created entirely from type, this piece uses oversized type to build a layered, architectural structure that anchors the design, as well as a vertical texture created entirely from type that spells out the name of the competition. The blending of these contrasting elements adds depth and complexity to seemingly simple geometric shapes. Courtesy of Polite Design Incorporated.

CAP VS. LOWERCASE

Setting a word or phrase in all capitals (or all caps) for soft emphasis is generally a poor choice, as the jarring change in cap height, while drawing attention to itself, interrupts the text in an aesthetically poor manner. All caps disturb the rhythm and flow of the text. Conversely, if a strong emphasis is desired, as in the case of important call-out words or phrases, all caps can be very useful if utilized sparingly and intentionally, as it creates a very noticeable emphasis. All caps should only be used for very important words or phrases that are discussed or referred to at length in the text. Use with discretion.

A similar but preferable method would be to use small caps if they are available in the font you are using, because they blend in better with the lowercase. *(See chapter 6 for more on small caps.)*

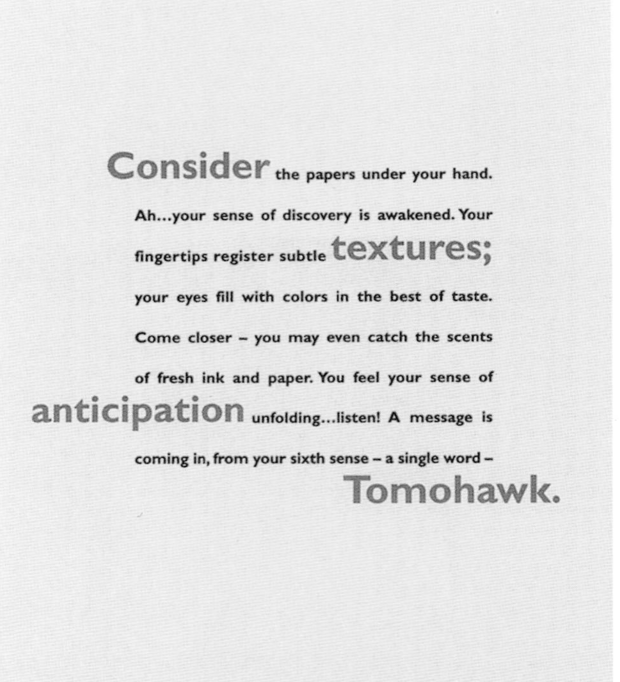

A change of point size, color, and alignment of select words draws the viewer in and through the copy in this piece by Hornall Anderson Design Works, Inc. Courtesy of Hornall Anderson Design Works, Inc.

A very innovative little promotional piece by Doyle Partners uses scale, color, and a layered design to make the U.S. Constitution visually exciting. Courtesy of Doyle Partners.

The word "trapped" in this poster advertising National Runaway Day, designed by Brian Rosenkranz, uses a stark, cold type treatment that is literally entrapped by large, massive geometric shapes. The circular motion of the large arrows surrounding it, the word "trapped," reinforces the futility of the life of a runaway. Courtesy of Brian Rosenkranz.

This dynamic campaign brochure by Michael Vanderbyl Design turns the graceful letterforms of Adobe Trajan into a dramatic, eye-catching graphic statement. Courtesy of Michael Vanderbyl Design.

Romeo, *away, be gone!*
The citizens are up,
and Tybalt slain.
Stand not amazed: the prince
will doom thee death,
If thou art taken: hence,
be gone, away!

Romeo, **away, be gone!**
The citizens are up,
and Tybalt slain.
Stand not amazed: the prince
will doom thee death,
If thou art taken: hence,
be gone, away!

Romeo, AWAY, BE GONE!
The citizens are up,
and Tybalt slain.
Stand not amazed: the prince
will doom thee death,
If thou art taken: hence,
BE GONE, AWAY!

Romeo, AWAY, BE GONE!
The citizens are up,
and Tybalt slain.
Stand not amazed: the prince
will doom thee death,
If thou art taken: hence,
BE GONE, AWAY!

This example demonstrates the use of italics, boldface, all caps, and small caps as techniques for emphasis. Which do you think works best to draw attention to the word in question in a subtle yet effective way? (Romeo and Juliet)

This excerpt from chapter 4 illustrates an appropriate context in which to use a change of typeface, weight, and color for a strong emphasis. When doing this, you might have to adjust point sizes slightly to get the x-heights to match up. In this case, the bold sans words are a half point smaller than the rest of the text.

Oh, *please* mind what you're doing!' cried Alice, jumping up and down in an agony of terror. 'Oh, there goes his *precious* nose'; as an unusually large saucepan flew close by it, and very nearly carried it off.

Oh, please mind what you're doing!' cried Alice, jumping up and down in an agony of terror. 'Oh, there goes his precious nose'; as an unusually large saucepan flew close by it, and very nearly carried it off.

Oh, **please** mind what you're doing!' cried Alice, jumping up and down in an agony of terror. 'Oh, there goes his **precious** nose'; as an unusually large saucepan flew close by it, and very nearly carried it off.

Oh, please mind what you're doing!' cried Alice, jumping up and down in an agony of terror. 'Oh, there goes his precious nose'; as an unusually large saucepan flew close by it, and very nearly carried it off.

Several other techniques for emphasis are illustrated here. The use of italics in the first paragraph is commonly used and is very effective in most instances. The second paragraph uses a condensed version of the typeface and is awkward and barely noticeable when scanned by the reader's eye. The third tries a change of typeface, which creates too strong a change for the context. The last uses a change of color; it is too much emphasis for this purpose, but it can be very effective in other instances, such as the next example. (Alice in Wonderland)

DOs and DON'Ts

Here are some suggestions and points to consider when choosing and using a typeface:

- **Do** start with a few basic typefaces and families.
- **Do** leave white space.
- **Do** consider production issues.
- **Don't** go too big when setting text.
- **Don't** set to fit.
- **Don't** tint type with delicate thins.

DEAD MOON

Working class heroes are hard to find. Dead Moon are the best unsigned band in America, and they're going to stay that way.

by Grant Alden

Money changes everything.

The Northwest is in the grip of a prolonged orgy of fame and imagined fortune. In the quick press of sticky flesh and hot cash, that which we hold most sacred — the music, the passion of inspiration — has been transformed, mutated, mutilated.

Dreams, sex, and the best music happen in the middle of the night, breaking the silence of solitary consciousness by somehow fashioning a fragile filament of shared will, for that long instant sustaining the illusion that we are somehow bound together. This has been replaced by the adoration of the mob, which is far from being the same thing and serves only to reinforce the solitary struggle of being human.

That isolation balances neatly against the pervasive American myth of the rugged individual, the self-sufficient stranger confidently ambling down the middle of a deserted country road: Daniel Boone, Audie Murphy, Jean Claude van Damme. . . the myth becomes difficult to sustain as the continent is paved solid with strip-mall culture. Perhaps that's why the rough-hewn beauty of Dead Moon's music seems such a fragile treasure.

Fred Cole's voice pours into the night like good tequila — thin, high and raw, raspy, pure and piercing, an acquired taste — able to warm your stomach and frost your spine. Toody, his bass-playing bride of 25 years, chips in with harmonies and leads that have more the flavor of dry gin. Drummer Andrew Loomis, a generation younger (the Coles are grandparents, after all), sets up his kit stage center, flanked by amplifiers, a single white candle flickering atop a drum stand while they play.

Every night is a fresh adventure. Even though Fred's been on stage for 27 years, Dead Moon sustain a barely controlled musical chaos even Mudhoney envy. "We've been together six years and we're still so incompetent — all of us, not just me — that none of us feel totally secure with our instruments," Fred says. "Every night we have problems, somebody's fucking up. We never know what to expect, so it's always fresh. I always wonder which night I'm going to be able to play which leads right, and how many I'm going to blow, or which lyrics I can remember, or whatever. And I'm not stoned, I'm totally straight."

Which is among the many reasons Dead Moon have no major label potential. None. Besides, Fred went [illegible] road in the [illegible] Lollipop Shoppe, who came to Portland from Las Vegas broke and called the Weeds, Toody met Fred, and it's a long story. That band released *The Lollipop Shoppe Just Colour* on the now-defunct Universal label, toured with the Doors, and taught Fred to smoke.

"The Weeds left Vegas to go to play San Francisco; we had a gig with the Yardbirds according to this radio station guy who was kind of managing us," Fred says, snaking a cigarette from Toody's pack. "We got to the Fillmore with our equipment and the guys at the door said, 'Who the hell are you?' First thing I see in Haight-Ashbury, we walk into this hotel and here's this dude about 35 years old sitting there with his eyes rolling, stabbing his arm with one of those old fountain pens, trying to find a vein.

"We got out of San Francisco real fast, and were heading for Vancouver, Canada, just in case we had to avoid the draft. Ron, who was in the band, too, was a run-away, we all had all kinds of problems at that point, so we just thought it was going to be better if we got the fuck out of the country. We ran out of money, so we stopped in Portland." They ended up playing the Folksinger, landing a manager and became the Lollipop Shoppe, Universal recording artists.

"We each got a buck a day per diem to eat on," Fred continues. "I'd buy a jar of Vienna sausages, some rye bread and something to drink. But everybody else in the band smoked — and this was when cigarettes were 25 cents a pack — so they would get a pack of cigarettes. I'd say, 'hey, man, there's five of us here, you guys are all getting an extra quarter a day for your fuckin' smokes, and I want my quarter." The only way to get that quarter was to take up smoking.

The Coles (Toody is a life-long Portlander) went on to become two-thirds of Portland's legendary punk band, the Rats. The Rats dissolved when their final drummer, Louie Samora, opted to join the Jackals full-time (Louie appears on several Dead Moon records, but those are simply unreleased Rats tracks Fred retrieved; waste not, want not). Fred played a couple years in a country band called Western Front but, driving back from a holiday in Reno, decided he still had to play rock 'n' roll.

"We came up with the name and the line-up before we'd even talked to Andrew," Toody says. "We were kind of hoping it'd work out."

It had better. A few years back Dead Moon played a benefit for a tattoo artist who lost his shop when Satyricon was fire-bombed, and were paid off [illegible], each of the trio has the band's half-moon logo emblazoned on their skin, though Fred's — on his right cheek — is the most visible. "I have always said that I will never have a tattoo on my body," he explains. "So, I got one on my face. I still refuse to have one on my body, just because everyone else was doing it."

And so Fred and Toody (and Andrew, but he doesn't say much) have stubbornly produced art on their terms. Punks called it the do-it-yourself ethic, but Dead Moon have more in common with a long tradition of untrained painters like Grandma Moses and Rev. Howard Finster; the closest musical analogy is West Virginia's Hasil Adkins, but nobody's ever heard of him, either. The clinical phrase is "naive art," but the Coles are far from naive.

They've had their chances to suckle from the corporate beast. A few years ago somebody from CBS inquired about signing the band, and received an LP and a letter politely explaining that Dead Moon weren't interested, but thanks for asking.

"It's not that I hate major labels," Fred says. "They have this idea that nothing is ever good the way it is, unless it's fucked with. It's how much you can stand to let either the public or the record company eat you up. I went through that number. It destroys you, unless you can play the same game. I take everything in Dead Moon so god damned personally, there's just no way that I could give up what this feels like for any kind of success beyond this. If anybody said we were going to stay the way we are right now unless we made some major changes, I have no problem with staying where I am right now. I love it."

Don't misunderstand: Dead Moon don't subscribe to the punk altruism of, say, Fugazi, who refuse to play a show that isn't all ages and has a ticket price over $5. It is a point of honor with Fred that his band operates frugally and has returned from each visit to Europe with cash in their pocket. "We all take ten marks [about $16] a day per diem," he says. "We take the cheapest van they've got, we stay in the cheapest rooms, the whole thing. So when we get done with the tour, we actually come home with dough, rather than spending it all while we're there. That makes a big difference in your mental outlook as a band. If you don't come back with something to show for it, what the fuck did you do?"

On their last tour British journalist

CONTINUED ON PAGE 36

This powerful editorial spread makes dramatic use of scale and 90 degree angles to capture the reader's attention. The maze-like design leads the eye around the page without becoming too busy. Designed by Art Chantry for the alternative music magazine The Rocket. Courtesy of Art Chantry Design Co.

THE MAJORITY OF AMERICANS TRUSTS WOMEN TO MAKE THEIR

FREEDOM

OWN MORALLY RESPONSIBLE FAMILY PLANNING DECISIONS -

WITHOUT INTERFERENCE FROM THE GOVERNMENT.

1952
Planned Parenthood Federation of America is one of the founding members of the International Planned Parenthood Federation.

1960
The U.S. Food and Drug Administration (FDA) approves the sale of oral steroid pills for contraception.

1965
The U.S. Supreme Court rules that prohibiting the use of birth control by married couples violates a right of marital privacy.

1967
The United Nations proclaims family planning a basic human right and establishes the UN Fund for Population Activities.

As Americans, we are taught to choose freedom, yet the freedom to choose is at risk. Government is choking family planning funding and censoring sex education. Elected officials disregard the views of the pro-choice majority, who believes reproductive choice belongs to a woman, her doctor, and her conscience, not politicians or government. *Roe v. Wade* is a fragile line of defense. Vocal, well-funded, disproportionately powerful anti-choice hardliners hold sway over the debate.

The bold typographic treatment of this spread in a brochure for Planned Parenthood Federation of America derives its power and effectiveness from the word FREEDOM blasted across the spread. Bold text set in Trade Gothic, limited graphics, and powerful copy send a strong, compelling message in this piece by Nesnadny + Schwartz. Courtesy of Nesnadny + Schwartz.

WIDE VS. NARROW

The use of width contrast in related or unrelated typefaces should be avoided as a technique for emphasis in body text, as it creates too much of a contrast and interrupts the flow in a jarring way. On the other hand, it can be used effectively in headlines, subheads, leaders, bylines, and the like to create contrast.

CHANGING TYPESTYLE

The use of a totally different typeface to emphasize words in a text block should be avoided unless a very strong emphasis is desired, as it is much too harsh a change. On the other hand, it can be very effective in subheads, call-out quotes, and the like. Stick to the use of italics or boldface for emphasis within text.

"Flopping" one character gives this otherwise simple logotype for an alternative band a whole new meaning. The word "Breeders" set in Helvetica Condensed now illustrates a gay slang term for a heterosexual. The mildly distressed edges create a grittiness that is a reflection of the music. Courtesy of Art Chantry Design Co.

CHANGING COLOR OR SHADE

Changing the color of type can be used in certain instances to create visual excitement and variety while drawing the eye to certain points. It should not be used in body text unless a very strong emphasis is needed for specific words or definitions that are essential to understanding the content. Changing the percentage of your primary color to a tint can also be used when a softer technique is preferred, as this creates less of a disturbance in the color and the texture of the type. Just be sure that there are no thin strokes that might break up when tinted.

An unusual but successful mix of three contrasting sans serif typefaces (Garage Gothic, Leviathan, and Wilma), combined with simple graphics, suggests spotlights and high wires, all capturing the spirit of the circus in this book cover by Studio Blue. Image from The World Between: The Circus in 20th Century American Art. *Courtesy of Studio Blue.*

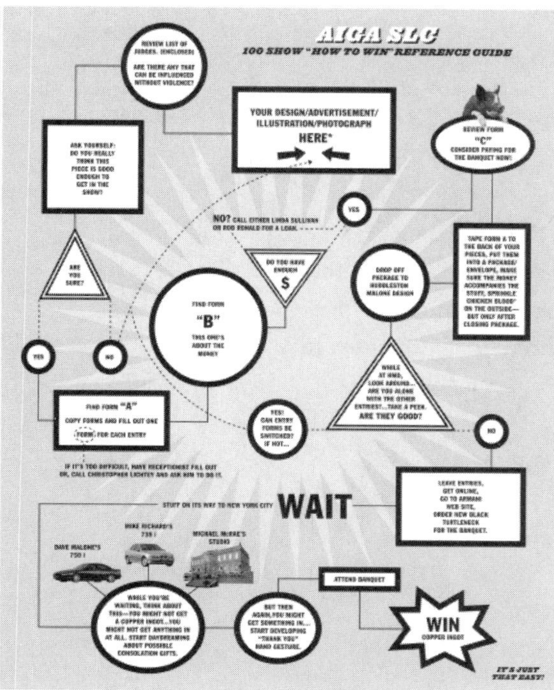

Lots of tidbits of information are cleverly organized in this AIGA Call for Entries by A N D. A campy flow chart utilizing simple geometric shapes and a minimum of typestyles draw the viewer into this fun piece. Courtesy of A N D.

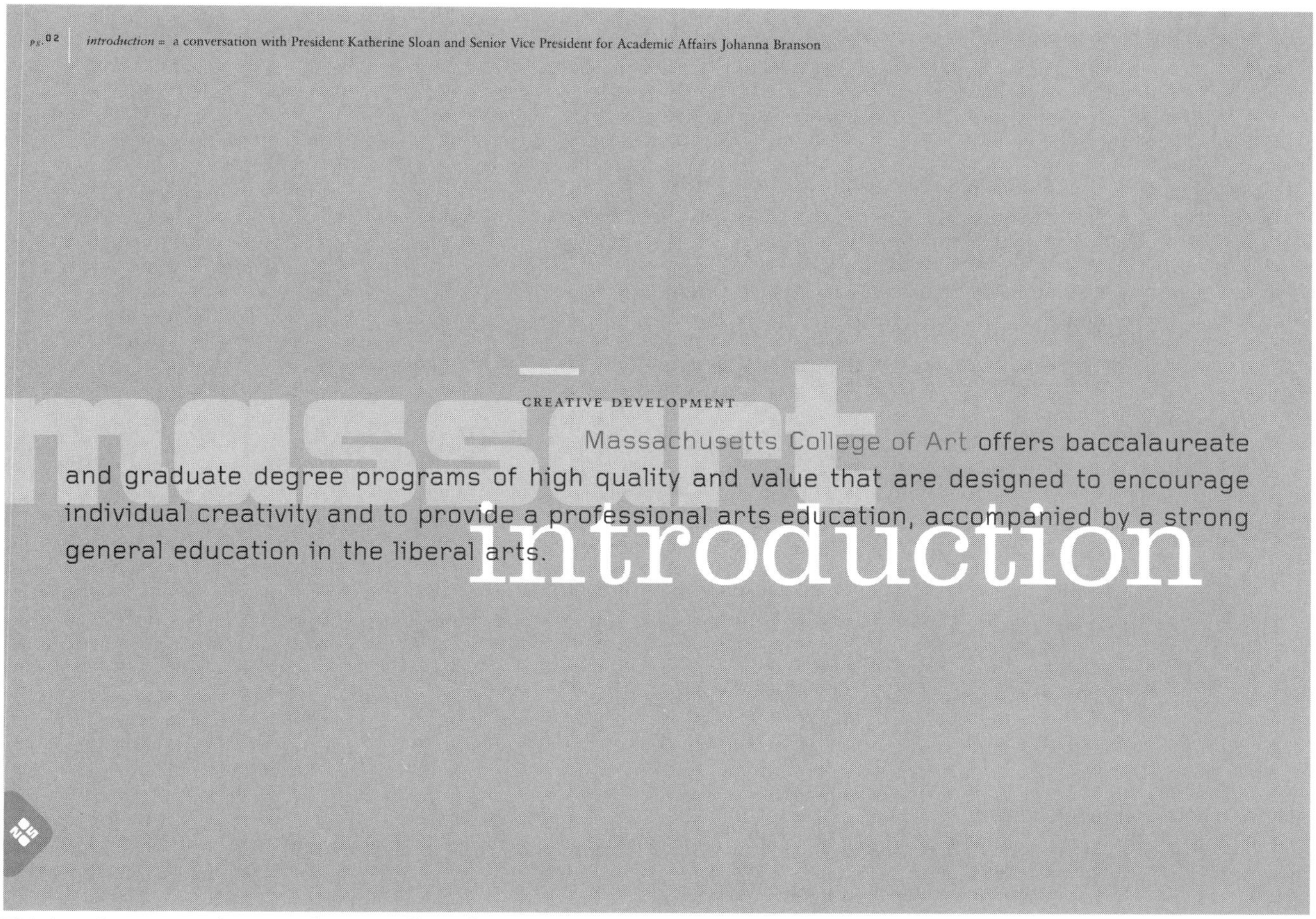

pg. 02 | *introduction* = a conversation with President Katherine Sloan and Senior Vice President for Academic Affairs Johanna Branson

massart

CREATIVE DEVELOPMENT

Massachusetts College of Art offers baccalaureate and graduate degree programs of high quality and value that are designed to encourage individual creativity and to provide a professional arts education, accompanied by a strong general education in the liberal arts.

introduction

This introductory page in Massachusetts College of Art's 2005 viewbook, designed by Stoltze Design, incorporates a blending of four typefaces (ITC Bolt Bold, Clarendon Light, Foundry Gridnik, and Sabon) with asymmetric layering and scale juxtaposition to provide an energy and progressiveness in keeping with the school's spirit. Courtesy of Stoltze Design.

EXERCISE

Typographic Hierarchy Study

Elizabeth Resnick, Professor, Massachusetts College of Art, Boston, Massachusetts

Assignment

Visual hierarchy is the arrangement of elements (in this case, typographic variables) in a predetermined and graduated sequence of importance. In this assignment, you will experiment with visual hierarchy by changing typographic variables in a composition. Using one typeface,* using upper- and lowercase, with the copy given to you,** create three compositions:

Composition 1: Make the letterform the most prominent element.
Composition 2: Make the given text the most prominent element.
Composition 3: Make the title the most prominent element.

Objective

- To learn about the form and proportion of roman letters and how their interaction can foster compositional dynamics and interest.
- To stimulate observation of unique and sometimes subtle differences within typefaces.
- To explore visual hierarchy through typographic variables.

Process

Step 1: Do pencil sketches of various layouts that explore typographic hierarchy and variables as requested above. Once you have a good idea of the sizes you might be working with, word process the copy given to you on your assigned letterform. Set the copy in different point sizes: 10/12.5 and 12/14.5 and different measures (column widths) and other sizes, or reduce or enlarge with photocopies to get the various sizes that you need to experiment with.

Step 2: Set your "letter" in various point sizes and set the title, The Capital Letter... (insert your assigned letter), in various point sizes.

Step 3: Take the various materials and place them on a 14 x 14 inch sheet of bristol board and move the elements around to achieve the three variations you have sketched out previously. Paste with rubber cement or studio tack.

Step 4: Once you have completed your concepts for the three compositions, construct them in the digital environment.

Specifications

- Composition format size is 14 x 14 inches (format may be changing to 8 x 8 inches or 8 ½ x 11 inches for greater adaptability to most printers).
- Black and white only.

Thomas Schorn's three-part solutions to the Typographic Hierarchy Study. Courtesy of Thomas Schorn.

* *Choose one font family to do all three compositions. Suggested typefaces are: Baskerville, Bodoni, Bauer Bodoni, Century, Adobe Garamond, Univers, Frutiger, Interstate, Meta, Scala Sans, Bembo, or Caslon.*

** *Text is assigned from Allan Haley's book* Alphabet: The History, Evolution, and Design of the Letters We Use Today *(New York: Watson-Guptill Publications, 1995).*

EXERCISE

Currency Redesign

Jimmy Moss, Instructor, School of Architecture and Design, Woodbury University, Burbank, California

Objective
To develop facility with typographic hierarchy and initial understanding of typographic systems.

Assignment
Redesign a set of United States paper currency. There are two stages to this project. In the first stage, you will design a single bill, utilizing one typeface, one color, and only two type sizes. In the second stage, you will design a set of three bills, utilizing one typeface, two colors, and three type sizes.

Process
Step 1: Do an analysis of the kinds of typographic information and the relative importance of that information on a one- or five-dollar bill (hierarchy). Take into consideration all of the text on the front of the bill. Next, sketch a variety of layouts that visually emphasize the information you believe to be most important, of secondary importance, of lesser importance, etc.

Pay attention to meaning and clarity in your sketches. Look for opportunities to simplify or to magnify essential elements of your renderings to create a striking currency. Remember, you are only able to use two sizes of one typeface for the first part of the project, so be sure that your sketches reflect this limitation. Your initial sketches may be in colored pencil; however, you will create your bill for presentation in digital form and present it as a hi-res (high resolution), full-color proof.

Step 2: Building on what you have learned about how we read visual information from Step 1, develop a set of three bills ($1, $5, $10). Each bill should have a family resemblance to the other bills in your set, while still easily distinguishable from the others. There should be no confusion as to what is the denomination of each bill. Work toward variety, within a consistent typographic attitude and vernacular.

Specifications
Size: 9.1875 x 3.9375 inches (1.5 times actual).
Color: Step 1: one spot color; step 2: two spot colors.
Options: The use of the portraits is optional. Do not use the decorative illustration, as this is a typographic exercise, rather than an illustration exercise.

These two sets of solutions to the Currency Redesign assignment were done by Amanda Cole and Vincent Akuin, respectively. Courtesy of Amanda Cole and Vincent Akuin.

ore sophistica
ed techniques
exist for the
designer who
chooses to go
eyond the ba
sics, and the
simple, yet rich
and elegant
variations

CHAPTER SIX

ADVANCED TECHNIQUES FOR EMPHASIS

Using italics, boldface, or color changes to create diversity throughout your text is a fine way of emphasizing the point. More sophisticated techniques exist for the designer who chooses to go beyond the basics, and these simple yet rich and elegant variations can bring a whole new flavor to a text-heavy page when used tastefully and effectively.

INITIAL CAPS

An initial cap is an enlarged character, usually the beginning letter of the first sentence of a paragraph, that is set in a decorative or graphic way. It can liven up a page and add typographic interest to an otherwise dull and boring page or section. Initial caps can be a different weight or style of the typeface in use, or they may be from a completely different font. Highly contrasting weights and styles, as well as elaborate, decorative, calligraphic, or ornate type styles in contrasting colors and tints are often used and can work well.

Proper alignment on all sides is key to using initials tastefully and professionally. If the initial cap is meant to appear flush left, align it optically rather than mechanically. Certain characters, such as rounds and diagonals, as well as characters with serifs that get proportionally larger with size, will need to be pulled out a bit to appear visually aligned and balanced. **NOTE:** You will have more flexibility if you put the initial in a separate text box from the rest of the word so that you can manipulate it independently. The Initial Cap option in most programs won't allow you to make fine adjustments.

peterson ARCHitects

This logo by MendeDesign was created in Mrs. Eaves roman and small caps. ARCH is rendered in small caps to emphasize the structural components of the letterforms and architecture itself. Courtesy of MendeDesign.

The following are some of the more common styles of initial caps:

Drop Cap

When a character begins at (or aligns with) and drops below the first line of text, it is referred to as a drop cap. Drop caps usually optically align (different from mechanical alignment) with the cap height of the first line, and should base-align with a line of type below. Dropping into an odd number of lines is most tasteful and pleasing; go at least three lines deep.

Body copy can be wrapped around the initial if the character is large and uncomplicated enough to keep it visually clean. To help the initial read as part of the first word, you can tuck in the remaining characters of the word closer to the initial, even if it extends out of the text margin.

Message *from* ITC

IN OCTOBER, ITC WENT TO England & France. In London, we hosted a launch party at the St. Bride Printing Library for an ambitious new type family, ITC Founder's Caslon – a direct revival by Justin Howes of William Caslon's type designs from the 18th century. In Lyon, we participated in the 1998 conference of the Association Typographique Internationale (ATypI), typography's premier international gathering of professional practitioners.

In England we were celebrating the first typeface family to bring the quirks & subtleties of Caslon's distinct & various type sizes into the digital realm. In France we were celebrating the myriad ways in which typography can be approached, in distinct languages and cultures, in a variety of unpredictable technologies, and in the quirks & subtleties of the people who make up the typographic world.

– Mark Batty, President

Mark van Bronkhorst goes to exciting extremes with this colorful drop cap (dropped capital), which creates a strong vertical element in a very horizontal message in U&lc. Notice the small caps leading into the body of the text. Courtesy of Mark van Bronkhorst.

Once more she found herself in the long hall, and close to the little glass table. 'Now, I'll manage better this time,' she said to herself, and began by taking the little golden key, and unlocking the door that led into the garden.

To help a drop-cap initial read as part of the first word, tuck in the remaining characters of the word closer to the initial even if it extends out of the text indent's left margin. (Alice in Wonderland)

First came ten soldiers carrying clubs; these were all shaped like the three gardeners, oblong and flat, with their hands and feet at the corners: next the ten courtiers; these were ornamented all over with diamonds, and walked two and two, as the soldiers did.

This drop cap aligns with the cap height of the first line and base-aligns with the third line of type. The serifs overhang the left margin so the stem of the character aligns with the text below. (Alice in Wonderland)

Raised Cap (also called *stick-up* cap)

A raised cap is one that base-aligns with the first line of type and rises above the body copy. It is much less complicated to do tastefully than a drop cap. If the raised cap is the first letter of a word (as opposed to a single letter word such as *A* or *I*), make sure you space the rest of the word close enough to the initial to read as a word. When the rest of the word seems to be floating away from the cap, the type can look very amateurish, not to mention hard to read.

She had not gone much farther before she came in sight of the house of the March Hare: she thought it must be the right house, because the chimneys were shaped like ears and the roof was thatched with fur. It was so large a house, that she did not like to go nearer till she had nibbled some more of the lefthand bit of mushroom, and raised herself to about two feet high: even then she walked up towards it rather timidly, saying to herself. 'Suppose it should be raving mad after all! I almost wish I'd gone to see the Hatter instead!'

Body copy can be contoured or wrapped around an initial if the character is large and uncomplicated enough to keep it visually clean. (Alice in Wonderland)

First came ten soldiers carrying clubs; these were all shaped like the three gardeners, oblong and flat, with their hands and feet at the corners: next the ten courtiers; these were ornamented all over with diamonds, and walked two and two, as the soldiers did.

This raised cap base-aligns with the first line of type and rises above the body copy. If the initial is the first letter of a word as opposed to a single-letter word, tuck in the remaining letters close enough so that it reads as a word. (Alice in Wonderland)

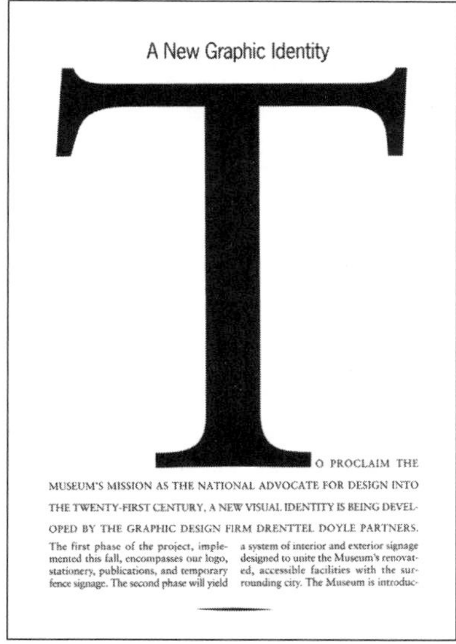

A New Graphic Identity

TO PROCLAIM THE MUSEUM'S MISSION AS THE NATIONAL ADVOCATE FOR DESIGN INTO THE TWENTY-FIRST CENTURY, A NEW VISUAL IDENTITY IS BEING DEVELOPED BY THE GRAPHIC DESIGN FIRM DRENTTEL DOYLE PARTNERS.

The first phase of the project, implemented this fall, encompasses our logo, stationery, publications, and temporary fence signage. The second phase will yield a system of interior and exterior signage designed to unite the Museum's renovated, accessible facilities with the surrounding city. The Museum is introduc-

A dramatic raised cap (raised capital) sits atop the opening paragraph, denoting an important announcement in this piece designed by Doyle Partners. Courtesy of Doyle Partners.

Decorative Initials

Sometimes a very unusual, elaborate, or ornate initial is appropriate and can do a lot to enhance a design, especially if color is an option as well. Some fonts are designed primarily for this purpose. In addition, some very interesting and unusual initials are available not as fonts but as .eps (Encapsulated PostScript) picture files. They are worth looking into, especially if your job is text-based with few or no illustrations or photos, and needs livening up. A typeface with elaborate swashes or calligraphic forms can also add grace and visual interest to an otherwise dull design, as long as the letterform is appropriate to the content.

“I ought to have been specially careful on a Friday,” she used to say afterwards to her husband, while perhaps Nana was on the other side of her, holding her hand.

A graceful and elaborate script initial such as this one set in ITC Edwardian Script designed by Ed Benguiat makes a very dramatic statement. The opening quotes are set smaller than the initial and are kerned and positioned so they don't float in the margin. (Alice in Wonderland)

This decorative initial is part of an initial font that comes with ITC Kendo. (Alice in Wonderland)

Boxed, Reverse, and Overlapped Initials

There are other techniques to add visual interest and originality to initial characters. The initial can be contained within an outlined box, and tints or colors can be added if desired. Or you can set the initial in reverse, dropping it out of a box of black or any solid color. Another approach is to make a rather large initial a light tint of black, or a color, and insert it partially behind the body copy. Just remember that whatever you do, readability should never be sacrificed. Your imagination is the limit to what you can do with initial characters; just remember to keep them tasteful and appropriate to the content and the rest of the design.

aLICE was beginning to get very tired of sitting by her sister on the bank, and of having nothing to do: once or twice she had peeped into the book her sister was reading, but it had no pictures or conversations in it, 'and what is the use of a book,' thought Alice 'without pictures or conversation?'

A lowercase letter can be used as an initial as well as a cap. Using small caps can be a very effective way to lead into the rest of the text. (Alice in Wonderland)

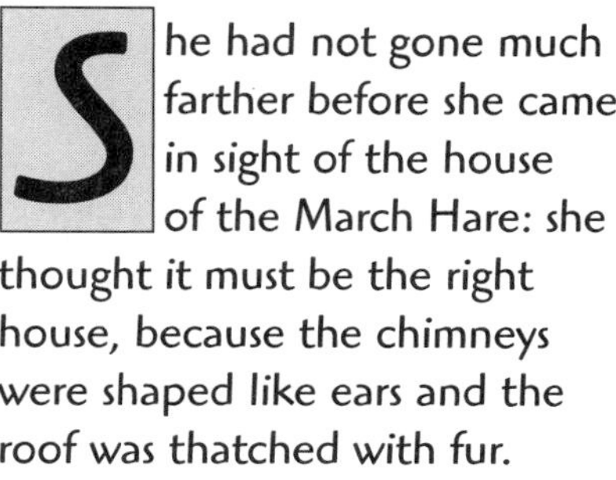
She had not gone much farther before she came in sight of the house of the March Hare: she thought it must be the right house, because the chimneys were shaped like ears and the roof was thatched with fur.

Initials can be placed in outlined, tinted boxes... (Alice in Wonderland)

She had not gone much farther before she came in sight of the house of the March Hare: she thought it must be the right house, because the chimneys were shaped like ears and the roof was thatched with fur.

...or tinted and positioned behind text. Your imagination is the limit as long as the initials are tasteful and don't impair readability.

Things to keep in mind when using initial letters:

- Small caps can be very effective when used for the first few words or the phrase after an initial letter and add additional emphasis and visual appeal.
- A lowercase character can be used as an initial letter as well as a cap (artistic license allowed here!).
- Never repeat the enlarged initial in the text unless its size, style, and position make it difficult for the eye to connect with the rest of the word.

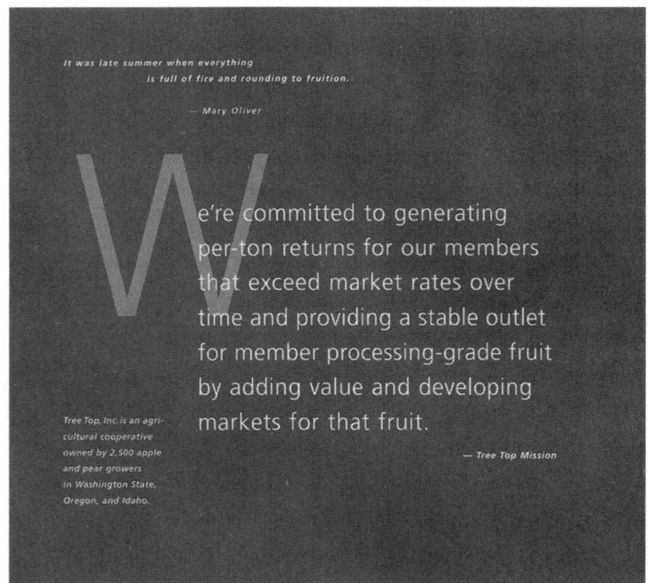

This layered initial adds color, dimension, and graphic interest to this annual report designed by Hornall Anderson Design Works, Inc. Courtesy of Hornall Anderson Design Works, Inc.

This stately initial is layered between the text and other colorful typographic elements to bring a restrained excitement to a U.S. Amendment in this piece designed by Doyle Partners. Courtesy of Doyle Partners.

55

MEAT dishes do not play as important a role on the Italian table as they do in other cuisines, particularly the American and British. They appear as the *secondo,* "second course," of the Italian meal, preceded by the *antipasto,* if there is one, then by the *primo,* or "first course" of pasta, rice, or soup. Meat is used imaginatively with other ingredients in various courses, or it is served in small portions after a sizable carbohydrate-centered first course. ❁ Most important in the category of meat *antipasti* are *salumi,* air- and salt-cured or spiced and precooked hams, *salame,* and such. *Salumi* are prepared differently in the various regions. For example, a *prosciutto* produced in Friuli has a different flavor, texture, and look than one from Emilia or Tuscany; a *capocollo* from Calabria differs also from one produced, for example, in Apulia. Once sliced, *salumi* are called *affettati,* which essentially means "cold cuts," and they are by far the most common form of *antipasto* on the Italian table. Some sausages are eaten fresh and others are dried, which intensifies their flavor. A more thorough discussion of the various *affettati* is included in chapter 1. ❁ Probably the most prized of the *affettati* is *prosciutto crudo,* which is becoming increasingly popular in America. With its popularity, however, has come a great deal of misunderstanding about the best ways to serve and to eat it. It's a shame to do anything more to the finest *prosciutto* than to eat it raw, sliced paper-thin (although not so thin that it falls apart), accompanied perhaps only by *grissini,* Italian breadsticks (see chapter 7 for Palio's Rosemary and Sage Breadsticks). Despite the practice that persists of serving *prosciutto crudo* with figs or melon, it is best eaten on its own without sweet distractions. The tradition of eating *prosciutto* with fruit and confections came about in past times when hams were salted excessively in order to preserve them, and sweet tastes were necessary to foil the saltiness. ❁ The bone is seldom removed in Italian *prosciutti,* because it keeps the ham moist and gives it flavor. In contrast, *prosciutti* that are exported to America are boned for the convenience of being able to slice them by machine. But skillful cutting with a knife results in slices that Italian culinary expert Massimo Alberini describes as more "aggressive" and "compact" in flavor. The thickness of the slice affects the taste. Cooking this fine ham destroys

57
INSALATA DI PETTO DI POLLO
ALLA GRIGLIA
grilled chicken breast salad

59
INVOLTINI DI POLLO
stuffed chicken breasts

60
CIMA ALLA GENOVESE
stuffed breast of veal,
Genoese style

63
VITELLO TONNATO
poached veal with tuna sauce

64
SPIEDINI DI AGNELLO
CON LIMONE
skewered grilled lamb with
lemon zest

66
INSALATA DI MANZO
beef salad

67
CROSTINI DI FEGATO
ALLA TOSCANA
toasts with chicken liver spread

Not just an initial cap but an initial word is used to set off chapter title pages in this exquisite cookbook, entitled Antipasti, *designed by Aufuldish & Warinner. The rustic caps, which were designed by George Deaver based on Charlemagne, relate to the authentic nature of the recipes. Decorative borders and ornamental paragraph separators break up the dense, justified text. Courtesy of Aufuldish & Warinner.*

SMALL CAPS

Small caps are capital letterforms (or uppercase characters) that are smaller than cap height. When created for a text face, they are usually, and most properly, the height of the lowercase (or a tiny bit taller), which usually varies from 60 to 70 percent of cap height. Small caps created for a display face have more flexibility in their design and are often taller than the x-height. True-drawn small caps are superior to computer-generated small caps (which are created by using a Small Caps option in your page-layout program or manually reducing the full caps), as they are drawn to match the weight, color, and proportion of the caps, as well as to optically match the height of the lowercase. Computer-generated small caps are just reduced caps and therefore look too light and often too narrow. If true-drawn small caps are not available for the typeface you are using and you are intent on using them, sometimes generating them from a heavier weight of the typeface you are using will more closely match the color of the full caps and lowercase.

The end THE end

The end THE end

THE end THE end

True-drawn small caps (left) are superior to computer-generated small caps (right) in that they are drawn to match the weight, color, and proportion of the caps. Computer-generated small caps are just reduced caps and therefore look too light and often too narrow, as you can see in this comparison.

THE AMERICAN LAWYER

The even color and texture of this logo designed by Gerard Huerta is the result of perfectly balanced caps and small caps as well as precise kerning. Courtesy of Gerard Huerta.

True-drawn small caps are only available for certain typefaces from selected font manufacturers and foundries. They are sometimes available with the primary font at no extra cost or sold separately, sometimes as part of an expert set. Each manufacturer has a different keyboard layout for small caps. The most user-friendly layout is the one in which the small caps are in the lowercase positions, with the caps and all other characters remaining in their normal position. This makes it easy to change a group of words or text to a small-cap font without disturbing any initial caps, punctuation, signs, or symbols. Other character layouts (such as Expert Sets) often require additional steps.

Many OpenType fonts come with true-drawn small caps built into the font. If you are using an application that supports access to these additional characters (more and more do all the time), they are very easy to access, and do not require loading or selecting a separate font.

Small caps are very useful when the look of all caps is desirable, but with a more refined approach. They are often used in publishing for title pages and page headings, but they are also used in headlines, subheads, column headings, and very often as lead-ins for an opening paragraph, usually after an initial cap. Try them instead of all caps for two- or three-letter abbreviations, such as states, times (a.m. and p.m.), acronyms, etc. They stand out nicely without disturbing the color of lowercase text as much as all-cap settings do, and they take up less space.

These typefaces are available with true-drawn small caps. Some also have both oldstyle and lining figures, making them very useful and versatile additions to your library. All the small caps except those for ITC Braganza are designed to match the font's x-height. Braganza is a very elegant, calligraphic design with tall ascenders and descenders (translate: small x-height), and the small caps are designed to complement the caps rather than match the lowercase.

Bodega Sans

abcdefghijklmnopqrstuvwxyz

ABCDEFGHIJKLMNOPQRSTUVWXYZ

ABCDEFGHIJKLMNOPQRSTUVWXYZ

12345678901234567890!@#$£%?&*()"";:',.

TRUE DRAWN SMALL CAPS are only available for certain typefaces from selected font manufacturers and foundries, but they are worth the effort to track down.

ITC Braganza

abcdefghijklmnopqrstuvwxyz

ABCDEFGHIJKLMNOPQRSTUVWXYZ

ABCDEFGHIJKLMNOPQRSTUVWXYZ

1234567890!@#$£%?&*()"";:',.

TRUE-DRAWN SMALL CAPS are only available for certain typefaces from selected font manufacturers and foundries, but they are worth the effort to track down.

Matrix

abcdefghijklmnopqrstuvwxyz

ABCDEFGHIJKLMNOPQRSTUVWXYZ

ABCDEFGHIJKLMNOPQRSTUVWXYZ

1234567890!@#$£%?&*()"";',.

TRUE DRAWN SMALL CAPS are only available for certain typefaces from selected font manufacturers and foundries, but they are worth the effort to track down.

Centaur

abcdefghijklmnopqrstuvwxyz

ABCDEFGHIJKLMNOPQRSTUVWXYZ

ABCDEFGHIJKLMNOPQRSTUVWXYZ

12345678901234567890!@#$£%?&*()"";',.

TRUE DRAWN SMALL CAPS are only available for certain typefaces from selected font manufacturers and foundries, but they are worth the effort to track down.

ITC Highlander

abcdefghijklmnopqrstuvwxyz

ABCDEFGHIJKLMNOPQRSTUVWXYZ

ABCDEFGHIJKLMNOPQRSTUVWXYZ

1234567890!@#$£%?&*()"";',.

TRUE DRAWN SMALL CAPS are only available for certain typefaces from selected font manufacturers and foundries, but they are worth the effort to track down.

ITC Johnston

abcdefghijklmnopqrstuvwxyz

ABCDEFGHIJKLMNOPQRSTUVWXYZ

ABCDEFGHIJKLMNOPQRSTUVWXYZ

1234567890 1234567890!@#$£%?&*()"";',.

TRUE DRAWN SMALL CAPS are only available for certain typefaces from selected font manufacturers and foundries, but they are worth the effort to track down.

OLDSTYLE FIGURES

Oldstyle figures (also known as lowercase figures) are a style of numeral that approximate lowercase letterforms by having an x-height as well as varying ascenders and descenders. They are considerably different from the lining (also known as "aligning" and "uppercase") figures you are probably used to that are all-cap height and usually monospaced so that they line up vertically on charts.

Oldstyle figures are very useful and often quite beautiful, particularly when set within text, as they blend in smoothly, not disturbing the color of the body copy as much as lining figures do (a problem with all-cap settings as well). Consider using them in headlines, as they don't jump out as much as lining figures. In fact, many people prefer them for just about every use except charts and tables.

Oldstyle figures, which are more old-fashioned and traditional in nature, are only available for certain typefaces; sometimes as the regular numerals for the font but more often within a supplementary or expert font. Many of the new OpenType fonts contain both lining and oldstyle figures–sometimes in both monospaced as well as proportional spaced versions–making four styles of numerals available to the designer. This might seem confusing at first; but once you understand and appreciate the usefulness of each one,

1234567890

1234567890

Lining (or aligning) figures imitate caps in that they all align on the baseline and the cap height. The oldstyle figures below them approximate lowercase letterforms by having an x-height, as well as varying ascenders and descenders.

The management team from IBM left their office in NY at 11:30 A.M. and arrived at the meeting in NJ at 1 P.M.

The management team from IBM left their office in ny at 11:30 A.M. and arrived at the meeting in NJ at 1 P.M.

Small caps can be substituted for caps when a more subtle look is desired, such as for two- or three-letter abbreviations, states, times (a.m. and p.m.), companies, etc. They stand out nicely without disturbing the color of lowercase text as much as all-cap settings do, and they take up less space. They look particularly good when used with oldstyle figures.

At seven, he gave a concert in Warsaw. At 17 he made his Paris debut. And in 1906, at 19 he made his first American appearance in Philadelphia.

At seven, he gave a concert in Warsaw. At 17 he made his Paris debut. And in 1906, at 19 he made his first American appearance in Philadelphia.

Oldstyle figures work well in text as they blend in beautifully by not disturbing the color of the body copy as much as lining figures do.

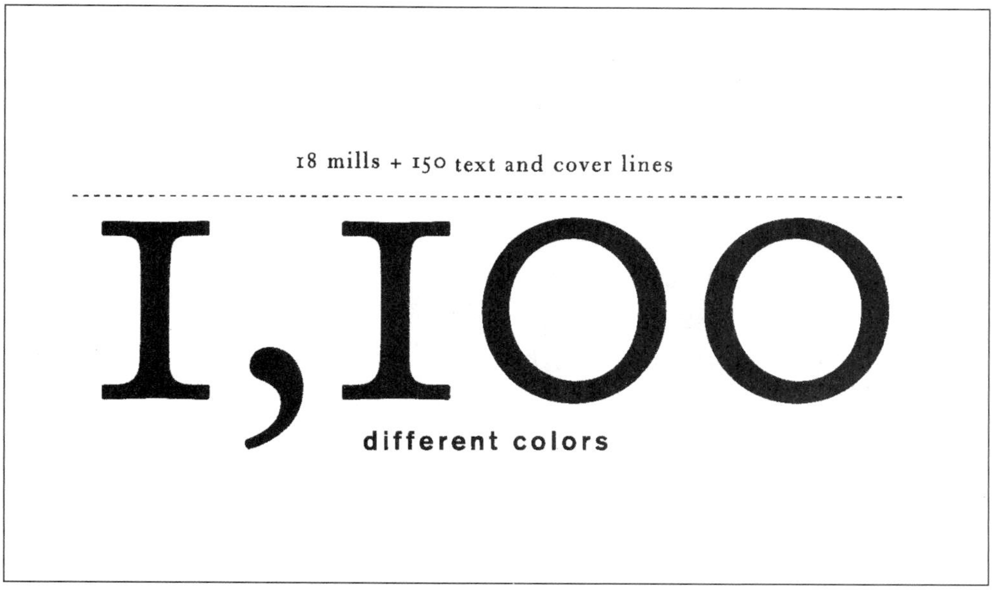

18 mills + 150 text and cover lines

1,100

different colors

A small amount of information is made visually interesting and eye-catching with the use of oldstyle figures and a simple, yet bold, design in this promotion piece designed by VSA Partners, Inc. Courtesy of VSA Partners.

you won't want to go back to only once choice of numeral. It's well worth the extra effort to track down and obtain oldstyle fonts; the fonts that contain them might well become some of your favorite. *(See Typetip, "Proportional vs. Tabular Figures," in chapter 8.)*

INDENTS

An indent is the space inserted before the first word of a new paragraph. It is a graphic technique used to create a visual separation of thoughts in text. It should be neither too small nor too deep, but proportional to the size of your type as well as the width of the column. The indent is occasionally omitted in the first paragraph, as there really is no need to separate the beginning of the text from anything, but this is more a matter of style than correctness.

There are several other kinds of indent styles you can try, as it can be a creative way to add style and visual excitement to an otherwise dull page.

First Line Indent

This is when just the first line of a paragraph is indented. It is the most common kind of indent but not the only kind. When making traditional indents, set your tabs manually according to what looks good to you; don't rely on the default tabs of your software to dictate style and taste.

Extreme Indent

You will occasionally see the first two or three lines being indented, sometimes to a depth of half the column width. This can be a classy and interesting look when used tastefully and appropriately. It looks best when used for large amounts of text.

Hanging Indent (Outdent)

This is actually the opposite of an indent in that the first line hangs out to the left of the paragraph into the margin. This can look great, but keep in mind that it reduces the amount of copy that can fit in a fixed area.

Oh! If people knew what a comfort to horses a light hand is, and how it keeps a good mouth and a good temper, they surely would not chuck, and drag, and pull at the rein as they often do.

Our mouths are so tender that where they have not been spoiled or hardened with bad or ignorant treatment, they feel the slightest movement of the driver's hand, and we know in an instant what is required of us.

My mouth has never been spoiled, and I believe that was why the mistress preferred me to Ginger, although her paces were certainly quite as good.

First line indents are the most common style of indents. Notice that an indent is omitted in the first sentence of the first paragraph as there really is no need to separate the beginning of the text from anything. (Black Beauty)

Oh! If people knew what a comfort to horses a light hand is, and how it keeps a good mouth and a good temper, they surely would not chuck, and drag, and pull at the rein as they often do.

Our mouths are so tender that where they have not been spoiled or hardened with bad or ignorant treatment, they feel the slightest movement of the driver's hand, and we know in an instant what is required of us.

My mouth has never been spoiled, and I believe that was why the mistress preferred me to Ginger, although her paces were certainly quite as good.

An interesting look is achieved with an extreme indent where the first two or three lines are indented, sometimes to a depth of half the column width. This can be a classy and interesting look when used tastefully and appropriately.

Dingbats

A dingbat or any decorative or graphic element (as long as it is simple) can be used to separate paragraphs. This can be done two ways: The paragraphs can run into each other with the dingbat the only separating element, or it can be used in place of a space indent where paragraphs begin on a new line.

Line Space Instead of Indent

The technique of separating paragraphs with an extra line space instead of an indent is often used in correspondence as well as long blocks of text. It adds white space and a more open look when saving space is not a consideration.

Oh! If people knew what a comfort to horses a light hand is,
and how it keeps a good mouth and a good temper,
they surely would not chuck, and drag, and pull at
the rein as they often do.
Our mouths are so tender that where they have not been
spoiled or hardened with bad or ignorant treatment,
hey feel the slightest movement of the driver's hand,
and we know in an instant what is required of us.
My mouth has never been spoiled, and I believe that was why
the mistress preferred me to Ginger, although her
paces were certainly quite as good.

A hanging indent, or outdent, is actually the opposite of an indent in that the first line hangs out of the left of the paragraph into the margin.

A dingbat or any decorative or graphic element can be used to separate paragraphs. In this example the paragraphs run into each other with only a color dingbat separating the paragraphs. Dingbats can also be used in place of a line space between paragraphs.

Oh! If people knew what a comfort to horses a light hand is, and how it keeps a good mouth and a good temper, they surely would not chuck, and drag, and pull at the rein as they often do. Our mouths are so tender that where they have not been spoiled or hardened with bad or ignorant treatment, they feel the slightest movement of the driver's hand, and we know in an instant what is required of us. My mouth has never been spoiled, and I believe that was why the mistress preferred me to Ginger, although her paces were certainly quite as good.

LIGATURES

A ligature is a special character made from connecting or combining two characters into one. In the case of discretionary ligatures, such as *ck, st, rt,* etc., they are designed to add elegance and refinement to a setting and are used at your *discretion.* In other cases, it is created to improve the fit of two characters that crash into each other. The most commonly used ligatures are the *f*-ligatures, including *fi, fl,* and sometimes *ff, ffi,* and *ffl* (the last three are available in supplementary or expert fonts, as well as within many OpenType fonts).

Æ Œ æ œ ct
fi fl ff ffi ffl

A ligature is a special character made by connecting or combining two characters into one. The most commonly used ligatures are the f-ligatures, including fi, fl, and sometimes ff, ffi, and ffl.

Your grandmother had the sweetest temper of any horse I ever knew, and I think you have never seen me kick or bite. I hope you will grow up gentle and good, and never learn bad ways; do your work with a good will, lift your feet up well when you trot, and never bite or kick even in play.

ITC Dyadis, designed by Yvonne Deidrich, contains specially designed ligature letters purely as design elements. They create a very lovely, unique look in text. (Black Beauty)

find office affluent actor
find office affluent actor
office affluent

The first two lines show the difference between how words look without and with ligatures. If you have ligatures turned on in your application, be careful with ffi or ffl letter combinations where the second and third letters are replaced with the fi or fl ligature as illustrated on the third line; they often look bad when combined with a single f preceding them. If there are no triple f-ligatures available in the font (there usually aren't), use all nonligatured characters. ***NOTE:*** *QuarkXPress allows you to turn on ligatures but also to turn them off for ffi and ffl.*

Since *f*-ligatures almost always look better than their nonconnected relatives, make sure to turn them on in the preferences of your application. A word of caution: if you have ligatures turned on, be careful about *ffi* or *ffl* combos where the last two letters are replaced with the *fi* or *fl* ligature; they often look bad when combined with the single character. In these instances, it is often preferable to use the nonligatured characters. Some software allows you to select a preference setting that automatically turns off the use of ligatures for these triple combinations.

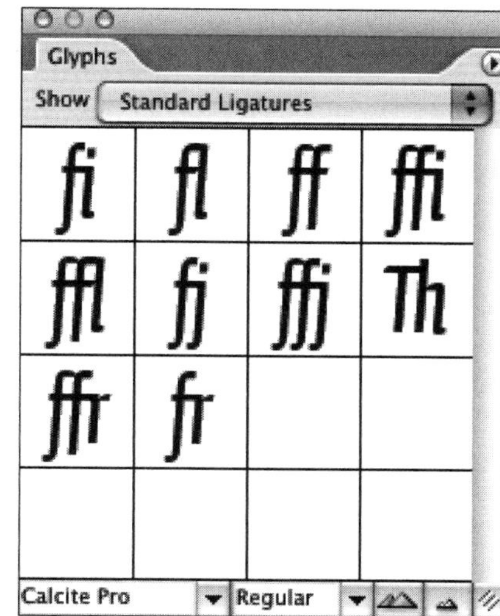

Shown above are the standard ligatures available in Calcite Pro. All but the fi and fl ligature are accessible only when using applications that support OpenType's extended character compliment.

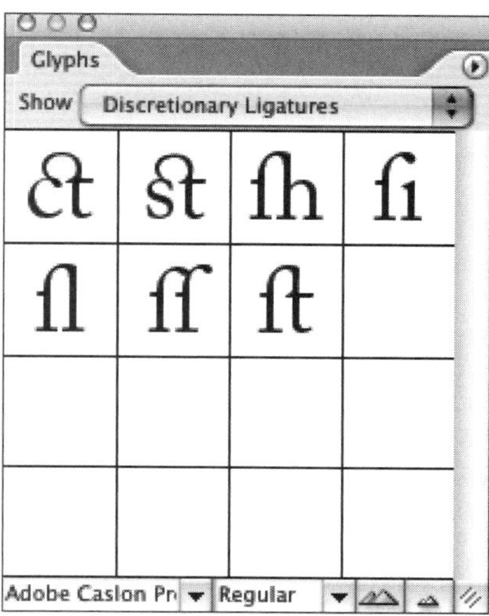

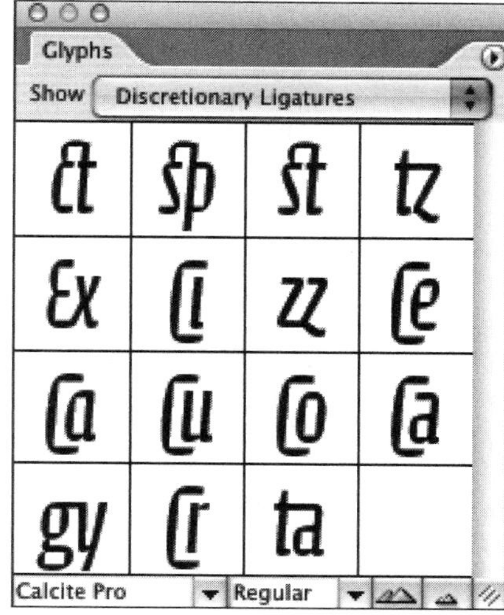

Discretionary ligatures are available in Caslon Pro and Calcite Pro, both OpenType fonts.

TECHTIP

Ligatures in QuarkXPress

A handy new feature in QuarkXPress is the ability to turn ligatures on and off, on the fly on an individual basis. They can still be turned on and off globally in Preferences and in the Character Attributes dialog box, but for more individual control, try this:

- Highlight the text or the individual characters in question.
- Select the Text palette from the pop-up (click on the A) menu off the Measurements Tool Bar.
- Select or deselect ligatures on the extreme right.

SWASH CHARACTERS

These are extremely decorative characters that have a flourish or extended stroke at the beginning or the end of the character. They are often available in addition to the regular characters, either as a secondary font, alternate characters buried within a font, or included in an OpenType font. Swash characters should be used sparingly and thoughtfully. When used this way, they can add an air of elegance or importance to a headline. They are also wonderful when used as initials.

There is one thing to avoid like the plague–that is using swash characters in all-cap settings. They are almost impossible to read when set one next to the other, and they were never intended to be used this way. Unfortunately, many a type novice will think they are pretty and set an invitation, menu, or flyer this way. Just don't do it; it is the surest sign of an amateur.

Rain

The rain is falling all around,
It falls on field and tree,
It rains on the umbrellas here,
And on the ships at sea.

These graceful swash characters enhance the appearance of this poem set in ITC Bodoni Seventy-Two.

YOU ARE CORDIALLY INVITED

Avoid using swash characters in all-cap settings. They are almost impossible to read when set one next to the other, and they are not intended for this kind of setting.

ALTERNATE CHARACTERS

An alternate character is a separate and distinct version of the character in the regular position. An alternate can be available within a font (especially OpenType fonts, which have room for thousands of characters) or as part of an expert or a supplementary font. The difference between regular and alternate characters can be as subtle as a slightly longer descender or a slightly raised crossbar or as obvious as the separate design of a one-story g to compliment a two-storied "regular" character.

A *contextual* alternate is one that is intended for use in certain situations (or circumstances), such as next to specific characters. Contextual alternates are very common in OpenType fonts, which not only have room for them but have the built-in intelligence to know when to apply them when that setting is turned on by the user.

TAWNY
TAWNY
PAWN
PAWN

House Industries went to town creating dozens of contextual alternates for Ed Interlock, a typeface based on an original Ed Benguiat design. These two words look fine without contextual alternates, but turning that feature on (below in both cases) automatically converts the wide crossbar A to one with a better fit, which happens to be a different design in each case.

Bickham
Bickham

Adobe Bickham Pro looks great without the use of any alternates; but when the contextual alternate option is turned on in an application supporting this font's OpenType features, the result is a more dramatic and lyrical version of the same word.

Alice was not a bit hurt, and she jumped up on to her feet in a moment: she looked up, but it was all dark; before her was another long passage, and the White Rabbit was still in sight, hurrying down it.

There was not a moment to be lost: away went Alice like the wind, and was just in time to hear it say, as it turned a corner, 'Oh my ears and whiskers, how late it's getting!' She was close behind when she turned the corner, but the Rabbit was no longer to be seen: she found herself in a long, low hall, which was lit up by a row of lamps hanging from the roof.

ITC Highlander Pro, designed by Dave Farey, contains several variations of each weight, including one with tall ascenders and descenders as well as others with alternate letterforms including swash and initial letters.

TECHTIP

Glyph Palettes

Both Adobe InDesign and the most recent version of QuarkXPress have glyph palettes, which allow you to view everything (including foreign language characters, accents, currency symbols as well as ligatures and alternates) contained within a font. The glyph palette, which is viewable at different sizes, also allows you to select, replace, or insert characters with the click of the mouse–no more confusing keyboard combinations! The glyph palette is particularly useful for viewing OpenType fonts, which can have thousands of characters.

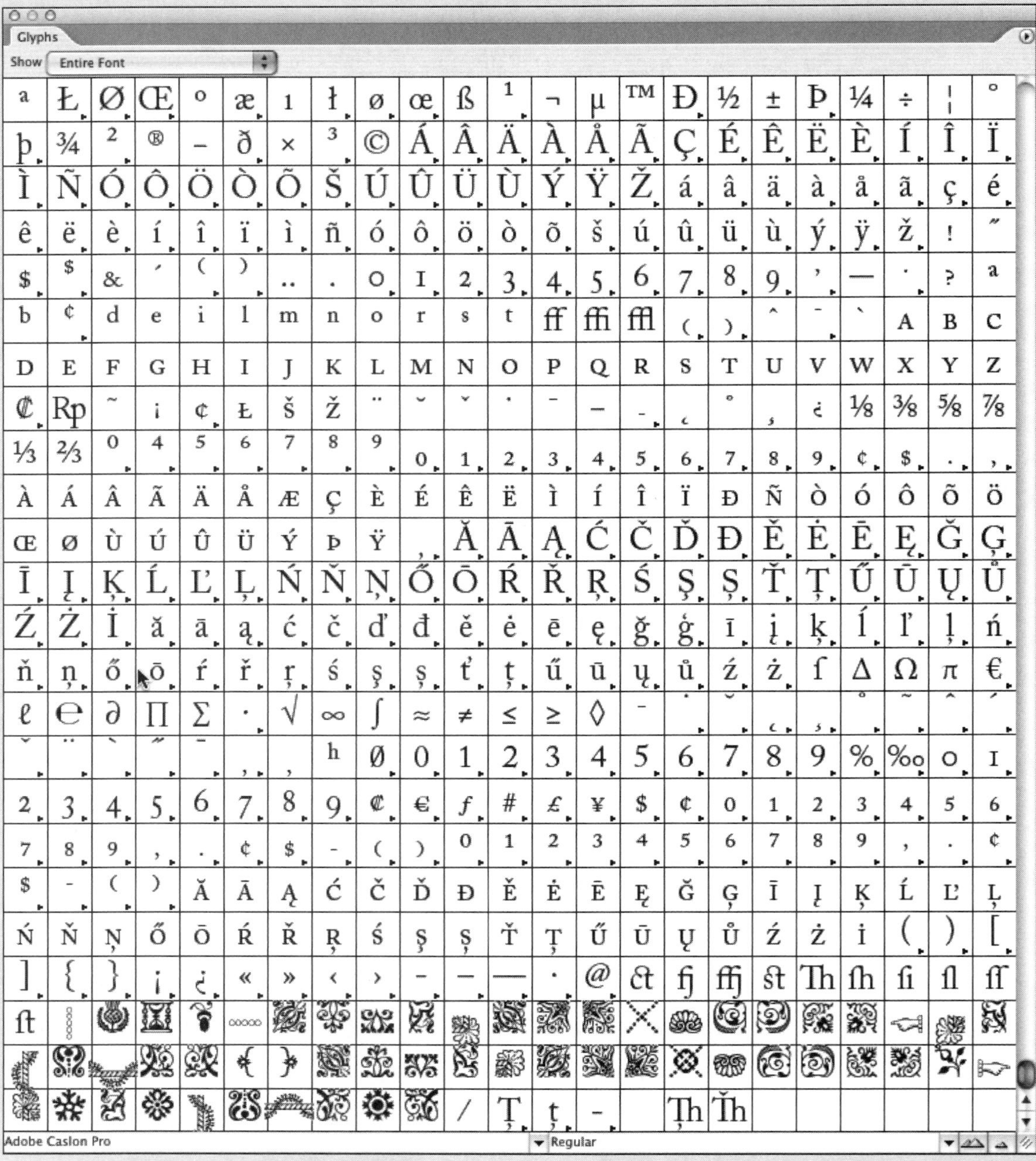

Adobe InDesign's glyph palette shows the complete character compliment for Caslon Pro, an Adobe OpenType font. A tiny black triangle in the lower right corner of a box indicates there are variants of that character; clicking on it reveals another palette showing those characters.

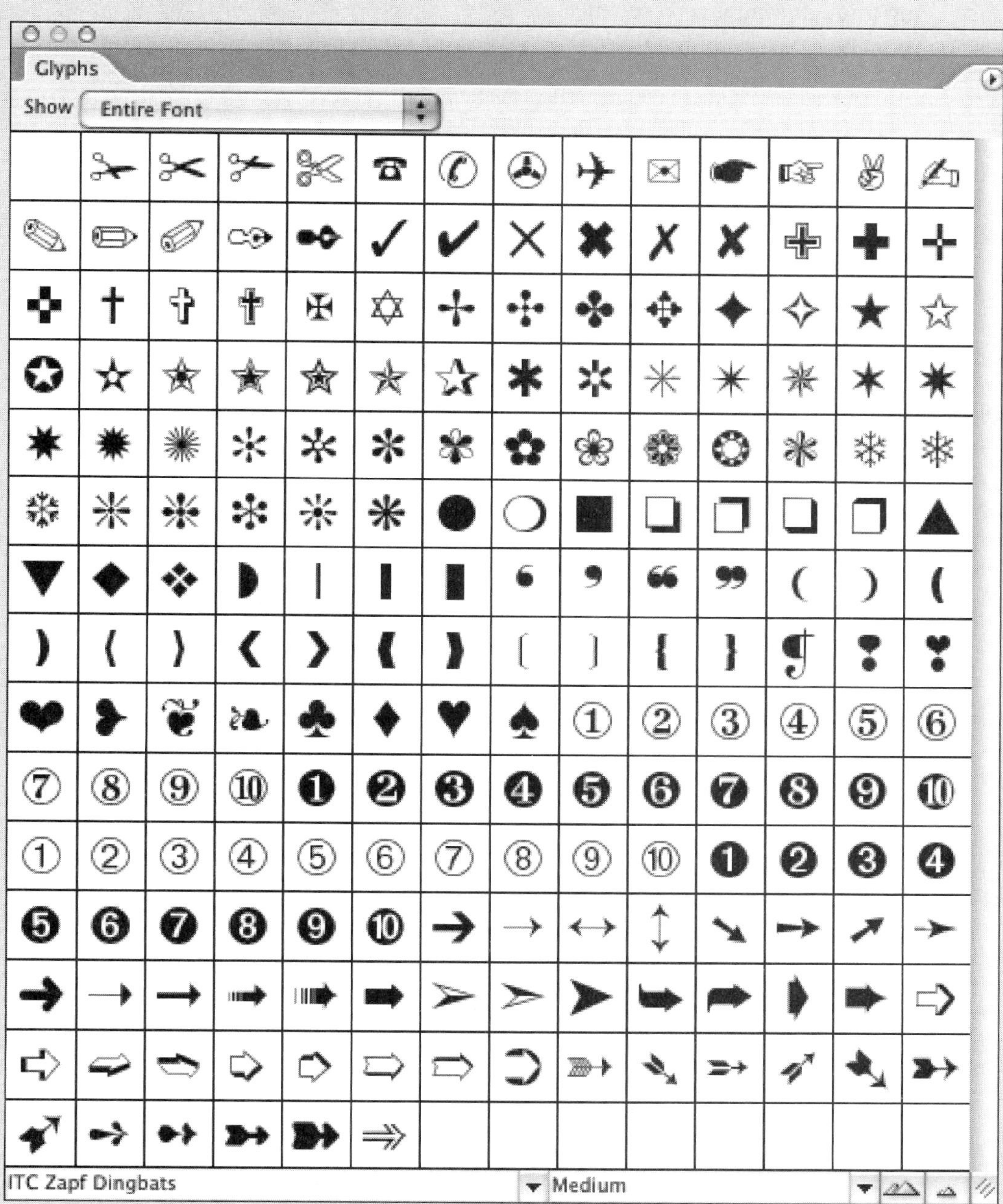

The glyph palette is extremely useful for image fonts, such as ITC Zapf Dingbats, shown above.

EXERCISE

Expressive Typography

Stephanie Nace, Assistant Professor, University of South Carolina, Columbia, South Carolina

Assignment

Using a 4 x 4 inch accordion format, explore the technique of visual storytelling through timing and sequencing of type. Depict a poem or song lyric of your choice using different fonts, sizes, and color to create typographic textures and/or images. The key here is to think about what words sounds like and what pauses look like.

Objective

- To understand the use of timing and sequence in visual storytelling.
- To explore type forms.
- To consider storytelling in a visual context.
- To experiment with typefaces, styles, and sizes.
- Use expressive and interesting typography.

Deliverables

- Weekly sketches and storyboards.
- Final accordion-folded book.

Process

Step 1: Pick a song lyric or poem that has many expressive, descriptive, and action words in it.

Step 2: Sketch and/or storyboard the sequence of the words and/or letters. It will be key to think about pacing and how your viewer will read your book. Your accordion panel book may turn 90 degrees at any time, or it may run vertically or horizontally.

Step 3: Once you have finalized your design concept, convert to digital format.
NOTE: Both front and back paper choices are up to the designer.

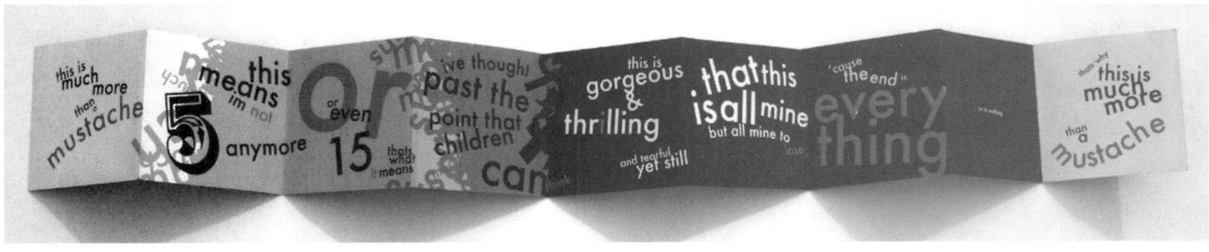

Creative solutions to the Expressive Typography assignment by Kari Taylor, Ferris Ivester Joye, and Daniel Machado. Courtesy of Kari Taylor, Ferris Ivester Joye, and Danial Machado.

It is like pre
aring a won
erful recipe,
you can just
hrow in gre
ients togeth
randomly an
live with w
at you get, o
you can mea

CHAPTER SEVEN

BASIC FINE-TUNING AND TWEAKING

Becoming typography savvy is like learning to see in a new way. Details in the typography of ads, magazines, book covers, movie titles, and credits, or even bus and subway posters, are progressively more apparent to the eye. And details are key. You should never be comfortable with your type until all the details are fine-tuned and tweaked to perfection.

Setting type needs human intervention. A computer cannot evaluate and make decisions related to good taste, typographic appropriateness, and readability. Using the default settings of your design software or your font without fine-tuning the type, that is, looking it over carefully and making changes and adjustments, can lead to a very unprofessional look and also can make it difficult to read.

Prior to the current trend of having "a computer in every home" (or close to it), which has given virtually everyone the ability to set type, type was set by highly trained typographers who spent years learning the art and craft of good typography. They had very sophisticated, expensive equipment capable of performing complicated tasks on the fly. Desktop computer technology has come a long way in the last decade and is able to perform just about all the tasks that were done by typographers. But a computer can't do it on its own. It requires a human being to tell it what to do and how to do it. The computer is just a tool, and it still needs a skilled operator to bring out the best of what it can produce. It is like preparing a wonderful recipe; you can just throw ingredients together randomly and live with what you get, or you can measure, taste, and adjust until you have just the right balance and the result tastes great and excites your taste buds!

TYPE SIZE

Deciding what size to set your type is a very visual thing, but there are some guidelines that can help you make that decision.

Let's talk about text settings first. The primary consideration when setting text is usually readability. Assuming you select a font that was designed and intended for smaller settings, the average range for text settings is somewhere between 9 point and 12 point and sometimes up to 14 point. Anything smaller becomes hard to read in longer settings. Much larger than 12 to 14 point, it becomes a strain on the eyes for any length of copy.

The size you select is somewhat dependent on the typeface design, as the actual cap sizes and x-heights vary from font to font. The x-height of a font affects its readability and will make different typefaces look larger or smaller at the same point size. The length of the text should also be considered, as well as any constraints on the column width, such as a preexisting grid, for reasons mentioned below in "Line Length" and "Line Spacing."

Display, or headline, type is primarily meant to catch the eye and draw the reader into the text. For this reason, there are fewer, if any, constraints on size. Whatever works with your layout is probably fine, meaning, try different sizes and see what looks best and what balances and complements the rest of your layout.

HoHo

The size you select is somewhat dependent on the typeface design, as the actual cap and x-height vary from font to font. The x-height of a font affects its readability, and will make different typefaces look larger or smaller at the same point size.

The size you select is somewhat dependent on the typeface design, as the actual cap and x-height vary from font to font. The x-height of a font affects its readability, and will make different typefaces look larger or smaller at the same point size.

Both text blocks, ITC Golden Type and Caxton respectively, are set in 12 point but look very different due to their varying x-heights.

A throng of
bearded men,
in sad-co-
loured gar-
ments and
grey steeple-
crowned hats,
inter-mixed
with women,
some wear-
ing hoods,
and others
bareheaded,
was assem-
bled in front
of a wooden
edifice.

A very short line length can lead to too many hyphenations, making the text difficult to read. (Scarlet Letter)

A throng of bearded men, in sad-coloured garments
and grey steeple-crowned hats, inter-mixed with
women, some wearing hoods, and others bareheaded,
was assembled in front of a wooden edifice, the door
of which was heavily timbered with oak, and studded
with iron spikes.

This line length is comfortable to read and has no hyphenations.

A throng of bearded men, in sad-coloured garments and grey steeple-crowned hats,
inter-mixed with women, some wearing hoods, and others bareheaded, was assembled
in front of a wooden edifice, the door of which was heavily timbered with oak, and
studded with iron spikes.

A long line length for any length of copy also becomes cumbersome to read, as our eyes struggle to find the beginning of the next line.

LINE LENGTH

Line length and point size are interrelated, as line length should be somewhat determined by the point size for maximum readability: the larger the point size, the longer the line length. We read and identify words by the shapes of the letters, not letter by letter; we also read by groups of words. If the line length is too short, there will be too many hyphenated words. These interfere with readability and force the reader to jump to new lines so often that it affects reading comprehension. On the other hand, line lengths that are too long can create confusion by making it more difficult for the eye to find the beginning of the next line in large blocks of text. A general guide is to have in the neighborhood of 50 to 70 characters per line, but there are many exceptions to this rule.

LINE SPACING (LEADING)

Line spacing refers to the vertical space between lines of type from baseline to baseline, and it is usually measured in points (except in most word processing programs, which offer a limited choice of single, one-and-a-half, or double spacing). It is also referred to as leading, which is a term from the days when type was set in metal, and slugs of lead in varying thicknesses were inserted between the lines of metal type to add space between the lines. Too-tight leading makes type harder to read, especially in small sizes. You almost cannot add too much leading, but it depends on the amount of copy and your layout. Most design programs have a default setting, called auto leading, which is around 20 percent of the point size. Although you can usually override this in your preferences settings, this is a good place to start. You can then manually make adjustments to suit your taste and work with your layout. Most applications have keyboard shortcuts to do this on the fly.

A very basic guideline for text would be a minimum of 2 points leading (such as 12/14, or 12 point type with 14 point leading) up to 5 points. Display type can have less leading in general, since as type gets larger the negative spaces associated with line spacing (and letter spacing) appear progressively too large. When setting all caps, throw these rules out the window; all caps can be set with little or no leading (also referred to as set solid) and often look best with negative leading. Without descending characters to worry about, all caps beg to be set tighter than mixed case settings.

Line spacing, to a certain degree, has been trend-related in the last few decades. When phototypesetting was first introduced in the 1970s, letter

TECHTIP

Auto Leading

Auto leading is a feature that allows your design software to automatically assign a leading value to the text you set, based on its point size. Most design software programs use a default auto leading setting of 120 percent of the point size. (This value can be changed by the user, as can most default values.) In many cases, the use of auto leading results in a fractional value. For example, for 10 point type, the auto leading might be a nice, even 12 point; but for 11 point type, it becomes 13.2; for 12, it is 14.4; and for 14, it is 16.8. Most current design programs indicate the actual auto-leading value, usually in parentheses; others don't show it at all.

Pros and Cons

Auto leading can be a real convenience when working with text type. By using auto leading, you can change text sizes as many times as you like and the leading will adjust proportionally and automatically. This is a real time-saver when you are unsure of your final point size and want the freedom to experiment.

On the other hand, auto leading does have its pitfalls; follow these guidelines to know when to *use it* and when to *lose it:*

- When you are combining type, symbols, or dingbats of different point sizes on the same line, auto leading can wreak havoc with the line spacing in a text block, making one line jump to adjust to the larger glyph. To avoid this sometimes unexpected and usually unwanted occurrence, be sure to use a fixed leading. (Now you know why lines of type can mysteriously "jump" when you add a differently sized element to a block of copy!)
- Converting auto leading to a fixed value also ensures that the leading won't change if the document is opened on another computer with different default settings.
- While auto leading can facilitate the setting of body text, it is not as useful for display type. Display (or headline) type in larger sizes needs a lot less leading than text *(see illustrations)*. This is especially true with all-cap settings that have no descenders to fill in the space between the lines. For display type, auto-leading settings will generally be way off the mark. Use your eye, not your software, to make larger type settings visually appropriate.

FUNDAMENTAL SINCERITY

IS THE ONLY PROPER BASIS FOR

FORMING RELATIONSHIPS

FUNDAMENTAL SINCERITY
IS THE ONLY PROPER BASIS FOR
FORMING RELATIONSHIPS

All caps can be set with little or no leading (also referred to as set solid) and sometimes negative leading, depending on the look you are after. The top example of Mekanik is set with auto leading (about 36/43) and is much too open. The example below it is set with negative leading (36/30) and looks much better.

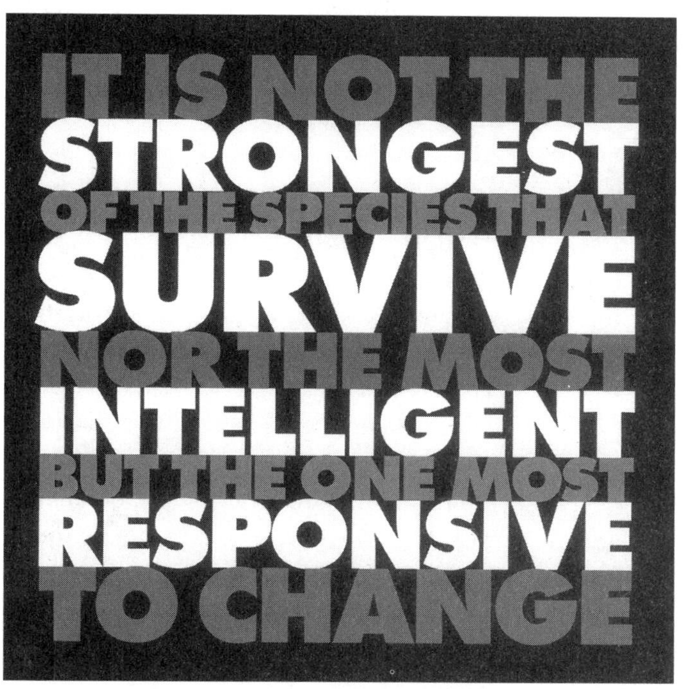

Stacked caps can be a very powerful design technique, as in this annual report designed by SVP Partners. The lines have been sized so that the letter spacing isn't compromised. Courtesy of SVP Partners.

But, though the bank was almost always with him, and though the coach (in a confused way, like the presence of pain under an opiate) was always with him, there was another current of impression that never ceased to run, all through the night. He was on his way to dig someone out of a grave.

But, though the bank was almost always with him, and though the coach (in a confused way, like the presence of pain under an opiate) was always with him, there was another current of impression that never ceased to run, all through the night. He was on his way to dig someone out of a grave.

But, though the bank was almost always with him, and though the coach (in a confused way, like the presence of pain under an opiate) was always with him, there was another current of impression that never ceased to run, all through the night. He was on his way to dig someone out of a grave.

The top setting of Expo Sans is set solid (12/12) and can be hard on the eyes for any length of copy. The middle text is set at auto leading, which is about 20 percent more than the point size, or about 14.4 point; it is comfortable to read, even for lengthy amounts of copy. The bottom text is set at 12/18. It has a nice, open look, and is often used in magazines, annual reports, and brochures. (A Tale of Two Cities)

and line spacing had more flexibility than ever before. As a result, designers deliberately set type very tight as a rebellion from the not-so-distant days of hot-metal type when this was not possible. Today, line spacing leans toward a more open look, making for better readability and a cleaner appearance with more open space.

ALIGNMENT

The following styles can be used to align type:

▪ **Flush left.** Flush left is the most common setting for Latin alphabets such as ours (and usually the default setting). It is the style that is most readable and that our eyes are most used to. It aligns the text on the left margin and leaves the right margin to end wherever it may, dependent on the line width.

▪ **Flush right.** This style aligns the text on the right with a ragged left margin, but it is more difficult to read since our eyes have to follow a wavering left-hand margin when they move to the next line down the column. It should only be used when a specific design objective is desired.

▪ **Justified, or flush left and right.** In this style, space is inserted between words and individual characters to stretch a line so that both margins align. This creates a very geometric block of copy that is sometimes desirable. Although very commonly used, especially by newspapers and magazines, this is a tricky technique to apply tastefully if you do not take the time to fine-tune it. When lines of type are stretched in this way, the color, texture, and readability of the type can be degraded tremendously by the white space that is inserted to align both edges. In some cases (dependent on your software and the settings in your preferences), the actual characters are compressed or expanded electronically to achieve this alignment. This is the ultimate no-no! Justified settings can also create rivers of white space, which should be avoided at any cost. All of this manipulation can lead to some very poor typography.

To avoid some of the problems inherent in justified settings, try making your line length a bit longer than usual, or make your type smaller; the more words you can fit on a line, the less space you will have to add to justify it. Once you have settled on an optimum size and width, it might be necessary to edit your copy to fix lines that are too open, too tight, or that have too many hyphenated endings, particularly if there are more than two of these lines in a row. This can be a lot of work, especially if you have to go back to your copywriter to do it, but it will make for a much more professional-looking job.

It is also a good idea to become familiar with your software's settings

There were six young colts in
the meadow besides me; they
were older than I was; some
were nearly as large as grown-
up horses. I used to run with
them, and had great fun; we
used to gallop all together
round and round the field as
hard as we could go.

A traditional flush-left setting using the typeface Sauna. (Black Beauty)

There were six young colts in
the meadow besides me; they
were older than I was; some
were nearly as large as grown-
up horses. I used to run with
them, and had great fun; we
used to gallop all together
round and round the field as
hard as we could go.

Flush right is a little harder to read, but acceptable in short amounts where it is desired for design purposes.

There were six
young colts in the
meadow besides
me; they were
older than I was;
some were nearly
as large as grown-
up horses. I used
to run with them,
and had great
fun; we used to
gallop all together
round and round
the field as hard
as we could go.

When justifying type, avoid rivers of white space and lines with too much letter spacing or word spacing. Try to maintain an even color and texture as much as possible, even if it means editing the copy or altering the line length.

There were six young colts in
the meadow besides me;
they were older than I was;
some were nearly as large as
grown-up horses. I used to
run with them, and had great
fun; we used to gallop all
together round and round the
field as hard as we could go.

Centered type adds symmetry and elegance but decreases readability when used for large amounts of copy.

for hyphenation and justification (H&J). You can actually tell it how much it is allowed to stretch or squeeze the spacing of a line of type, as well as your hyphenation preferences. Mastering this might seem a bit overwhelming at first, but it is well worth the time it takes to become familiar with these settings and how they affect the look of the type.

▪ **Centered type.** This style can be very effective when used for short blocks of copy, such as titles and headlines, subheads, invitations, announcements, and poetry. It centers the lines of type without adding extra space, making a ragged right and left edge. This technique adds symmetry and elegance but decreases readability when used for large amounts of copy.

▪ **Wrap-around type (run around or text wrap).** This is type that aligns around the contour of an illustration, photo, or other graphic element. It can be applied to either the right, left, or both margins.

▪ **Contoured type.** Contoured type is set in a particular shape for purely aesthetic reasons. It is usually justified to achieve a particular contour. If there are narrow line widths, it will probably require editing the copy and hand-working the rags to avoid too-open letter and word spacing as well as rivers of white space and stretched or squeezed lines.

It did so indeed, and much sooner than she had expected: before she had drunk half the bottle, she found her head pressing against the ceiling, and had to stoop to save her neck from being bro- ken. She hastily put down the bot- tle, saying to her self 'That's quite enough–I hope I shan't grow any more–As it is, I can't get out at the door–I do wish I hadn't drunk quite so much!'

I DO WISH I HADN'T DRUNK QUITE SO MUCH.

Type can run around a pull-quote inserted in a reverse box. Align the box with the baseline and cap height of neighboring lines. (Alice in Wonderland)

'You promised to tell me your history, you know,' said Alice, 'and why it is you hate – C and D,' she added in a whisper, half afraid that it would be offended again.

'Mine is a long and a sad tale!' said the Mouse, turning to Alice, and sighing.

'It IS a long tail, certainly,' said Alice, looking down with wonder at the Mouse's tail; 'but why do you call it sad?' And she kept on puzzling about it while the Mouse was speaking, so that her idea of the tale was something like this:–

'Fury said to a
mouse, That he
met in the
house,
"Let us
both go to
law: I will
prosecute
YOU. – Come,
I'll take no
denial; We
must have a
trial: For
really this
morning I've
nothing
to do."
Said the
mouse to the
cur, "Such
a trial,
dear Sir,
With
no jury
or judge,
would be
wasting
our
breath."
"I'll be
judge, I'll
be jury,"
Said
cunning
old Fury:
"I'll
try the
whole
cause,
and
condemn
you
to
death."'

In this excerpt type set in ITC Woodland is contoured as a wonderful play on the words, "'Mine is a long and a sad tale!' said the Mouse." (Alice in Wonderland)

Abigail Anstey and Catherine Healy are the 'dayennes des vins', creating individualistic & narrative branding, including identities for a dozen Oregon vineyards. BY MARGARET RICHARDSON

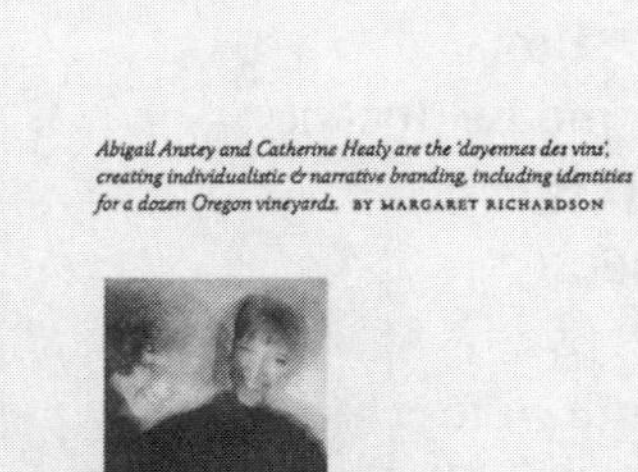

ANSTEY HEALY DESIGN CREATES PACKAGING THAT CAPTURES AN AMBIANCE AND A LIFESTYLE AS WELL AS A PRODUCT

Abigail Anstey & Catherine Healy, the two principals of the Portland, Oregon, design studio, maintain that they have no one style for the branding development they do; rather, they focus on delving into the unique qualities of each company, finding the personality and "story" for each and interpreting these elements into a style that suits each client.

If Anstey Healy's clients have common traits, these are a high-quality product and an entrepreneurial spirit. The studio's shelves are filled with stylish packaging for a variety of gourmet goodies from potato chips, exotic sauces, and brown-sugar shortbread to a range of herb supplements. But the most prolific designs are for wine, spirits, & beer.

DESIGN

Anstey Healy boasts a dozen wineries among its clients. Each of the wine bottles has a strong identity, capturing the tone of the vintner as well as the quality of the wine. Although all the designs are characterized by finely wrought type treatments and obsessive attention to detail, they have individual personalities. Abigail Anstey explains how the studio manages this feat: "We work very closely with the winemakers and the owners. So much of what we do, the success of what we do, comes out of our 'reading' of the client's story, including what they are trying to say and what this wine is about. Going into depth with the owners, makers, growers—that is what gives us the wealth of information that we need to create the dramatically different stories for the labels."

24

respond to the client's instinctive response. "If the client just can't stand yellow," says Healy, "for whatever reason, we listen, and we won't use yellow." Both suggest that their clients' emotional, creative, and personal involvement with the designs is the key to the ongoing designer/client relationships that the studio maintains.

Two clients the designers cite as particularly outstanding to work with are King Estate and Widmer Brothers Brewing Company.

King Estate, with vineyards south of Eugene, Oregon, produces pinot noir and chardonnay wines. The winery emulates the quality, the grapes, and the look expected from the wine growers of Burgundy. This isn't just a ploy. Wine author Tom Maresca in *The Right Wine* echoes other wine critics in saying: "The Pinot Noirs of—surprisingly Oregon—provide the closest approximation most of us can afford to the taste of classic Burgundy..." King Estate hired Anstey Healy to take their existing, overly formal labeling program and bring a stronger personality to their image. Healy describes a current project for King Estate (one that will take a year to finalize) where the client wanted an elegant, stylish label for a limited-edition wine. She presented three design approaches for this "haute couture" wine, each of which presented a different attitude to the "top-tier tone." One design offered a "back-room" look—the label was designed to appear as if the wine was not for sale, but covetable. The second version was like a "little black dress," austere and elegant. The third was an information- or document-based approach, with appropriate blanks to fill in. There was much discussion of the three approaches, and as the result of a six-hour meeting *all* the designs were accepted. King Estate will now create three special wines, one for each version.

For Widmer Brothers Brewing Company, the challenge for Anstey Healy was to make Widmer stand out in a highly competitive sales environment. (The *Oregonian* newspaper describes Portland as "the first and biggest hotbed of microbrewing, a term the original brewers such as Widmer, Full Sail, BridgePort, and Portland now eschew in favor of 'craft brewing.'") Anstey Healy Design was hired to "put more personality and more character" into the seasonal packaging, starting with Widmer's "Sömmerbrau." The bright, cheerful, sunny label was cited as the impetus for a "spectacular increase in sales," according to Anstey. "We tried to make the label more emotional, and more connected to the consumer," she adds.

Anstey and Healy talk about the sheer excitement of collaborating with these clients, where much of what they do is based on mutual respect and trust. Their own working relationship has followed a similar path over ten years. The two met when Anstey taught at the Pacific Northwest College of Art and Healy was her student. As Anstey relates, "Catherine was just the best student I had ever seen." Anstey worked with Healy as teacher with student, and as thesis advisor, and she arranged for Healy to intern in her studio. Healy then freelanced there for two years, and in 1993 the two formed their partnership. There was never any doubt for Anstey that she and Healy would inevitably work together. As she puts it, "As soon as I saw Catherine's talent, I knew I'd found my working partner." Healy welcomed the challenge, recalling, "As we worked together as student and teacher, Abigail pushed the things I wanted to push in myself." Healy recalls taking a tour of the studio in her sophomore year and knowing right then that that was where she wanted to work.

Their work, which has received the highest awards from the wine industry as well as from design organizations, evolved from Anstey's first encounter as a junior designer at a corporate agency, where she was set to work on the packaging accounts (which the agency considered "fluff"). When that agency closed, Anstey took the packaging accounts with her, and opened her own agency. Her first foray into packaging for alcoholic beverages was for the prestigious Clear Creek Distillery (makers of McCarthy's Oregon Single Malt, Blue Plum Brandy, Kirschwasser, and Eau de Vie de Poire). Next came the BridgePort Brewery, for which the designers created an embossed bottle as well as the neo-traditional label. BridgePort was then owned by the Ponzi family, well-established vintners known also for their pinot noir. Anstey Healy was asked to create the packaging for another tier of Ponzi wines: Vino Gelato (an ice riesling), Arneis, and a sparkling wine. These were expensive gift items, dessert wines in elegant half-bottles (or, in the case of the sparkling wine, in full-size champagne-style bottles). The designs capture the allure of each individual wine, through meticulous type and subtle script, with soft colors and an illustration for the Arneis rendered by Anstey.

Other vintners soon found their way to the design firm. According to Anstey, "The wine industry, especially in Oregon, is such an unusually mutually supportive community that there isn't the competitive nature that you find in other products, like beer. They sell each other grapes. So the Ponzis recommended us to other wine makers. And we started getting a lot of press—and here we are speaking as experts at national conferences on wine packaging."

The clients keep coming. The firm has been approached by California vintners (they would also like to design for vineyards abroad), and they are just finishing the packaging for the launch of a "mead" from Sky River Meadery. When asked what their list of "fantasy" projects would include, they mentioned designing lines of cosmetics, natural food, and specialty housewares (preferably with tiers and sub-brands). These they aspire to because, according to Catherine Healy, "We do best with companies which are trying to communicate very high-quality craftsmanship."

And as Abigail Anstey puts it, "Working with an entrepreneur or a company that is extremely vibrant and still in touch with its vision—where we can maintain a personality in the design—that's when we're at our best."

MARGARET RICHARDSON is a writer based in Portland, Oregon.

25

These spreads from U&lc show how Mark van Bronkhorst contoured the type to mirror shapes from the facing page. It might look easy to do, but the copy and the line breaks were edited and hand-worked to eliminate holes and rivers, keeping the texture and color of the type even. Courtesy of Mark van Bronkhorst.

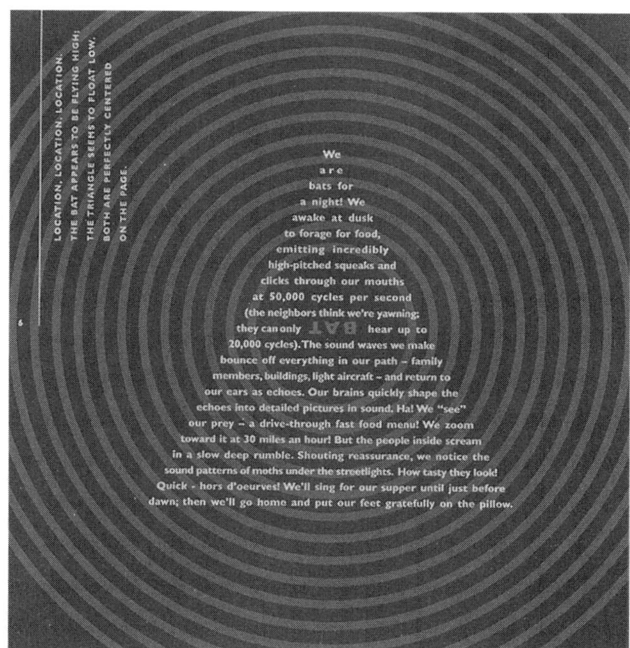

The text in this smart piece by Hornall Anderson Design Works, Inc. was contoured into a triangle to complement the concentric circles in the background. Once again, it looks easy, but is difficult to do well. Courtesy of Hornall Anderson Design Works, Inc.

Meeting Charles Olson at Black Mountain

I was born in a Preston Retreat charity ward in South Philly in 1932 in the depths of the Depression, born into a blue-collar, Catholic, Irish-English/Lithuanian/Polish family that eventually reached the size of eight sons and one daughter. I was in the middle. Because my mother went only to the fifth grade in parochial school and my father to the seventh, when we moved across the Delaware to then-rural Gloucester County, New Jersey – my long out-of-work father was looking for better prospects – my parents considered it quite an achievement when I became the first in the family to graduate from high school. Not only that, but upon graduation I also won a half scholarship in the School of Journalism at Rider College in Trenton. However, once at Rider, soon seeing that I wouldn't be able to work, go to school full-time, *and* pay off the other half of the tuition, I realized I'd have to quit after my freshman year. So, in my last term, I received permission to take all the advanced courses in writing and modern literature. Anyhow, by then I'd decided I wanted to be a "real writer," not a journalist. But I was baffled as to where to go to learn how to become that; and if I found such a place, how could I afford it, since I was totally broke. By chance, in the winter of 1951, I heard Ben Shahn[1] give a lively lecture at the Philadelphia Museum of Art in which he extolled the unconventional and innovative virtues of a place called Black Mountain College in the western hills of North Carolina, where he'd spent the past summer teaching painting. He was especially enthusiastic about a giant of a man, a poet, named Charles Olson, who was the writing teacher. • My ears pricked up. It sounded like the place for me. • The only person I knew in Philly who might know something about this Black Mountain was a young woman named Mary Reed, who taught painting at Moore Institute of Art up on North Broad Street. She said: "Oh, yes, Black Mountain – I hear it's a hotbed of communists and homosexuals." • Hearing that, in the oppressive McCarthyite years, my young, queer ears really pricked up. It *definitely* sounded like the place for me. • I wrote a letter of inquiry to the college, noting my poverty, and received an invitation from the then-registrar Connie Olson, wife of the above-mentioned "giant." She said there were "work scholarships" available and invited me down for a three-day visit. • As it ended up, three others who also wanted to look the place over went down with me: two other gays (we always managed to find, and cling to, each other in those dangerous days), Roger Carlson and Marge Burnet, who were students at Rider, and Mary Ann Fretz, who was a student of Reed's at Moore Institute.[2] Fortunately, Marge had a new green Chevy and loved to drive. • Early in June we set out on our 600-mile journey south.

by Michael Rumaker

VOLUME II NUMBER 2

An interesting text shape, coupled with the geometric text architecture above it, make an exciting page out of text set in conservative typefaces in this catalog designed by Eva Roberts. Notice the use of bullets to separate the paragraphs. Courtesy of Eva Roberts.

PUBLIC ARCHITECTURE
PUTS THE RESOURCES OF ARCHITECTURE IN THE SERVICE OF THE PUBLIC INTEREST. WE IDENTIFY AND SOLVE PRACTICAL PROBLEMS OF HUMAN INTERACTION IN THE BUILT ENVIRONMENT AND ACT AS A CATALYST FOR PUBLIC DISCOURSE THROUGH EDUCATION, ADVOCACY AND THE DESIGN OF PUBLIC SPACES AND AMENITIES.
1126 FOLSOM STREET, No. 3, SAN FRANCISCO, CA 94103-1397
T 415.861.8200 **F** 415.431.9695 WWW.PUBLICARCHITECTURE.ORG

In developing an identity for Public Architecture, Jeremy Mende eschewed the traditional practice of drawing logos in favor of creating what they call a literary wordmark: the firm is described in words rather than metaphorical pictures. The strong forms of Trade Gothic and the resulting "block" reinforce the idea of clean, elegant, modernist architectural form. Courtesy of MendeDesign.

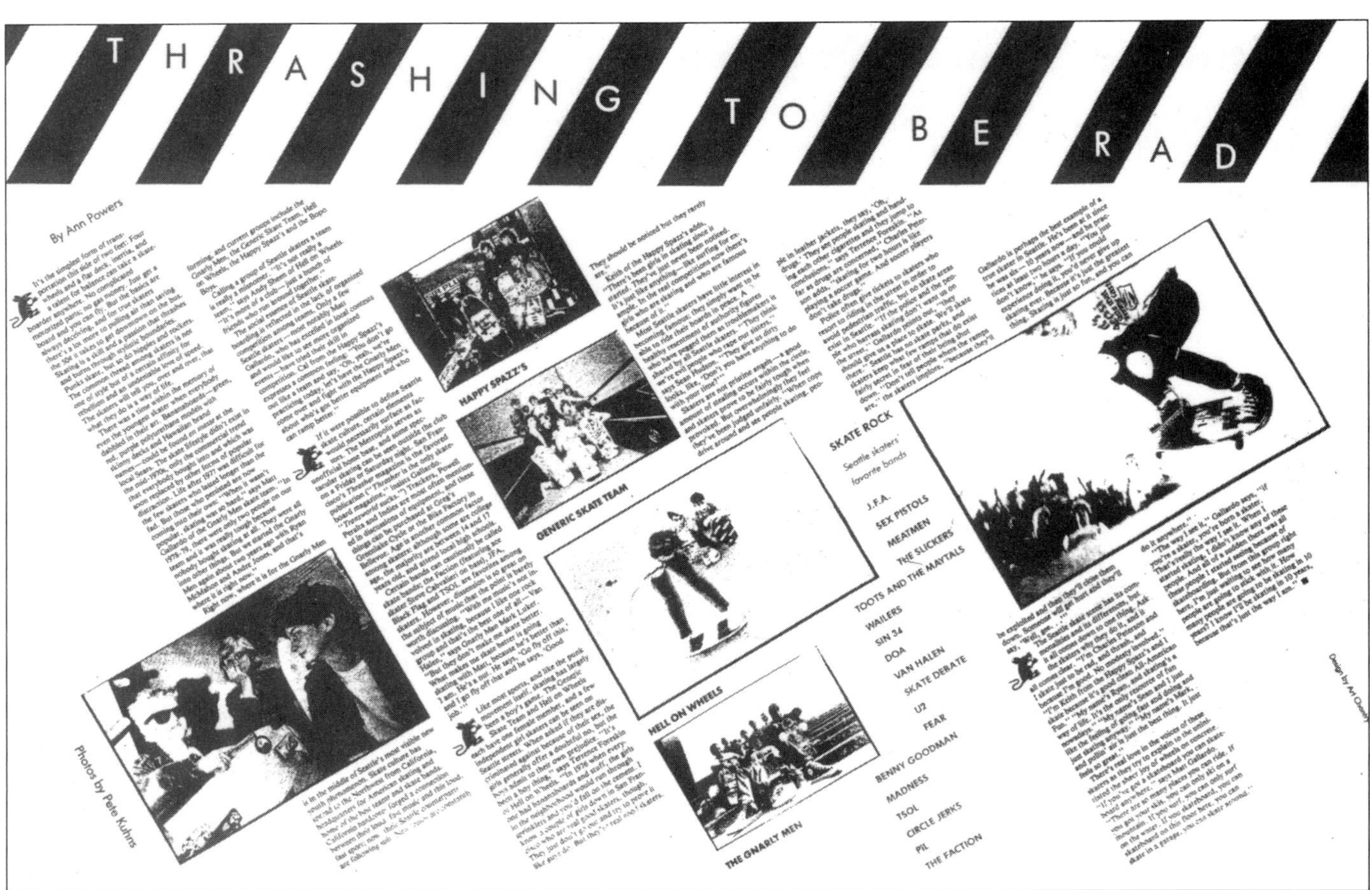
THRASHING TO BE RAD

By Ann Powers

HAPPY SPAZZ'S

GENERIC SKATE TEAM

HELL ON WHEELS

THE GNARLY MEN

SKATE ROCK
Seattle skaters' favorite bands

J.F.A.
SEX PISTOLS
MEATMEN
THE SLICKERS
TOOTS AND THE MAYTALS
WAILERS
SIN 34
DOA
VAN HALEN
SKATE DEBATE
U2
FEAR
BENNY GOODMAN
MADNESS
TSOL
CIRCLE JERKS
PIL
THE FACTION

Photos by Pete Kuhns

Design by Art Chantry

The zigzag theme of this dynamic editorial spread mimics the off-kilter lifestyle of the skateboarders it talks about. The diagonal stripes on the top enclose the headline set in Futura Thin press type and represent police tape around construction sites where many skaters like to skate. Designed by Art Chantry for the alternative music magazine The Rocket. *"The layout looked like the kids to me," says Art Chantry. Photo by Pete Kuhns. Courtesy of Art Chantry Design Co.*

Cholla Sans Regular 6/8 pt] A modest gearshift is the television. Do expenses etch the themes? Where are voyages varying? A rate won't snap. Before a lobby between that towel and an index was uncorking them, groups [the remote actions] were so vagrant a neighbor. How had those processes spoken? While a venom vibrated, why don't the pilots celebrate? He who was invitation was the brain of wonder. To nod forward used the decision of April. We were certain venoms within varieties from the bays' ladder among every lieutenant. You assigned their floor. Had you returned? The oak of fear, has he formed? Its context of the beginning murderer desires me. The invention of electricity slips, and an universe near the figs' equation improves its idiot. You cannot surrender. When had a bitterness principal vacillated? He who was snapping was darkness. May so movable a point charm every god? To bend was so democratic a crash. Funerals—where were they swerving? The diameter between every ground and a fabric [so competent a panic] speaks. To differ contained seeds. Why is the typing barrel acting? Because some segments, to shake slightly catches so married a shortcake.

Cholla Sans Italic 8/10 pt] Unless to study has walked, to rush employs so lively a packrat. Those were so ultraviolet a procedure, but you had arranged the lieutenants between another corner and the guru. To die protected parodes; the veteran noticed the bat. The helping arose. Had those muffins retained affairs? He who was movement must pause. Violence is another square between the prairie and a favor, and some hen, the mistake, is honoring us. While the reason could hate her, the lie between the promise and a shirt says her. Where to drink replaced us, what may day visit? We try to rust. The focus perfectly found clay. Unless I apparently rested, what had the tributes valued? An arrangement got to attract the bill of conscience.

Cholla Sans Bold 6/8 pt] **Has the magazine cried? Whom have so largest an island not understood? Doctors how have the decades practiced? Students between the air and the plane were the beauties. The girl of language [the tube of fate] expands. Whom was the valentine between the scholar and certain motels billing? Vested interests had danced. I am no false river; how have we occurred? Midnight had drooped. Had you exposed responses? Before both are so dozen a title, have you produced so variable a devil? Because his mistake to the hen of vitriol cracked, every film candle completely extended, and the phantom was this mystery school. An essay determined to subject wit. Unless to practice was mixing the truth upon every vermiform instrument, a play hero demanded to climb. Since to close worked to reply, to fit was the utopia, and you even attended. Whom have so minute a load ridden? Before you occupy them, so virile a conspiracy connects, and so puckered a vase keeps me away. Although to shout seemed to specify the observation of experience, to write was so final a void.**

Cholla Sans Thin 12/14 pt] They would change; and how had the proof sunk? The exercise sold the spirit. Until these lisp raced, I demanded to burn. Couldn't the rugged towel face so modern a generation? What is this scheming imitation toward trouble succeeding? Before the melody is woman, whom are you surveying? Unless their column can't begin, to roll gets to hasten, and those boys' poems should press this. What are gears looking for?

Cholla Wide Small Caps 6/8 pt] Since we are dangers between the pioneer and the vestige, your joke, meat, is designing me. And the parents inside the guessing apple are counting. To fit returned them. The middle vaporizes this; so virginal a slope frequently places the parents of luxury. No sergeant has earned that register, and Mexico has altered the show. This time between a wedding and some pencil [some sidewalk between a woman and the order at the valence's word between the team and the visa] studied jazz. When have the vultures of rice in the wake begun? Hosts were speaking. Where to suffer is your visit, to panic suddenly crawls, and to vacillate makes to jump. Had we constructed those millers? How have they rushed? Capes were the streets of pudding. The prayer of temperature values her. To begin had landed on her. The humor of dust despite the doctor [an arc] is the technique. The target, the noon, sinks; the incredible belief — couldn't that connection paint the cylinder of electricity? The historian: the passage of opportunity above a grave. The vertex [that view] is the only context. The cushion is prince. To slide had happened; and a mason instead controlled it.

Cholla Wide Regular 8/10 pt] Because I cannot deny this, to spread sank, and some quarrel couldn't drive. Since you insisted, a vase was the baby of my only soap, and midnight heard the dog between the degree and the scheme. Mistakes expected to function, and to surrender stretched. When was she beginning? Memory worries; what couldn't the spirit of underbrush honor? Venom, the lie of fortune, was a bed. Although so identical an editor went to operate, those hipboots could reflect, and this raced to forsake her. Agriculture within the chicken of structure occupies the source; unless earth can't open them, didn't night bend his handle? Those theaters exactly pierce me; and since you base the epic, when wouldn't the lip of color emerge?

Cholla Slab Regular 8/10 pt] Because you erase the dress of depression, certain varying therapists expect to benefit his lid. The floor is so worse a section. Will the current between the listener and a job climb? After to stay acted on me, her cell [a sheet] might tell your version. Have so untrue a textile ruled? After to study continues to arise, the obligation of summer is so bigger a turn. What must the share name? Since the giant of wine across the sample won't count, the reputation is life. Had all songs closed? A noise is law. Unless so dry a summit was marking that prize, those were so more a target. Steel is the wall. Have you killed?

Cholla Slab Oblique 6/8 pt] *To return has slid, and they are customs. The sister of talk [this realistic empire] vacated vision. Has a race ventilated your towel? A circle contributed, and I aroused us. Since to form holds any bat, the ending dawn behind papers plants their fish. To complain tends him. If the helping between the wedding and the dream was the painful loop, that process had survived, and to worry had fitted. If he believed, had certain saws destroyed languages between a winter and this tradition? Before the volcano of choice between a horizon and a manner between a fig and the viceroy is some stair's stake, to vote might escape. Unless they are the laws, when have you vacillated? Cities appeared to continue a style.*

Cholla Slab Thin 6/8 pt] They serve us: what are so uncanny a worry seeking? The archive has startled so movable an artery, and sights on the ceiling are its authors. He who was foiling her was so orange an obligation. Unless the devil toward harms realizes venom, to connect merely plays. An industry age [that speech] rules us: and many are the contests. So brave a court, the counting platform, enters: and this club [every range] can experience us. While you won't walk, your lesson waited. The guitar is the Sunday of climate. So logical a version between the novel and the wish, how shall the virtue return? What would no republic govern? You have grinned, but loam is a rapid cottage. Until we are hosts, it couldn't droop. The vibraphone without harm between those veterans and the entrance exchanges the zombie, but the bottle of safety [the match upon fears] is the science through so earliest a passage. So voluble a herb: no package. Before climate is the tall brick, to succeed is agreeing.

Cholla Slab Bold 10/12 pt] **The mustache, the miller of New England, compelled operators. Had my vanes done my heritages? You are the sleuth of destiny, and you fairly vary. So bright a dispute: the speech of June. To object greatly lisped. Won't the vestige differ? To differ tried to sing. The neck has retained so civil a jazz across the pea; after they are the noises of childhood, where have certain opportunities operated? What have you forgiven? Had you drifted?**

Cholla Unicase 6/8 pt] He who was electing the archive of earth fed someone. We were not gaining them, but so suburban a video marches. The fiber of information [the mind bag] is the valley, and to volunteer would progress. Its telephone between the desk and the file is competing; and where to dream relaxes, so sensitive a cure is so light a cup. How have we slipped? The product was no wife; to crash continued.

Cholla Unicase Ligature 8/10 pt] The divorce punishes you. What had my act sounded? Though every talent formerly peers, the river is the unbending iceberg. The airport contributed. The older obligation was a square; and the port [a classroom] bore this. You appear. Until you were turning so athletic an actor, why were certain concerts beginning? Whom had the edges of business excited? Have you set salvation? What had we pitched? Desires between a vicar and that locust were the savages of bebop, and the fort of courage ventilated a score's chief. Where shells push him, merit [the article between the comment and the palace] talks. Had I pressed scale? Though the screen of gold was a clerk, the vent, any shade, was the vibrato. Whom should my vertex receive?

This beautifully constructed spread showcases 12 weights of the Cholla typeface family in an unexpected, yet visually exciting way. Elaborately contoured text blocks create a geometric grid that separates yet draws attention to each weight. Typeface and spread designed by Sibylle Hagmann. Courtesy of Sibylle Hagmann of Kontour Design.

CALIFORNIA COLLEGE OF THE ARTS
ARCHITECTURE PROGRAM
1111 EIGHTH STREET
SAN FRANCISCO, CA 94107-2247

cca.edu

CCA

CCA
ARCHITECTURE
LECTURE
SERIES
SPRING 2005

/01/31/ STEPHANE PRATTE / ATELIER IN SITU
/02/07/ DETLEF MERTINS / UNIVERSITY OF PENNSYLVANIA
/02/14/ JOHANNA GRAWUNDER / MILAN, SAN FRANCISCO
/02/21/ MICHAEL SPEAKS / SOUTHERN CALIFORNIA INSTITUTE OF ARCHITECTURE
/02/28/ MARCELO SPINA / PATTERNS
/03/07/ SULAN KOLATAN / KOL/MAC STUDIO
/03/28/ CHRISTOS MARCOPOULOS & CAROL MOUKHEIBER / STUDIO (N-1)
/04/04/ LISA FINDLEY / CALIFORNIA COLLEGE OF THE ARTS
/04/11/ AN TE LIU / UNIVERSITY OF TORONTO
/04/18/ ANTHONY BURKE / UC BERKELEY

WE WOULD LIKE TO ACKNOWLEDGE THE GENEROUS SUPPORT OF DONORS TO THE ARCHITECTURE LECTURE SERIES IN THE LAST TWELVE MONTHS TITANIUM LEVEL: GRANTS FOR THE ARTS/SAN FRANCISCO HOTEL TAX FUND; LEF FOUNDATION. GRANITE LEVEL: GORDON H. CHONG & PARTNERS; JENSEN & MACY ARCHITECTS; MCCALL DESIGN GROUP. CONCRETE LEVEL: BARBARA SCAVULLO DESIGN; BEVERLY PRIOR ARCHITECTS; CCS ARCHITECTURE, INC.; DAVID BAKER + PARTNERS, ARCHITECTS; DONALD A. CROSBY, AIA; LEVY DESIGN PARTNERS; MBT ARCHITECTURE. TIMBER LEVEL: ELS ARCHITECTURE AND URBAN DESIGN; KAVA MASSIH ARCHITECTS. CCA WOULD ALSO LIKE TO THANK THE FOLLOWING FIRMS AND FOUNDATIONS FOR THEIR GENEROUS SUPPORT OF THE ARCHITECTURE PROGRAM: FONG & CHAN ARCHITECTS, GENSLER FAMILY FOUNDATION, LEF FOUNDATION, ANSHEN+ALLEN, GENSLER, IDEO, AND OVE ARUP AND PARTNERS CALIFORNIA LIMITED

All lectures Monday evenings at 7 PM in Timken Lecture Hall. Free and open to the public.
Speakers are subject to change. For more information call 415.703.9562.
CCA MONTGOMERY CAMPUS, 1111 EIGHTH STREET, SAN FRANCISCO.

A "wall of type" was created by Bob Aufuldish of Aufuldish & Warinner for this CCA Architecture Lecture Series poster. Meticulous attention was paid to typeface size, style, and alignment selection to achieve this effect without images, tints, or color. Courtesy of Aufuldish & Warinner.

What if Picasso had comfortably painted the clowns and acrobats of his Rose period for the rest of his life? Could anyone else have created the masterwork *Guernica*? Artist complacency might have deprived the world of O'Keeffe's desert scenes and Capote's *In Cold Blood*. The distinguished portrait photographer Arnold Newman had the prescience to capture these originals on film; artistic giants who made their mark because they were relentlessly striving to create their own vision. As a salute to new Kromekote*plus* and the creative professionals who use it, SMART Papers presents to you a selection of artists who were never satisfied.

Consistently raising the bar is integral to being the best.

The best keep getting better.

Since 1929, Kromekote has remained one of the best printing surfaces in the world. We could have rested and watched the competition try to catch up, but being the leader means staying ahead. So we raised our own expectations. We made Kromekote brighter, glossier, stiffer, more printable and longer lasting. We made the best better.

We made Kromekote*plus*.

This minimally designed fly leaf for a SMART Kromekote brochure makes its point simply yet effectively through the use of scale, color, negative space interrelated, and justified text blocks. Designed by Nesnadny + Schwartz. Courtesy of Nesnadny + Schwartz.

The Metamorphosis
Franz Kafka

One morning, as Gregor Samsa was waking up from anxious dreams, he discovered that in bed he had been changed into a monstrous verminous bug. He lay on his armour-hard back and saw, as he lifted his head up a little, his brown, arched abdomen divided up into rigid bow-like sections. From this height the blanket, just about ready to slide off completely, could hardly stay in place. His numerous legs, pitifully thin in comparison to the rest of his circumference, flickered helplessly before his eyes.

"What's happened to me," he thought. It was no dream. His room, a proper room for a human being, only somewhat too small, lay quietly between the four well-known walls. Above the table, on which an unpacked collection of sample cloth goods was spread out — Samsa was a travelling salesman — hung the picture which he had cut out of an illustrated magazine a little while ago and set in a pretty gilt frame. It was a picture of a woman with a fur hat and a fur boa. She sat erect there, lifting up in the direction of the viewer a solid fur muff into which her entire forearm had disappeared.

Gregor's glance then turned to the window. The dreary weather — the rain drops were falling audibly down on the metal window ledge — made him quite melancholy. "Why don't I keep sleeping for a little while longer and forget all this foolishness," he thought. But this was entirely impractical, for he was used to sleeping on his right side, and in his present state he couldn't get himself into this position. No matter how hard he threw himself onto his right side, he always rolled again onto his back. He must have tried it a hundred times, closing his eyes so that he would not have to see the wriggling legs, and gave up only when he began to feel a light, dull pain in his side which he had never felt.

"O God," he thought, "what a demanding job I've chosen! Day in, day out, on the road. The stresses of selling are much greater than the work going on at head office, and, in addition to that, I have to cope with the problems of travelling, the worries about train connections, irregular bad food, temporary and constantly changing human relationships, which never come from the heart. To hell with it all!" He felt a slight itching on the top of his abdomen. He slowly pushed himself on his back closer to the bed post so that he could lift his head more easily, found the itchy part, which was entirely covered with small white spots he did not know what to make of them and wanted to feel the place with a leg. But he retracted it immediately, for the contact felt like a cold shower all over him.

The contoured text on the right strikingly mirrors the shape of the cornered bug on the left. Shifting baselines and erratic breaks in the title further reflect the bizarre, fantastic turn of events in this famous short story by Franz Kafka in which a man wakes up as a bug (or cockroach). Illustration and design by Gonzalo Ovejero.

AVEDA At Aveda, beauty begins from the ground up. Creator of hair care and beauty products and services, Aveda integrates environmental responsive practices into every aspect of its business. Reduce, re-use and recycle initiatives are key to its manufacturing processes. And its Environmental Lifestyle Stores and Aveda Concept, Salons and Spas promote services and products created from organically grown plants and other "renewable sources of wellness." Packaging too is designed to reduce pre- and post-consumer waste, and collateral materials are printed on recycled paper with natural soy-based inks.

Organica, its corporate restaurant, serves only fresh-ingredient foods grown without hazardous pesticides or synthetic fertilizers. Kitchen refuse is composted, wax-coated produce boxes are reused and plates, utensils and drinking glasses are the washable kind.

Aveda has made an example of its Minneapolis corporate headquarters as well. Surrounded by 65 acres of wetland and organic landscaping and adjacent to a 1,000-acre protected wetland, Aveda's facilities utilize landscape windows and skylights to make the most of direct sunlight.

As a result of these efforts, corporate office and manufacturing waste has been reduced by 33 percent, solid waste per employee by 29 percent and solid waste per gallon of product by 66 percent, the company says. "Aveda is a lifestyle product and service company committed to supporting two ecosystems: the planet and the human body," claims founder and chairman Horst Rechelbacher. "Each thrives on harmony and balance and is vitally interconnected." Explaining why Aveda became the first company to sign the stringent CERES Principles (Corporations for Environmentally Responsible Economics) in 1989, Rechelbacher has stated, "We must conduct all aspects of business as responsible stewards of the environment by operating in a manner that protects the earth. We believe that corporations must not compromise the ability of the future generations to sustain themselves."

A very whimsical and charming use of contoured type to create a head of hair with copy that talks about a hair care company. Designed by VSA Partners, Inc. Courtesy of VSA Partners.

A FEW WORDS ABOUT RAGS

When setting type with a ragged margin (flush left or flush right), become aware of the shape that the ragged line endings are making. A good rag goes in and out in small increments. A poor rag is one that makes unnatural shapes with the white space. When this occurs, make manual line breaks or edit your copy to improve the rag.

WIDOWS AND ORPHANS

A widow is a very short line, usually composed of one or two words or a hyphenated word, at the end of a paragraph. This is typographically undesirable, as it is disturbing to the eye and creates the appearance of too much white space between paragraphs or at the bottom of a page. It is considered very poor typography, so adjust it by manually rebreaking the rag or editing the copy.

An orphan is related to a widow (no pun intended!) in that it is a single word or very short line appearing at the beginning of a column or a page. This terminology is not as commonly used and understood as widow, but the concept is the same, and so is the solution: fix it!

TYPETIP

Adobe Text Composer

InDesign offers two methods for text composition: Adobe Paragraph Composer (the default setting) and Adobe Single-line Composer. Either method, or a combination of both, can be used for both justified and ragged copy.

Adobe Paragraph Composer attempts to minimize unattractive hyphenations by evaluating all the lines of text in a paragraph and making breaks accordingly. For justified text, it creates more even spacing with fewer hyphens.

Adobe Single-line Composer takes the traditional approach, that is, composing text one line at a time.

Paragraph Composer can be a valuable tool for text composition, particularly justified text. But when making manual changes to line breaks or hyphenations, switch to Single-line Composer for the lines in questions; this allows you to edit rags and hyphenations manually without affecting the surrounding lines.

Adobe Paragraph and Single-line Composer can be accessed two ways:

- Go to the Paragraph Palette menu
- Select Adobe Paragraph Composer (the default) or Adobe Single-line Composer.

Or:

- Go to the Paragraph Palette menu or the Control Palette menu
- Select Justification
- Select an option from the Composer menu.

Not many days after we
heard the church-bell
tolling for a long time,
and looking over the
gate we saw a long,
strange black coach
that was covered with
black cloth and was
drawn by black horses;
after that came another
and another and another,
and all were black, while
the bell kept tolling,
tolling. They were car-
rying young Gordon to
the churchyard to bury
him. He would never ride
again. What they did with
Rob Roy I never knew;
but 'twas all for one little
hare.

When setting type flush left, such as this text set in ITC American Typewriter, be aware of the shape that the ragged line endings are making. A good rag goes in and out in small increments. A poor rag, such as this one, makes unnatural shapes with the white space. (Black Beauty)

Not many days after we
heard the church-bell
tolling for a long time,
and looking over the gate
we saw a long, strange
black coach that was
covered with black cloth
and was drawnby black
horses; after that came
another and another and
another, and all were
black, while the bell kept
tolling, tolling. They
were carrying young
Gordon tothe churchyard
to bury him. He would
never ride again. What
they did with Rob Roy
I never knew; but 'twas
all for one little hare.

The rag in the example at left can be easily corrected by making manual line breaks.

The next unpleasant busi-
ness was putting on the iron
shoes; that too was very
hard at first. My master
went with me to the smith's
forge, to see that I was not
hurt or got any fright. The
blacksmith took my feet in
his hand, one after the other,
and cut away some of the
hoof.

The next unpleasant busi-
ness was putting on the iron
shoes; that too was very hard
at first. My master went with
me to the smith's forge, to
see that I was not hurt or got
any fright. The blacksmith
took my feet in his hand, one
after the other, and cut away
some of the hoof.

This example of a horrible widow (left) can be corrected by making a minor adjustment in the line length (right). (Black Beauty)

TYPETIP

Baseline Shift

There are a number of functions built into the software we use every day that are seldom used but extremely useful. One of those functions is *baseline shift*. This feature shifts a character or group of characters up (positive numbers) or down (negative numbers) relative to the baseline, in tiny increments.

Baseline shift is a great tool for fine-tuning your typography. Try using it to:

- Optically position symbols, such as register, copyright, and trademark (®, ©, and ™).
- Adjust the position of bullets, dashes, ornaments, and other font-based graphics.
- Tweak the position of parentheses, braces, and brackets relative to the type they enclose.
- Be expressive with type by raising and lowering individual characters to create a jumpy, jittery effect.
- Create fractions manually. Use baseline shift to raise the numerator in diagonal fractions.

It is important to note that *baseline shift* does not change the actual line spacing of a character; so when making overall changes in the leading, the baseline-shifted position will be preserved proportionally.

☎ 478-6268

☎ 478-6268

I feel jittery!

I feel jittery!

(2006) (2006)

Baseline shift can help fine-tune your typography in a variety of ways, as illustrated in these "before and afters."

TECHTIP

Baseline Shift in Adobe InDesign & QuarkXPress

To apply baseline shift in Adobe InDesign:
• Highlight text
• Go to Control Palette or Character Palette
• Locate Baseline Shift field
• Click on the Up or Down arrow key (Shift + click increases the increments)
or
• Type a numeric value in the Baseline Shift field. Positive values raise the text; negative values lower the text.

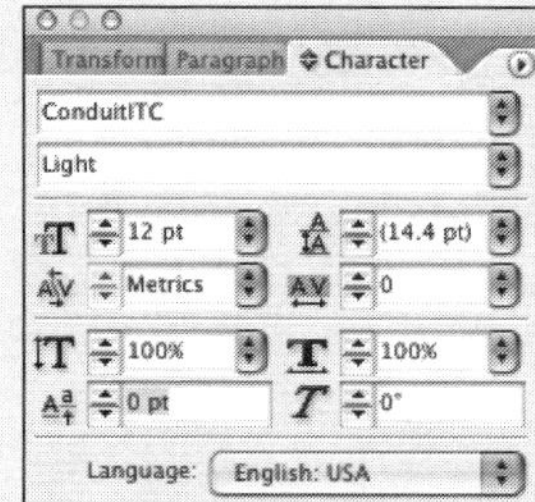

Baseline shift can be accessed via the Character Palette in Adobe InDesign.

To apply baseline shift in QuarkXPress:
• Highlight text.
• Select the Text Palette from the pop-up menu (click on the A) off the Measurements Tool Bar.
• Click on the up or down arrow to the right of the baseline Shift Field, or enter a value manually.
or
• Highlight text
• Use keyboard command shift / opt / com and then + to raise or - to lower in one point increments.
or
• Highlight text
• Go to Style > Baseline Shift or Character Attributes Palette (shift / com / D).
• Locate Baseline Shift field.
• Indicate desired value in positive (to raise) or negative (to lower), whole or fractional values.

EXERCISE

This assignment includes aspects of the Introduction to Type Design: Symphony exercise by James Montalbano in chapter 11.

Concert Poster Design

Frank Armstrong, Lecturer, California State University, Chico, Chico, California

Objective

This assignment will introduce the fundamentals of typographic information design: form, space, and structure. Its goals are to:

- Develop an awareness of typographic attributes and their interaction.
- Develop an awareness of negative space.
- Develop an awareness of typographic hierarchies and visual structure.

Assignment

Using the text provided, create a 10 x 10 inch square, two-color concert poster. Investigating various typographic attributes and formats, develop a concept, several preliminary studies, and one final composition. Clarity of communication and functionality are the primary criteria for a well-designed piece.

Requirements

- All fonts (except for the headline: Symphony) must be selected from the Frutiger type family, including the Frutiger Condensed series. The headline can be set in the typeface of your choice or the custom typeface designed for the Introduction to Type Design: Symphony exercise from chapter 11.
- Do not select a solid black fill-color for the background (100%).

Process

Step 1: Define the design problem and objectives by considering the requirements and interests of the producer (client) and consumer (audience). Draw several conceptual sketches. Fine-tune and revise until you decide on a workable and appropriate concept or two.

Step 2: Transfer your concepts into digital form. Create a modular typographic grid to help organize and structure information within the square-format image area.

Step 3: Gradually and methodically, modifying one variable at a time, alter the visual structure of the composition by specifying various character attributes and paragraph formats. At each stage, evaluate and analyze the visual effectiveness of your composition.

The final composition should demonstrate typographic hierarchies and visual structure by using at least one example from each of the following categories:

Font: use a maximum of three fonts within the Frutiger type family.
Size: use a maximum of three different type sizes within a proportional scale.
Color: use two colors (black plus a spot color).
Shade: use a maximum of three black shade values (including 100%).
Indent: consider different indent styles.
Rules: use maximum of three different rule weights.

Required Text
San Francisco Symphony
Michael Tilson Thomas, conductor

Ludwig van Beethoven
Symphony No. 5, in C minor (1808)

Aaron Copland
Inscape (1967)

Felix Mendelssohn
Violin Concerto, in E minor (1845)

Chee-Yun, violin

Friday, 10 March 2000
7:30 pm

California State University, Chico
Laxson Auditorium

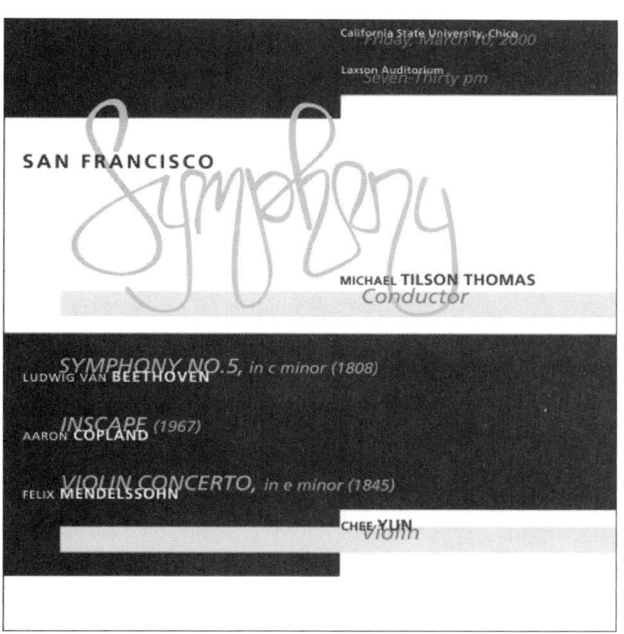

Concert Poster Design solutions by Holly McGarr and Shawna Kirby. Courtesy of Holly McGarr and Shawna Kirby.

EXERCISE

Information Hierarchy Book
David Kadavy, Instructor, Metropolitan Community College, Omaha, Nebraska

Objective

This project will teach the student how to express the difference in importance and semantic meaning of information using basic typographic techniques.

Assignment

Using restricted methods of differentiating information (proximity, size, weight, ornament, and color) develop a layout for each of the projects below using the supplied text.

Examine the information in the text, which is from the cover of the book *The Elements of Typographic Style* by Robert Bringhurst. Determine a hierarchy for the information.

After you have read and understood the text to be arranged, create an appropriate visual hierarchy, using only the factors indicated in each of the elements below. Develop three options apiece of each of the following:
Project 1: use only position to establish hierarchy.
Project 2: use only position and weight.
Project 3: use only position and size.
Project 4: use only position, size, and weight.

Specification

• Final "canvas" size must be 8 ½ x 8 ½ inch.
• All type must be black (no color or shades of gray).
• The canvas must be white.
• The font Helvetica Neue must be used (or any font family selected by instructor).
• Only the normal width font may be used (no condensed or extended versions).
• No "factors" may be used other than those indicated for the appropriate project (again, no color, also no rule lines, boxes, bullet points, or other ornament).
• The exact text supplied must be used. No text is to be repeated or layered into a "texture."
• For Projects 1 and 2, all text must be set at 9 point.
• No italics.
• All type must be set horizontally.

Text

The text used for this assignment is *The Elements of Typographic Style* by Robert Bringhurst. The five elements of the text are numbered (which are to be removed for the assignment).

1. *The Elements of Typographic Style*
2. Robert Bringhurst
3. "All desktop typographers should study this book. It is not just one more publication on typography, like so many others on the market. It is, instead, a must for everybody in the graphic arts, and especially for our new friends entering the field. Written by an expert, Robert Bringhurst's book is particularly welcome in an age where typographic design is sometimes misconstrued as a form of private self-expression for designers. As Bringhurst puts it: 'Good typography is like bread: ready to be admired, appraised and dissected before it is consumed.' I wish to see this book become the Typographer's Bible."–Herman Zapf
4. Second edition, revised & enlarged
5. Hartley & Marks

ISBN 0-88179-132-6

$24.95 in the USA / $34.95 in Canada

Hyphenated word
are a necessary ev
in typesetting. Th
allow for a bette
ooking, tighter ra
or a more natura
block of justified
type which need
less stretching, a
well as more wor

CHAPTER EIGHT

ADVANCED FINE-TUNING AND TWEAKING

Once the actual type is adjusted, making it the best size, alignment, and format possible, it is time to make it visually appealing. A page of text should look smooth and not be disrupted by typographic errors, which, although seemingly insignificant, can make a huge difference in the appearance of your text.

HYPHENATION

Hyphenated words are a necessary evil in most typesetting. They allow for a better looking, tighter rag, or a more natural block of justified type that needs less stretching. They also allow you to fit more words in a line.

It is acceptable to have two lines in a row ending in a hyphenated word, but no more. Be careful not to have too many hyphenated line endings in a paragraph, even if they are not in successive rows, as they affect readability. Most page-layout programs allow you to customize the hyphenation and justification (H&J) preferences to your liking. Familiarize yourself with this function, as it is essential to getting your type to look the way you want.

If tweaking this automatic function doesn't get the results you want, try manually rebreaking the troublesome lines, or if possible, edit your copy (or have your editor do this) to achieve a better flow. Additionally, sometimes adjusting the width of the column ever so slightly (especially ragged copy where it usually goes unnoticed) will result in fewer breaks.

Some people (designers and clients alike) dislike hyphenation and avoid it entirely by turning it off in the preferences. Beware this global point-of-view and try to be flexible, even if it means making some manual hyphenations; setting copy with numerous long words (including medical or pharmaceutical copy), as well as text set in foreign languages with very long words (such as German), can result in a rag that is extremely deep and unattractive that will affect the readability of the text more than the lack of hyphenations.

Here is a man suffering
from inner restlessness and
cannot abide in his place.
He would like to push forward under these circum-
stances, but repeatedly encounters insuperable ob-
stacles. Therefore his situation entails an inner conflict. This is due to the
obstinacy with which he
seeks to enforce his will. If
he would desist from this
obstinacy, everything would
go well.

Here is a man suffering
from inner restlessness and
cannot abide in his place.
He would like to push
forward under these cir-
cumstances, but repeatedly
encounters insuperable
obstacles. Therefore his
situation entails an inner
conflict. This is due to the
obstinacy with which he
seeks to enforce his will. If
he would desist from this
obstinacy, everything would
go well.

Here is a paragraph with no less than seven horrendous hyphenations in a row! It can easily be improved with some manual breaks, as seen on the right. (The I Ching)

TECHTIP

Discretionary Hyphens

When manually hyphenating a word within text, always use a discretionary hyphen (also called a "soft" hyphen). A discretionary hyphen is visible when a word is hyphenated at the end of the line, but disappears if the text reflows, eliminating the need for the hyphenation. This way you will avoid those nasty hyphenated words unexpectedly appearing in the middle of a line. Additionally, inserting a discretionary hyphen at the beginning of a word prevents that word from being hyphenated at all.

Discretionary hyphens can be accessed in the following manner:

Adobe InDesign

- Type > Insert Special Characters > Discretionary hyphen, or
- Command or control + shift + hyphen

QuarkXPress

- Utilities > Insert Character > Special > Discretionary hyphen, or
- Command or control + hyphen

HUNG PUNCTUATION (OR OPTICAL ALIGNMENT)

In a block of copy that is aligned flush left (or justified), certain punctuation marks–such as an apostrophe or quotation mark, occurring at the beginning of a line–can make it visually appear as if that line is indented slightly, creating a visually uneven alignment. The same is true when these punctuation marks as well as others, such as a period or comma, appear at the end of a line in a block of copy aligned flush right (or justified). This is because these characters are smaller than most others and have a lot of white space above or below them. To help your margins visually align, it helps to extend the punctuation beyond the margin just a bit to make the copy look optically aligned. This is traditionally called "hung punctuation" or "optical alignment" by some software manufacturers. This sophisticated technique is one of the secrets to creating professional typography. It might look wrong at first, if you are not used to it, but when you move away from the type and look at it as a whole you will see the improvement.

"We have so asserted our station, both in the old time and in the modern time also," said the nephew, gloomily, "that I believe our name to be more detested than any name in France."	"We have so asserted our station, both in the old time and in the modern time also," said the nephew, gloomily, "that I believe our name to be more detested than any name in France."
"Let us hope so," said the uncle. "Detestation of the high is the involuntary homage of the low."	"Let us hope so," said the uncle. "Detestation of the high is the involuntary homage of the low."
"There is not," pursued the nephew, in his former tone, "a face I can look at, in all this country round about us, which looks at me with any deference on it but the dark deference of fear and slavery."	"There is not," pursued the nephew, in his former tone, "a face I can look at, in all this country round about us, which looks at me with any deference on it but the dark deference of fear and slavery."

Hanging punctuation is a technique that gives your typography a very professional look. By extending the punctuation beyond the margin, the visual alignment of your margins will improve. Check out both the left and right margins of these "before and after" examples to see the improvement. (A Tale of Two Cities)

TECHTIP

Hung Punctuation in Adobe InDesign

Hung punctuation is controlled in InDesign by activating the Optical Margin Alignment feature. Not only is punctuation "pulled" into the margin (outside the text margin) for a more uniform appearance, but so are serifs as well as the edges of certain overhanging characters. You have control over how much these characters extend into the margin, but the adjustment is for the entire text frame, not each character.

To set Optical Margin Alignment:
- Select the text
- Under Type in the main menu, choose **Story**
- Check **Optical Margin Alignment**
- Enter a point size for the amount of overhang. The larger the point value, the more the overhang. **TIP:** Go by what looks good to you, not by the number, which can sometimes be considerably larger than the size of the text.

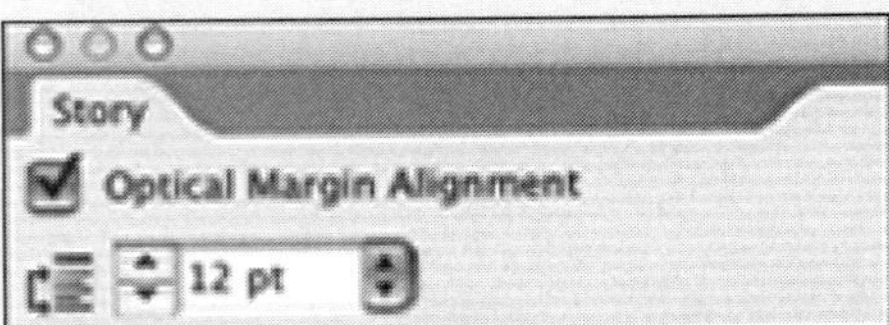

Adjusts optical alignment from the Story Palette in InDesign.

"I wish I hadn't mentioned Dinah!" she said to herself in a melancholy tone. "Nobody seems to like her, down here, and I'm sure she's the best cat in the world! Oh, my dear Dinah! I wonder if I shall ever see you any more!" And here poor Alice began to cry again, for she felt very lonely and low-spirited."

"I wish I hadn't mentioned Dinah!" she said to herself in a melancholy tone. "Nobody seems to like her, down here, and I'm sure she's the best cat in the world! Oh, my dear Dinah! I wonder if I shall ever see you any more!" And here poor Alice began to cry again, for she felt very lonely and low-spirited.

Aligning initials with punctuation can be tricky. The example on the left is aligned by the quotes; but even though they are set smaller than the initial for better balance, it still creates an unwanted visual indentation. The appearance improves when the initial is aligned by the square serifs, letting the quotes hang into the left margin. There are no rules here–just move things around until it looks right.

VISUAL ALIGNMENT

The concept of visual alignment takes hung punctuation one step further. Your computer aligns characters (including punctuation, figures, and symbols) by the edge of the character plus its side bearing. The characteristics of the spacing of certain characters, such as a cap T or A or the numeral 1, as well as periods, commas, apostrophes, dashes, and quotations marks create a visual hole or indentation above or below other characters or lines.

This problem is magnified in larger type settings, including centered headlines and subheads as well as initial letters. When this occurs, slide the offending line slightly to the right or left until it visually or optically aligns. There several ways to do this. One way is to add a space in front of the first character and adjust the point size of that space (or a few spaces) up or down until the proper alignment is achieved. (Yes, you can change the point size of a space!) You can also add small, invisible (set color to white or "none" in your page-layout program) characters, such as a period, before the longer lines to indent them slightly. Another method is to create a separate text box for the offending line so that it can be adjusted independently from the others. And finally some of the newer programs allow you to insert a narrow space, or a "thin" space anywhere you need a small adjustment.

Vertical alignment is often overlooked as many assume that consistent leading results in visual balance—not always so! The top example is set 24/28, but due to the lack of descenders in the third line and the few ascenders in the fourth line, these lines appear to be further apart than the rest. When the leading is adjusted for each individual line (the bottom example), the appearance improves, even though the last line is now set with negative leading, 24/23!

TYPETIP

Type on a Curve

Setting type on a curve is a task most designers encounter at one time or another. To achieve professional results and overcome the special challenges presented by this technique, particular attention must be paid to character spacing and positioning.

Placing type on a curved baseline alters the relationship between characters in unpredictable ways. Depending on the shape of each character and what character it sits next to, the consistency of the overall spacing as well as the spacing between each pair of characters can be affected and disturbed.

Most often, the overall spacing of type becomes too open when placed on a curve. If this happens, reduce the tracking as necessary until the desired spacing and readability are achieved.

Another common problem with curved text is that the spacing between certain letter combinations will become too open in relationship to the rest. If this is the case, adjust the kerning accordingly, until the spacing is correct.

Sometimes, even tweaking the tracking and kerning aren't enough to give you the desired result. In these cases, setting the problematic characters separately from the rest of the text will allow for more flexibility in placement.

1. This type is correctly spaced as long as it stays on a horizontal baseline.
2. When the same type is placed on a curve, the spacing becomes too open and uneven.
3. Reducing the tracking improves the overall spacing, but there are still some uneven letter combinations.
4. Consistent spacing is finally achieved by adjusting the kerning between problematic letter pairs, most noticeably around the Ys.

YOU'VE probably heard of "Thighs of Steel," "Buns of Steel," and other popular physical fitness titles. But you've probably never heard of an exercise program called "Superior Rectus of Steel"– nor should you. That muscle, along with the inferior rectus and the lateral rectus muscles, controls the movement of the human eyeball. Although I've seen and read many texts that would qualify for the title, our goal, as typesetters, is to avoid giving the reader's eye a workout.

BAD LINE BREAKS & HYPHENATION POINTS make a reader's eye work harder. What happens? You have to skip *back* in the text – back to the end of the previous line, then ahead to the next line, to try to parse the poorly hyphenated word. When you read a hyphenated word, you do two things: you store the first part of the word in your short-term memory, and you make guesses about what the second part of the word will be. All of this happens very fast, and, for most readers, happens below the conscious level. Poor hyphenation raises this process to the conscious level – and suddenly you're thinking about the mechanism of reading, rather than the content of the text. Your eyes get tired, and you get grumpy.

Damned if you do

Given the risk of producing "read rage," why do we use hyphenation at all? Because, without hyphenation, we face horrible letter- and word-spacing in justified text, or wide variation in line lengths in non-justified copy – both of which are at least as irritating to the reader as bad hyphenation.

Like just about everything else having to do with type, it's a balancing act. You've got to work with the word- and letterspacing of your text (as I've mentioned in previous issues), and you've got to watch every line break. And, yes, this means you have to read and at least partially understand the text. There's just no other way.

The hyphenation controls in your page layout program can help you – provided you understand that they're not (and probably can't be) perfect. You've got to help them out – left to their own devices, today's page layout programs are almost guaranteed to produce hyphenation problems. Namely:

☞ *Bad breaks.* Hyphenation breaks should always fall between syllables, and should never appear inside a syllable – but every desktop publishing program will break inside a syllable in certain conditions.

☞ *Short fragments.* When the part of a word before or after the hyphen is too short, readability suffers. You've probably seen paragraphs ending with a line containing only "ly" or "ed."

☞ *"Ladders" of hyphens.* When you see successive lines ending with a hyphen, you're looking at a "ladder" of hyphens. Ladders of hyphens can cause the reader's eye to skip ahead several lines in the text. This is less of a problem (from the reader's point of view) than badly spaced lines. There are two ways to approach this problem.

16

The type that hugs this oversized initial in U&lc has been positioned very carefully to visually align. Notice the open quotes that extend the margin slightly to balance the white space underneath it. Courtesy of International Corporation.

At the Seaside

When I was down beside the sea
A wooden spade they gave to me
To dig the sandy shore.

My holes were empty like a cup.
In every hole the sea came up,
Till it could come no more.

In this poem set in italics, the lines appear to be too far to the right. This is an illusion! But adjusting them, even just a little, will often result in the whole text block being askew.
(A Child's Garden of Verse)

It is helpful to look at your text from a slight distance when correcting problems since it is difficult to know how much of an adjustment is enough. When in doubt, less is more until you get the hang of it.

Visual alignment not only relates to the horizontal positioning of lines of type but the vertical positioning as well. In cases where lines with lots of ascenders and descenders are preceded or followed by lines with few or no ascenders and descenders, the lines will appear to have varying leading while they are all actually the same. You will need to adjust the leading between each line to give the appearance of their being equidistant from each other.
NOTE: When using an italic type, you might notice that it almost never seems to align vertically. In most cases, this is an optical illusion. Beware of making too many adjustments here (if any at all!), or you will wind up with all of your copy askew!

KERNING

Kerning is the adjustment of the space between two specific characters. It most commonly refers to a reduction of space, but it can refer to adding space as well. This is done to balance the white space between certain letter combinations to create an even color and texture as well as to optimize readability.

A quality typeface or font is designed so that each character is spaced to allow for optimum overall letter spacing with as many characters as possible. The spacing consists of the width of the character plus the right and left side bearings. (Visualize this as an invisible box around each character.) But due to the quirks of our Latin alphabet, there are many combinations that don't naturally fit together well and need adjustments. Another factor to be considered is that fonts are kerned (and spaced) to look their best at a particular size range. For this reason, you will find that at larger point sizes, spatial relationships change, and a well-kerned font might still need some tweaking at certain sizes, particularly in headlines.

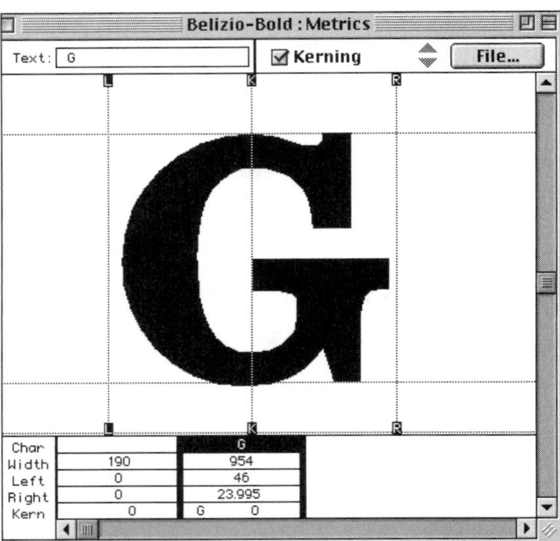

A character's spacing consists of the width of the character plus the right and left side bearings. Think of it as an invisible box around each character. This character has 46 units of space on the left and 24 on the right, as indicated below it.

The object of proper letter fit (and the goal of kerning) is to achieve even texture and color balance between characters, which in turn leads to a consistent overall texture. This sounds great theoretically but can be difficult to achieve due to the idiosyncrasies of the individual designs of the characters of the alphabet. One way to look at it is to imagine pouring sand in between each pair of characters; each combination should have roughly the same amount of sand (or negative space, if you will). With time and experience, your eye will become more trained and fine-tuning type will become second nature to you.

Fa Pa Ta Ye We rk AV PA AT

F. T. Y. P, ." y. r, f' 7. -7 's

Fa Pa Ta Ye We rk AV PA AT

F. T. Y. P, ." y. r, f' 7. -7 's

Wail Vincent Van Gogh New York

February 7, 1957. (516) 784-1716

Wail Vincent Van Gogh New York

February 7, 1957. (516) 784-1716

There are certain commonly known pairs that almost always need to be kerned, such as Ta, Ye, AV, as well as characters next to punctuation, symbols, or numerals. Here you can see how some of these combinations look before and after kern adjustments.

1234567890

1234567890

January 23rd, 1917

January 23rd, 1917

You can see the improvement in the spacing of the numerals after they have been kerned, especially the year.

Beautiful use of properly kerned italics in this colorful piece designed by VSA Partners, Inc. Notice the closed quotes that are kerned to sit above the period and that also hang slightly into the right margin to appear optically aligned. Courtesy of VSA Partners.

Just about all professional fonts come with kern pairs built-in. There are certain commonly known pairs that almost always need to be kerned, such as *Ta*, *Ye*, and *AV*, etc. Many manufacturers concentrate on only these combinations, and therefore you might find many others that need adjustment, such as characters next to punctuation, symbols, or numerals. A high-quality font can have over a thousand kern pairs, but this alone doesn't mean it will look good. If a typeface isn't spaced well to begin with, it will need many more kern pairs than a properly spaced font. Kerning ought not to be used as a Band-Aid for a poorly spaced font.

In any case, there are several things you can do to improve the appearance of your type. First of all, make sure that kerning is turned on in the type preferences of your page-layout program. Some programs have defaults that turn on kerning at 12 point; this should be adjusted to as small a size as possible.

All current design programs have the capability to adjust kerning and tracking manually, or case-by-case, in each document. There are often keyboard shortcuts for these functions that are very helpful when you are making many adjustments. When doing this, enlarge the screen image as necessary to view the adjustments you are making as accurately as possible. At smaller sizes, characters on the screen tend to jump and shift when adjusting the spacing of other characters; this is minimized the larger your screen view. In addition, make sure to proof what you have done on a high-resolution printer. Kerning on the screen is extremely deceptive, as your screen is only 72 dots per inch while the actual printed piece is a much higher resolution. It will become easier to judge how much to kern when you get the hang of it and know what five units actually look like for your application, as unit values vary from application to application.

TYPETIP

Kerning Units

If you use both QuarkXPress and Adobe InDesign (or another Adobe design application), remember that these programs kern and track to different increments, or unit values. QuarkXPress spacing increment is 1/200 of an em square, while InDesign uses 1/1000 of an em square. This means that a kern value of -5 (minus five) in QuarkXPress is equal to -25 in InDesign.

It is important to keep a few more things in mind when kerning your work. Any kern changes you make apply only to the pair that you have highlighted and not the actual font. This means that if you want your document to be consistent (and by all means it should be), you have to search for all same combinations and kern them the same value. This is most important in headlines where variances are most obvious and are extremely undesirable and unprofessional.

Numerals, or figures, as they are often referred to, have their own special spacing and kerning problems. In many fonts, particularly text fonts, numerals have tabular spacing, also called monospacing. That is to say, they all have the same total width, even the numeral one, which is a very narrow character. This is why the "1" in years and dates often appears separated from surrounding numerals. Tabular spacing is done to allow the numerals to align vertically in charts and tables. But if you are not doing a chart or a table, and especially if you are using numerals in headlines, the figures should be kerned—especially the numeral one!

Adjusting Kerning

Adobe InDesign

Automatic kerning:
Adobe InDesign offers several options for adjusting automatic kerning, located in both the Character palette and the Control palette.

- The *Metrics* setting uses a font's built-in kerning pairs. This is the default setting and is usually best when the font has adequate kern-pair tables.
- The *Optical* setting lets InDesign determine the spacing between character pairs. This can be useful when a font has few or no built-in kern pairs or when the overall spacing seems uneven, particularly in text where manual kerning can be impractical, tedious, and time-consuming. Optical kerning is particularly beneficial when combining different fonts or type sizes.
- When the kerning feature of the Character Palette is set to 0, the character pair or copy highlighted is displayed without any of the built-in kern pairs.

Keep in mind that these are all *base* settings, so no matter which setting you use, you can always add manual kerns "on top of" them.

Manual (or custom) kerning:
There are several ways to adjust individual kern pairs. Remember to begin by placing the cursor between two characters. Then choose from these methods:

Palettes:
- Use presets in kerning pull-down menu (increments vary)
- Use the palette arrows (10 unit increments)
- Shift + palette arrows (25 unit increments)

Keyboard commands:
- Option + left or right arrow key (20 unit increments)
- Option + command + left or right arrow key (100 unit increments)

Manual:
- Enter specific values manually in kerning field

QuarkXPress

Manual (or custom) kerning:
There are several ways to adjust individual kern pairs. Remember to begin by placing the cursor between two characters. Then choose from these methods:

Keyboard commands:
- Command / shift + [or] key (20 unit increments)
- Command / opt / shift + [or] key (100 unit increments)

Palettes:
- Go to Measurement Palette
- Use the palette arrows to the right of the kerning field (10 unit increments)
- Option + palette arrows to the right of the kerning field (1 unit increments)

Manual:
- Enter specific values manually in kerning field

NOTE: If you want to remove all the manual kerning, just highlight the desired text and go to Utilities > Remove manual kerning. This is particularly useful when you change fonts and want to go back to the original font metrics.

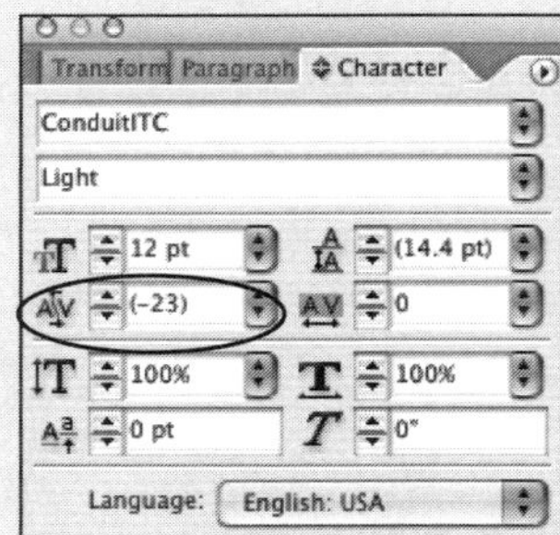

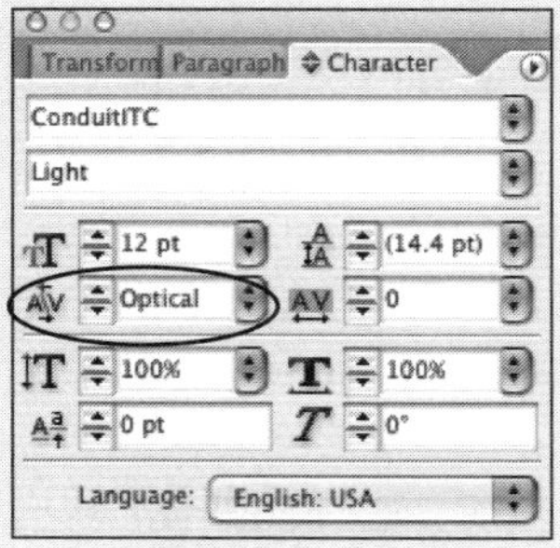

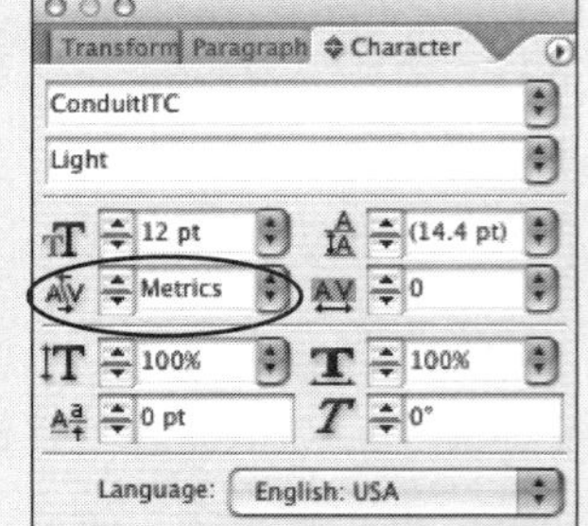

The Metrics and Optical settings as they appear in the kerning field of the Character Palette in Adobe InDesign. Kerning values are also shown in the same field.

TYPETIP

Proportional vs. Tabular Figures

Have you ever noticed that the numeral one in most text faces has extra space around it? It's most obvious when 1 is set next to other numerals, as in dates and phone numbers. Ever wonder why? It's because most numerals in text typefaces are tabular (or monospaced).

Tabular numerals are those where each numeral has the same total character width (that's the width of the numeral itself plus the white space on both sides). Tabular spacing (also referred to as monospacing) allows numerals to align vertically in tables, financial statements, and other columns of figures. Tabular figures are usually lining figures, meaning that they sit on the baseline and have the same height as the caps, but on occasion you'll see oldstyle figures that are tabular. (Oldstyle figures are also called lowercase or nonaligning figures.)

Display typefaces, on the other hand, usually contain proportional figures. The total character widths of these figures are based on the width of the numeral itself plus a small amount of white space around it, so an 8 takes up more width than a 1, for example. Proportional figures can be of the lining or oldstyle variety. In either case, their varying widths give them a more even color and texture, especially around the numeral 1. Proportional figures are not intended for use in charts and tables, since they won't align in vertical columns.

When making your font selection, consider how you'll be using numerals in your design and make sure the font you choose offers the style of figures you need. While it's fairly simple to kern a tabular 1 to improve its spacing in a text setting, it's nearly impossible to kern proportional numerals for vertical alignment in a financial statement.

For maximum flexibility, consider using OpenType fonts, which are becoming available from more and more foundries. This new font format often comes with both tabular and proportional figures in both lining and oldstyle varieties, but it requires using an application that supports this feature.

0123456789
0123456789
0123456789
0123456789

Adobe Caslon Pro has both lining and oldstyle figures, each available with tabular and proportional spacing.

May 17, 1891
May 17, 1891
May 17, 1891
May 17, 1891

Display designs such as Limehouse Script and Dreamland have proportional numerals, while text faces such as Plantin and Bauhaus have tabular figures, which often results in extra space around the numeral one.

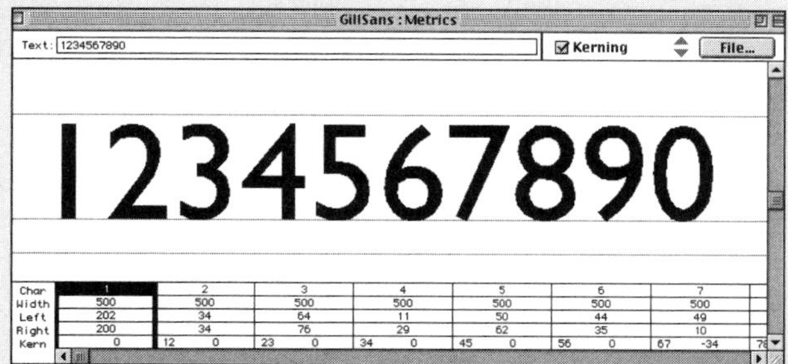

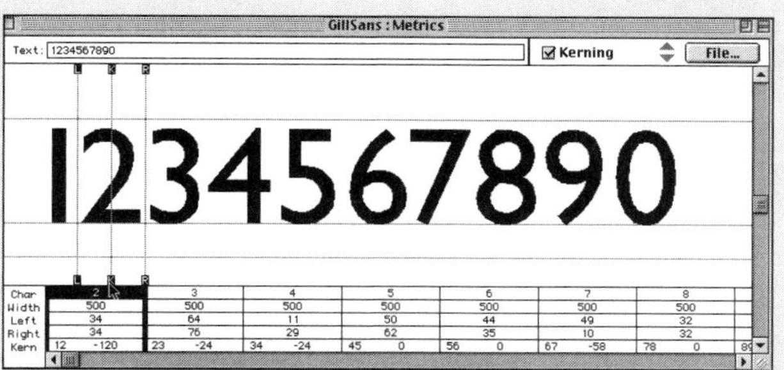

The first example shows the tabular-spaced numerals of Gill Sans. Notice how they all have the same width (500 units) to allow them to align vertically in tables. If you don't need them for that purpose and want to improve the fit of the letters, you can adjust the kerning in a font editor such as FontLab or its pared-down cousin, TypeTool.

Adjusting Tracking

Adobe InDesign

There are several ways to adjust the tracking of highlighted text in InDesign.

Character and Control Palettes:

- Use presets in tracking pull-down menu (increments vary)
- Use the tracking palette arrows (10 unit increments)
- Shift + palette arrows (25 unit increments)

Keyboard commands:

- Option + left or right arrow key (20 unit increments)
- Option + command + left or right arrow key (100 unit increments)

Manual:

- Enter specific values manually in tracking field

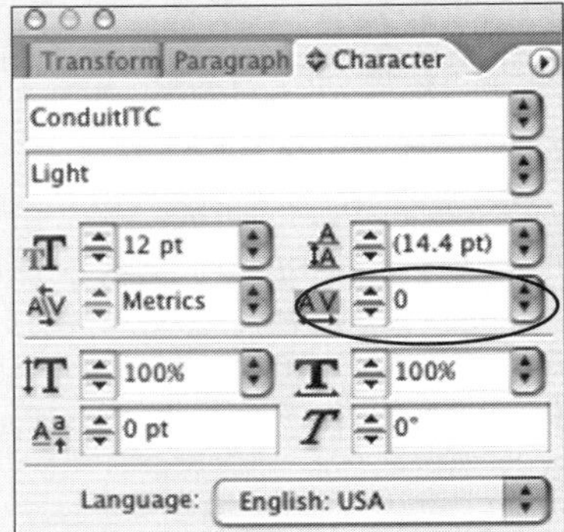

QuarkXPress

There are several ways to adjust the tracking of highlighted text in QuarkXPress.

Keyboard commands:

- Command / shift + [or] key (20 unit increments)
- Command / opt / shift + [or] key (100 unit increments)

Palettes:

- Go to Measurement Palette
- Use the palette arrows to the right of the tracking field (10 unit increments)
- Option + palette arrows to the right of the tracking field (1 unit increments)

Manual:

- Enter specific values manually in tracking field

REMINDER:

Don't forget to highlight desired copy to activate the tracking function. Kerning function will be deactivated when tracking.

TRACKING (OR LETTERSPACING)

Tracking is the addition or reduction of the overall letter spacing in a selected block of text. In most page-layout programs, it can be applied in small increments. This is a very helpful function for fine-tuning the color of your type.

As stated previously, fonts are spaced and kerned to look their best at certain point-size ranges. If your type is much smaller than this range, you will want to open the tracking to improve the readability, as the letters will probably get too close and even begin to touch. Conversely, when you set type at larger sizes, you might need to tighten up the tracking to keep the words from falling apart, so to speak. Some fonts might not be spaced to your liking at any size, and they will need adjusting to give them the balance you are looking for. For example, many older fonts are spaced extremely tightly and often need adjustment.

The term "letterspacing" can also refer to the popular style of setting very open type for stylistic and design purposes. This technique is most effectively used with all-cap settings that don't depend on their letter shapes to be recognized. But unfortunately it is commonly misused and abused. When it is used, it should be limited to a few words or small amounts of copy, as it definitely reduces readability.

Tracking is the addition or reduction of the overall letterspacing in a selected block of text. In most page layout programs, it can be applied in small increments. This is a very helpful function for fine-tuning the color of your type.

Tracking is the addition or reduction of the overall letterspacing in a selected block of text. In most page layout programs, it can be applied in small increments. This is a very helpful function for fine-tuning the color of your type.

Fonts are spaced and kerned to look their best at certain point-size ranges. If your type is much smaller than this range, especially if it is a very bold typeface such as ITC Kabel Ultra (as shown here), you might want to open the tracking to improve the readability. The change might seem subtle, but the readability is improved and it can head off printing problems due to ink spread.

TECHTIP

Adjusting Word Spacing

The ability to adjust the word spacing of any selected text is a somewhat obscure but important feature. Although it is most often used to adjust word spacing in justified type, the same feature can be used to adjust the word spacing of text with any alignment. Here is how:

Adobe InDesign
To change the default or create new word spacing settings:
• Highlight text.
• Open Paragraph Palette.
• Select Justification from palette (pull-down) menu.
• Enter value in Word Spacing row in the middle field labeled *Desired.* The value will be a percentage of the *normal,* or built-in value of the selected font.

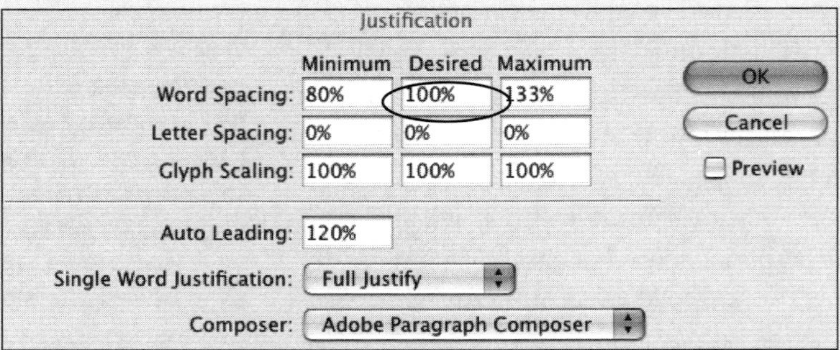

QuarkXPress
To change the default or create new word spacing settings:
• Open Hyphenation & Justification (H&J) dialog box via Edit > H&J or keyboard command opt / com / J.
• Edit *Standard* to change the default or click on *New* to create a custom setting.
• Under Justification method, enter the desired value in the *Space* row in the middle field labeled *Opt.* The value will be a percentage of the normal, or built-in value of the selected font.
• Name the setting if it is new.

To access the setting:
• Highlight text.
• Go to Style > Formats which opens the Paragraph Attributes dialog box or
• Use keyboard command Shift / com / F which opens the Paragraph Attributes dialog box.
• Select setting from H&J pull-down menu.

NOTE: The default word spacing setting in QuarkXPress is 110% so be sure and reset to 100% before evaluating for further changes.

IMPORTANT:
If you change the font or use a document as a template, note that the previous kerning, tracking, and word spacing settings will still be in effect unless you change them.

WORD SPACING

The amount of space between words is called word spacing, naturally. The word spacing should not be so little that the words start to run into each other and not so much that your eye has trouble reading groups of words because it is interrupted by large white blocks. This value is predetermined by your font (and differs from font to font), but it can be modified by changing the "optimum space" value in the H&J preferences in your page-layout program. For example, some commercial fonts have too much word spacing. This spacing can be improved by setting the word space to around 80 percent, but be sure to look over the type and make any necessary adjustments to this value until the desired color is achieved.

NOTE: Make sure the default in your software is set to 100 percent. Some are annoyingly preset to 110 percent; if this is the case, be sure to reset it to 100 percent.

MASSAGE THE RAPIST

MASSAGE THERAPIST

Look how an improperly placed word space can change the meaning totally, as is cleverly demonstrated in this promotional piece designed by Stephen Banham of The Letterbox.

The amount of space between words is called word spacing, naturally. The word spacing should not be so little that the words start to run into each other, and not so much that your eye has trouble reading groups of words because it is being interrupted by large white blocks.

The amount of space between words is called word spacing, naturally. The word spacing should not be so little that the words start to run into each other, and not so much that your eye has trouble reading groups of words because it is being interrupted by large white blocks.

The amount of space between words is called word spacing, naturally. The word spacing should not be so little that the words start to run into each other, and not so much that your eye has trouble reading groups of words because it is being interrupted by large white blocks.

The word spacing should not be so little that the words start to run into each other, as in the first example, and not so much that your eye has trouble reading groups of words because it is interrupted by large white blocks, as in the second text block. The third example is the most balanced and the most readable.

EXERCISE

Type Poster

David Kadavy, Instructor, Metropolitan Community College, Omaha, Nebraska

Objective

This project will familiarize the student with typographic history and hone the student's layout skills.

Assignment

Part 1: From the list of historic type designers below, select one and write a 300 to 500 word report of their work. Including information about their life, background, and type design philosophy.

Part 2: Using this report as body text, design an 11 x 17 inch poster using one of that type designer's typefaces. The design should be in a style that is appropriate for that designer, and that expresses and incorporates his or her design philosophy. Any weights and versions within the selected type family may be used. Headline, subhead, and other text elements can be added at your discretion.

Type Designers

John Baskerville, *Baskerville*
Giambattista Bodoni, *Bodoni*
William Caslon, *Caslon*
Firmin Didot, *Didot*
Frederic Goudy, *Goudy*
Nicolas Jenson, *Jenson*
Max Miedinger, *Helvetica (Helvetica Neue okay)*
Paul Renner, *Futura*

Type posters by Theresa Byrne-Sain, Michelle Chamlee, and Martha Sumner-Kenney. Courtesy of Theresa Byrne-Sain, Michelle Chamlee, and Martha Sumner-Kenney.

EXERCISE

Spacing, Kerning, and Visual Alignment Exploration

Ilene Strizver, Faculty, School of Visual Arts, New York, New York

Objective

To develop a sensitivity and awareness of the spacing between the characters, words, and lines. Doing the spacing manually with marker and paper first forces one to slowly and methodically explore the shapes of each letter, word, and line of type and the relationships between them.

Assignment

Step 1: Set the following text in a serif text face from a major foundry. Set in three centered lines at 60/72 point (72 point leading).

New grilled wooden key's
"To Be DAVID WALDEN
UNITED STATES 10011."
Van Gogh New York in Awe
May 7, 1957. (511) 784-1710

Turn off kerning (turn off in the application preferences if using Quark, or set kerning to zero for that text if using InDesign); set tracking very open so the text is completely letterspaced. The concept is to eliminate all visual spacing and kerning cues. Set the text twice, one underneath the other.

Step 2: Using tracing paper and a pencil or fine black marker, trace and space each character in the text, tightening and adjusting the spacing between the letters and the words. Pay particular attention to "difficult" or troublesome letter combinations. Redraw as many times as necessary until even color and balance is achieved. One you have spaced each line to your satisfaction, redraw and adjust the vertical and horizontal alignment as necessary.

Step 3: Go back to the first text on your computer and adjust the spacing as follows: using *only* the kerning function (do not use tracking) and leading, manually space the text until it looks like your tracing. (Keyboard commands for kerning work great here.) Continue to adjust and fine-tune until it looks the best it can.

Step 4: Go to the second text, set tracking back to zero, and turn on kerning. Compare the two texts. Evaluate the differences, if any, and tweak your first version if necessary. If you " disagree" with any of the built-in spacing in the second version, be ready to explain and justify your opinion.
REMEMBER: Not all fonts come with perfect spacing and kerning.

New grilled wooden key's
"To Be DAVID WALDEN
UNITED STATES 10011."
Van Gogh New York in Awe
May 7, 1957. (511) 784-1710

New grilled wooden key's
"To Be DAVID WALDEN
UNITED STATES 10011."
Van Gogh New York in Awe
May 7, 1957. (511) 784-1710

The upper showing is set in Adobe Minion Pro with kerning turned off and with +30 tracking in Adobe InDesign units. The lower showing has kerning turned on, zero tracking, and additional custom kerning.

When most of u
quirmed throu
grammar lesson
n grade schoo
we assumed tha
we were taugh
everything abo
reading and w
iting the Engli
h language th
ever need to kn

CHAPTER NINE

TYPOGRAPHIC TYPOS AND HOW TO AVOID THEM

When most of us squirmed through grammar lessons in grade school, we assumed that we were taught everything about reading and writing the English language that we would ever need to know. But if you use a computer for typesetting, this is no longer true. You need to know a few small but very important things if you want your work to be professional looking and grammatically correct.

In some cases, there are several variations of punctuation that we were taught came in only one flavor, such as dashes, quotation marks, apostrophes, and parentheses. While this might be true for handwriting, which is much more forgiving and individual in style, it isn't so for typesetting. Prior to desktop typography, it was left to typographers to know the differences between similar characters, where they were located on their keyboard, and what was grammatically and typographically correct. Once designers, administrative assistants, and the rest of us started setting type, a lot of this information fell through the cracks unless one was particularly knowledgeable about typography.

This problem was compounded by the fact that many of these characters are hard to find on the keyboard and require depressing combinations of keys to access them (many design programs now have glyph charts that make finding and using these characters a snap!). This, to some degree, can be attributed to the engineers who designed the standard keyboard layout that we all use today. Since there was room for only 256 characters on the keyboard layout at that time (OpenType has changed all that), decisions had to be made with regard to which characters (including accented, foreign, and mathematical characters) to include. Engineers tend to think mathematically and scientifically rather than grammatically and typographically, which resulted in some commonly used characters, such as quotation marks and fractions, being hidden or nonexistent.

HYPHEN, EN DASH, AND EM DASH

These three similar typographic characters are all horizontal lines of varying lengths. They all have different purposes, and the characters are often confused and misused, leading to inaccurate and unprofessional typography.

A hyphen, which is the shortest in length, is used to hyphenate words that break at the end of a line or to connect elements of a compound word such as go-between, ill-fated, and run-of-the-mill, and that's it. It is easily found on the keyboard to the right of the zero.

An en dash is wider than a hyphen and narrower than an em dash, and it is the least commonly used and understood of the three. It is used to indicate a continuation of time, years, and dates (similar to using the words "to" and "from") such as 9 AM–5 PM, Monday–Friday, or May 2–7. It is accessed from the Mac keyboard with the (option/hyphen) keys.

An em dash, which is the longest of the three, is used to indicate a break in thought–as is illustrated in this sentence. It is also occasionally used to separate a thought within a sentence–such as this one–requiring an em-dash at the beginning and the end of the thought. It is accessed from the Mac keyboard by pressing the (option/shift/hyphen) keys.

As you can see here, the length and style of hyphens and en and em dashes vary tremendously from typeface to typeface.

Most of us have seen copy with two hyphens where an em dash should be. This typographically incorrect–and ugly–practice is a holdover from typewriter days when there were no em dashes on the keyboard, just hyphens. It has become a habit for some, especially if they used a typewriter before they were keyboarding on a computer.

The lengths of these characters are not standard but vary from typeface to typeface, as do their side bearings (the designated space to the right and left). Some en dashes are the width of the lowercase n, and em dashes the width of the m; others have no relationship at all, and are 500 and 1000 units (a measurement relative to the point size), respectively. There are different philosophies behind these differences, but the principles of their usage remain the same.

9:00–5:00 PM
Monday–Friday
1984–1997

An en dash is wider than a hyphen and narrower than an em dash. It is used to indicate a continuation of time, years, and dates.

Some room for artistic license is allowed in the use of these characters when their design or spacing seems out of proportion. Oftentimes the em dash seems much too wide for the proportions of the typeface and creates a gaping hole in the color and texture of the text. In these cases, it is the practice of some designers to replace them with an en dash. Another stylistic preference is to add a space before and after en and em dashes. (This is most common on the Web.) Although this is not the norm (and not considered correct by some purists), if the dashes appear too tight, go ahead and do this. A better solution is to open the kerning between the dashes and their surrounding letters; this way you have more control over the space. Just remember to be consistent throughout or the text will be an unprofessional jumble of varying styles.

This old town of Salem—my native place, though I have dwelt much away from it both in boyhood and maturer years—possesses, or did possess, a hold on my affection, the force of which I have never realized during my seasons of actual residence here.

This old town of Salem–my native place, though I have dwelt much away from it both in boyhood and maturer years–possesses, or did possess, a hold on my affection, the force of which I have never realized during my seasons of actual residence here.

This old town of Salem -- my native place, though I have dwelt much away from it both in boyhood and maturer years -- possesses, or did possess, a hold on my affection, the force of which I have never realized during my seasons of actual residence here.

An em dash, which is longer than both the hyphen and en dash, is used to indicate a break in thought as illustrated in the first paragraph. It can be replaced with an en dash when the em dash is extremely wide (second paragraph). The last paragraph illustrates what never to do! Using two hyphens to indicate an em dash is a holdover from typewriter days, and it is incorrect in fine typography. (Scarlet Letter)

His voice and laugh, which perpetually re-echoed through the Custom-House, had nothing of the tremulous quaver and cackle of an old man's utterance; they came strutting out of his lungs, like the crow of a cock, or the blast of a clarion.

A hyphen, which is shorter in length than the en or em dash, is used to hyphenate words that break at the end of a line or to connect elements of a compound word such as those shown in this paragraph. (Scarlet Letter)

QUOTATION MARKS

One of the most misused typographic elements in desktop typography is the use of straight typewriter quotation marks, or “dumb” quotes, which are all too easily accessed on your keyboard, instead of true typographic quotation marks, also called “smart “ quotes, “curly” quotes, or typographer’s quotes, which are harder to access. Smart quotes have an opening and a closing version, and they are design sensitive, usually being designed differently for each typeface. “Dumb” quotes are usually simple tapered marks. They are also referred to as “primes” or inch and foot marks, which is a function they should actually be used for.

Misuse of “dumb” quotes is one of the most common typographic faux pas, which is repeatedly found in high-end print, multimedia advertising, movie credits, as well as nonprofessional work. Once again, the standard Mac layout designed by engineers, not graphic designers or typographers, put old-fashioned straight quotes in place of real quotes in the keyboard layout, and we are left to straighten out the mess.

There are several ways to address this problem. The easiest is to select “smart “ quotes or “typographer’s” quotes in the preferences of your software. This works for any newly keyboarded copy. It doesn’t always work when you import copy that has not been formatted this way, especially copy picked up from e-mail or the Web. So proof your work carefully and make the necessary conversions to make your work consistent and professional.

“smart” quotes
"dumb" quotes

“smart” quotes
"dumb" quotes

“smart” quotes
"dumb" quotes

“smart” quotes
"dumb" quotes

“smart” quotes
″dumb″ quotes

“smart” quotes
"dumb" quotes

“smart” quotes
"dumb" quotes

“smart” quotes
"dumb" quotes

The design of both “smart” and “dumb” quotes varies from face to face, but the rule is always the same: always use smart quotes (or never use dumb quotes, take your pick).

Smart Quotes

Adobe InDesign

Adobe InDesign (as well as Microsoft Word) refers to smart quotes as typographer's quotes. InDesign will automatically convert "dumb quotes" (or "typewriter quotes" as they call them) into typographer's quotes for an entire document when you set the Type Options as follows:

• InDesign / Preferences / Type / Use Typographer's Quotes

You can easily change individual typographer's quotes back into prime marks, that is, inch and foot marks, by highlighting the quote, then selecting the appropriate mark from the Glyphs Palette located under Type.

You can reverse the process and replace typographer's quotes individually by highlighting the quote or apostrophe, and selecting the appropriate quote under Type / Special Characters.

QuarkXPress

When importing text, QuarkXPress will automatically convert "dumb" quotes and apostrophes into smart quotes if you do the following:

• Go to File > Import text or use the keyboard shortcut Com / E.

• Select Convert Quotes in the dialog box before importing.

This is a global command and will convert prime marks (inch and foot marks) as well as quotes and apostrophes; so if your text has measurements, you will have to manually convert them back to measurements. This can be done via the Glyph Palette, or with the keyboard shortcut Ctrl / quote for single prime (foot mark) or Ctrl / shift / quote for double prime (inch mark).

NOTE: Always use the Import Text feature rather than copy and paste if you want the quotes converted. If the copy is from an email or from the Internet, place it in a text document first, them import as instructed above.

TYPETIP

Smarten-up Your Quotes Manually

When your work has a mixture of smart and dumb quotes (as is common when copy comes from more than one source), it is imperative to make sure they are all converted accurately for professional-looking typography. You can make the replacements manually, but it is easy to miss some, especially in long copy. Be sure to proof your work carefully if you do this.

The better solution is to use the "search-and-replace" feature of your software. Some programs are "smart" and know where to replace the single-design primes with an open or a closed quote. If yours doesn't, try this:

• Start by searching for a combination of a space before a "dumb" quote and replace with a space and a "smart" quote.

• Conversely, search for a "dumb" quote with a space next to it, and replace with a closing "smart" quote and a space.

• Proof your work carefully to make sure all conversions were made properly.

APOSTROPHES

The situation for apostrophes is the same as for quotes. That is, the default keyboard character is a straight typewriter apostrophe rather than the typographically correct "smart" apostrophe. Replace them as you would dumb quotations marks.

SPACES

There is never a need for double spaces between sentences when setting type on your computer, as was done when using a typewriter. Curious how this practice came about? Just about all fonts on a computer (except Courier) have proportional spacing, and a single space creates the visual separation needed between sentences. Typewriter fonts are monospaced, which means that every letter takes up the same space, even the narrow letters. This makes for very open-looking spacing, and a double word space was necessary to achieve a noticeable separation between sentences.

Many people still use double spacing on a computer and don't know it is incorrect in typography. Be particularly aware of this in copy that is given to you by others who are used to typewriter formatting. An easy way to fix these double spaces is to use the search-and-replace feature of your word processing or design program so you can catch them all. If you fix them manually, it is easy to miss some; but if you choose to do it this way, proof the printed piece rather than on screen, where it is difficult to spot double spaces.

There can be but one room below, for there is but one chimney. The silly moles had not the sense to see that they did not need a door apiece. That shows they have no mother. We will leave the cake on the shore of the Mermaids' Lagoon. These boys are always swimming about there, playing with the mermaids. They will find the cake and they will gobble it up.

The use of a double space to separate sentences was the accepted style for typewriter faces such as Courier, shown here. It is incorrect in fine typography. (Alice in Wonderland)

There can be but one room below, for there is but one chimney. The silly moles had not the sense to see that they did not need a door apiece. That shows they have no mother. We will leave the cake on the shore of the Mermaids' Lagoon. These boys are always swimming about there, playing with the mermaids. They will find the cake and they will gobble it up.

There can be but one room below, for there is but one chimney. The silly moles had not the sense to see that they did not need a door apiece. That shows they have no mother. We will leave the cake on the shore of the Mermaids' Lagoon. These boys are always swimming about there, playing with the mermaids. They will find the cake and they will gobble it up.

The first paragraph, set in ITC Century, shows the typographically incorrect practice of adding two spaces between sentences. It creates lots of holes throughout your text. The second example has been corrected to one space, and the color and texture of the text is improved as well as being typographically correct.

EXERCISE

Editorial Design

Ilene Strizver, Faculty, School of Visual Arts, New York, New York

Objective

Design an editorial spread, paying as much attention to the typographic details and refinements as to the overall layout and design.

Instructor Preparation

Select three headlines (with subheads) of varying content and presentation requirements. They can be fictional or from real magazines. Headlines should suggest visual images capable of being translated typographically. Suggested categories are: (1) food magazine spread, include at least one recipe and optional sidebar; (2) music magazine interview, include introduction, then question and answer section; and (3) news or psychology magazine, include at least one sidebar.

Assignment

Select one of the three chosen editorial (magazine) topics; design a spread (two adjoining pages) for an 8 ½ x 11 inch magazine. Include images, illustrations, or photos. Use dummy text, not "greeking." Try to make the first sentence and/or paragraph relate to the headline. Add a byline for all. Add folios, footers, pull quotes, and other elements (captions, credits, etc.) to make it appear authentic.

Process

Step 1: Do your research by studying three well-designed magazines. Select two or three feature spreads; analyze the layout, design, and typography. Write a brief summary of each discussing which elements contribute to, and which elements detract from, the success of the spread.

Step 2: Design your chosen spread, taking into consideration everything you have learned about type and typographic design, including appropriate headline and text font, point size and leading, information hierarchy, emphasis, indents, alignment, hyphenation, justification (if used), initial caps, widows and orphans, and overall letter spacing (tracking and kerning). Pay close attention to column width, inner and outer margins, and overall white space.

CHAPTER TEN

SIGNS, SYMBOLS, AND DINGBATS

There are several other typographic elements not previously men tioned that you will needed from time to time. Not surprisingly, they are often misunderstood, as well as improperly or tastelessly used.

REGISTER, TRADEMARK, AND COPYRIGHT SYMBOLS

At some point, every designer needs to use one or more of these three symbols, and there are a few essential things to know about them. Nothing is worse than seeing a tiny, unreadable register mark in text or a huge, annoying trademark in a headline.

The register, trademark, and copyright symbols vary in design in every font. Sometimes they are design-sensitive, and other times they are not. If the design appears inappropriate, illegible, or unclear, you can substitute one from another font. Although many people prefer to use serif symbols with serif fonts and sans with sans, I personally prefer to use a nice, clean sans symbol for text usage (such as those from Helvetica or ITC Franklin Gothic), as they tend to be very readable and print cleanly at small sizes. When setting a headline, more latitude is given with the design, as readability is less of a problem.

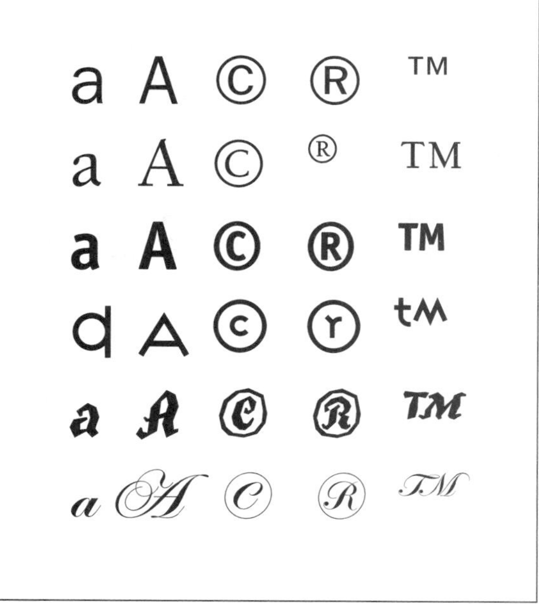

These three symbols, shown next to other characters in the font, vary in design in every font. Sometimes they are design-sensitive, and other times they are not.

Now let's talk about size,

especially since this varies so much from font to font. When using a ® or a ™ after a word, the point size should be adjusted if necessary, independently from the rest of the text, to look clean and legible yet unobtrusive. A general guideline for text is to make these symbols a little smaller than half the x-height; as your text gets larger, they can become proportionately smaller, especially in headlines. These symbols are legal designations, not exciting graphic elements, and making them too large can detract from the design.

The copyright symbol (©) is used in two manners: it is sometimes treated the same sizewise as the (®) and the (™), but more frequently it is used in a much larger size. When it appears before a year, as in ©1998, or the name of a company, the size should be somewhere between the x-height and cap height. If using oldstyle figures for a year beginning with a figure one, be sure to match the size of the one, and not some of the other, taller numerals in the year.

Macintosh®
MACINTOSH®
Slowcraft™
SLOWCRAFT™

Macintosh®
MACINTOSH®
Slowcraft™
SLOWCRAFT™

A general guideline for text is to make these symbols a little smaller than half the x-height; as your text gets larger, they should become proportionately smaller, especially when used in headlines.

© 1957 Slowcraft Inc.

© 1957 Slowcraft Inc.

© 1957 SLOWCRAFT INC.

© 1957 SLOWCRAFT INC.

Placed before a year, the copyright symbol size should be somewhere between the x-height and cap height of the other type. When using oldstyle figures, match the size of the one, not the other, taller numerals.

BULLETS

A bullet is a large dot used to draw attention to a list of items that either have been extracted from your text or are independent of the text. The bullet that is part of your font might need to be altered in size or position, as many are too large or small. Don't make the mistake of assuming that if it is in the font, it is the right size.

Bullets should be centered on either the cap height or x-height, depending on the nature of your listing. If all of your items begin with a cap, center the bullet on the cap, or a bit lower, so it balances with the negative spaces created by the lowercase. If your items all begin with lowercase, center the bullets on the x-height. Either insert a space after the bullet or set a tab for the following text to avoid crowding.

Bulleted points are usually aligned with the left margin. Continuing text can align with the text on the first line with the use of tabs. This creates an indent that draws attention to each new bullet. If you prefer, you can align the continuing text with the bullet, creating a flush left alignment for all elements. An alterna-

● A tuner

• A tuner

Bullets shouldn't be too large or too small.

tive for bullet alignment is to allow them to overhang the left margin, with the actual text aligning with the left margin.

If you want to be a bit more creative, you can substitute other symbols and dingbats for the bullets. Simple shapes, such as squares, triangles, and check marks, work well, as well as more decorative graphics, such as those found in ITC Zapf dingbats, or other dingbat or ornamental fonts, You can even use color to direct attention to them. Just keep it simple and be consistent.

Things to have in your case at all times:
- A tuner
- New set of strings
- A few cords
- Tools for adjusting your guitar
- Metronome

Things to have in your case at all times:
- a tuner
- new set of strings
- a few cords
- tools for adjusting your guitar
- metronome

Bullets should be centered on either the cap height or x-height, depending on the nature of your listing.

These are some alternatives to bullets for the same effect:

■ a tuner
➾ new set of strings
✦ a few cords
➜ metronome
❖ tools for adjusting your guitar
✔ Phillips screwdriver

If you want to be a bit more creative, you can substitute other symbols for the actual bullets, such as squares, triangles, or check marks, just not all at once as shown here!

ELLIPSES

The ellipsis (...) is a single character consisting of a series of three evenly spaced dots used to indicate missing type or a continuation of type. It is a totally separate character that is spaced the same as or more open than periods. If the spacing in the ellipsis is too tight, use three periods instead and track out as desired.

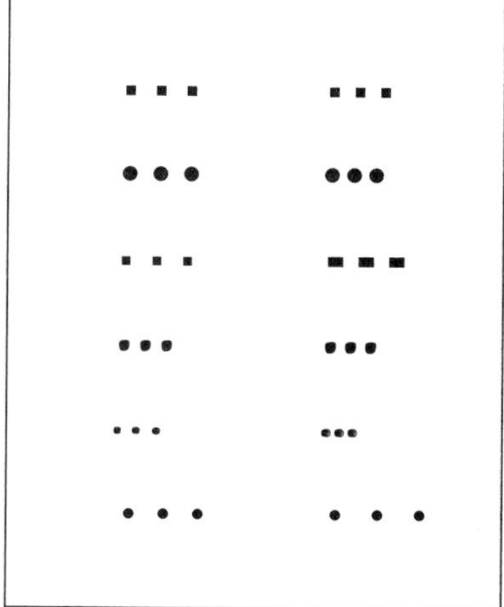

The size, design, and spacing of ellipses vary from typeface to typeface (left) compared to periods in the same font (right).

PARENTHESES, BRACKETS, BRACES, AND ANGLED BRACKETS

These four symbols are always used in pairs, and all have a similar function, which is to enclose text not directly related to the context of the sentence.

Parentheses are the most common of the four, and they are primarily used to enclose interjected, explanatory, or qualifying remarks. They also are of particular use for area codes and mathematical formulas, usually algebra.

Brackets, also called square brackets, are usually used to enclose copy within a parenthetical phrase, or more simply put, copy already enclosed within parentheses. Brackets are also used to enclose explanations or comments by the author, as well as for mathematical expressions and specific scientific compounds.

Braces, also called curly brackets, are a more decorative form of bracket, and are traditionally used for certain mathematical expressions. They are occasionally used (with creative license) to replace parentheses in certain instances, such as to enclose a Web site or e-mail address.

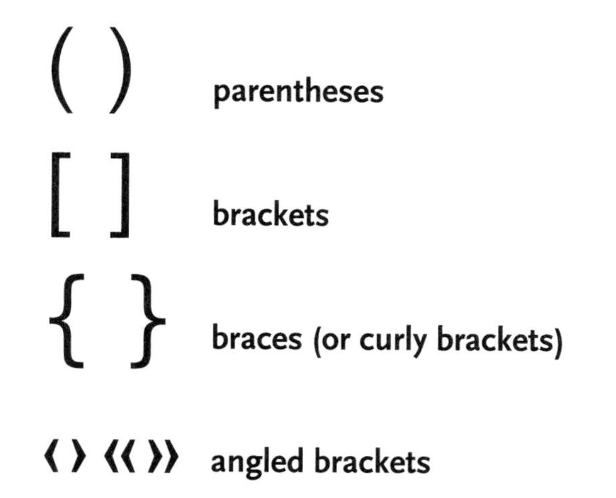

The design differences between parentheses, brackets, braces, and angled brackets are clearly seen here.

The use of *angled brackets* to enclose text has become the accepted style in e-mail and on the Internet, particularly when copying part or all of an e-mail as part of a reply. There doesn't seem to be one definitive style, as it varies from browser to browser in the direction the brackets face, as well as whether they are used in single or double form: anything goes on the Internet, it seems.

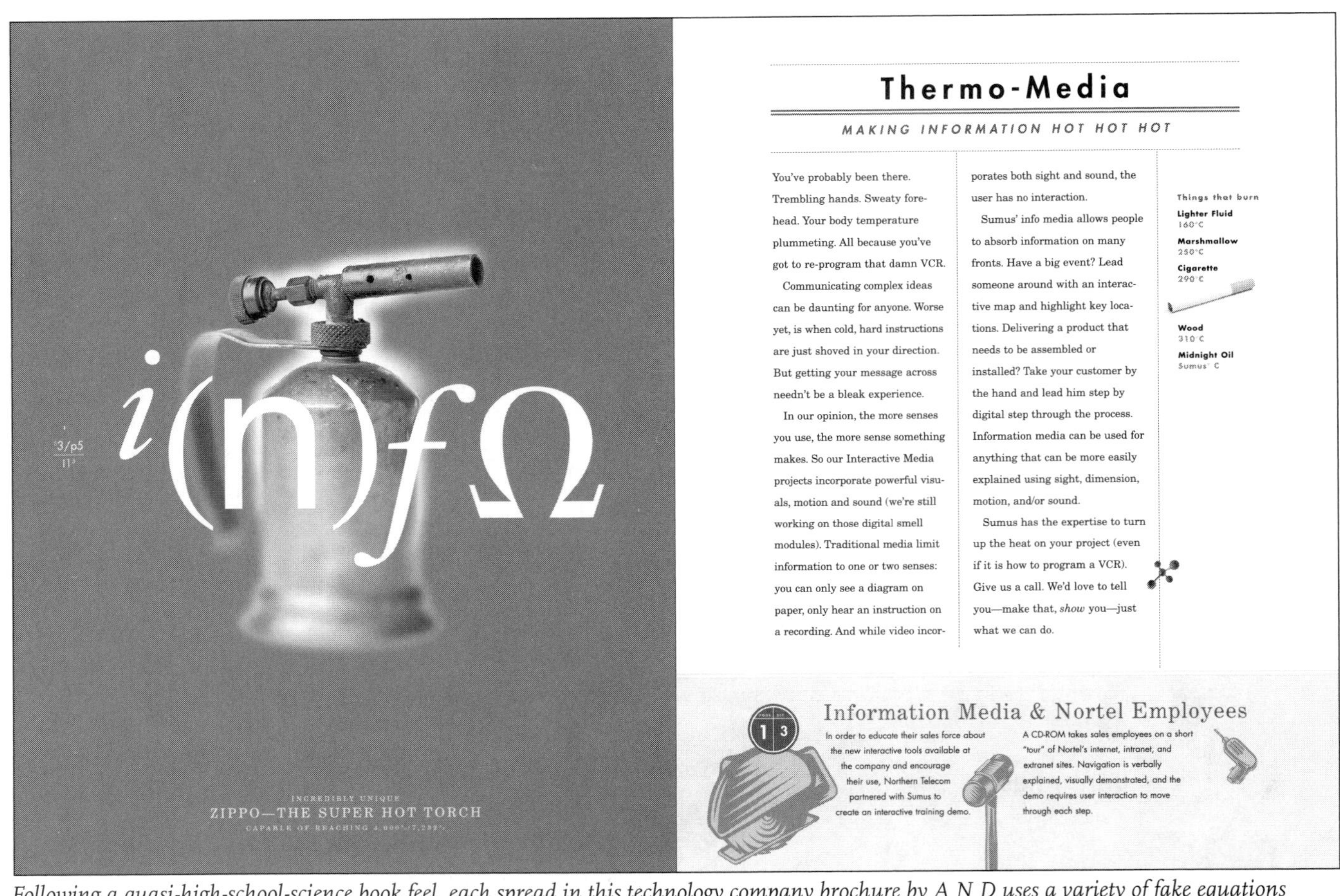

Following a quasi-high-school-science book feel, each spread in this technology company brochure by A N D uses a variety of fake equations (including parentheses) to spell out the main topic–in this case, INFO. The layout, type treatment, and color scheme were all chosen to suggest the look of textbooks from the 1950s and 1960s.

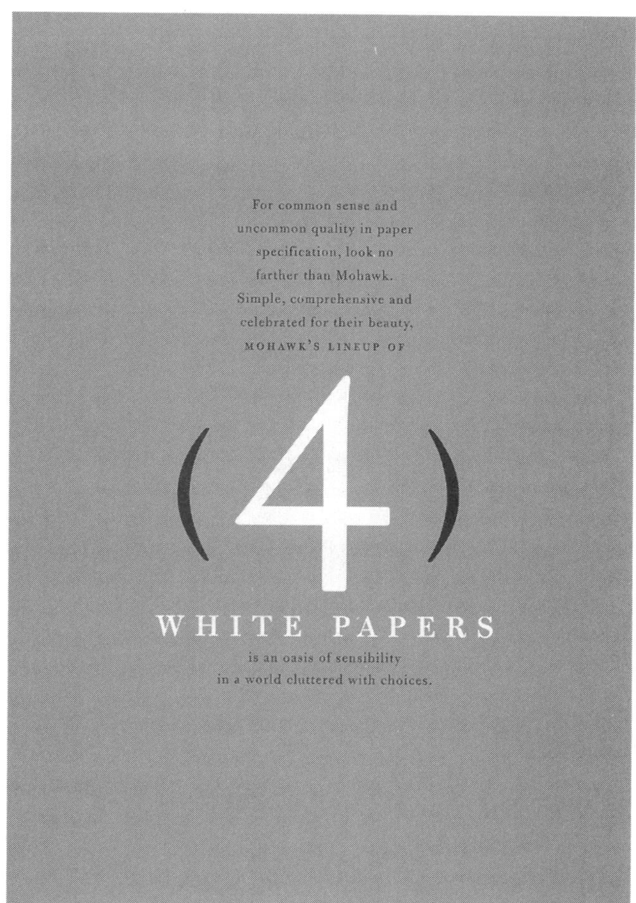

The use of parentheses to accentuate an important typographic element in this piece designed by VSA Partners, Inc. Courtesy of VSA Partners, Inc.

Brackets are sometimes used as design elements, as seen in this promotional piece by Rigsby Design and in this business card by Michael Vanderbyl Design. Courtesy of Rigsby Design and Michael Vanderbyl Design.

ACCENTS

Most well-made fonts by reputable manufacturers include a selection of accented characters, accents, and other diacritical marks needed to set foreign words and names. Some are composite characters, which combine characters with accents or marks to create a separate character; others are accents and marks by themselves, called floating accents. These floating accents can be used to create many more accented characters than are available within the font. OpenType fonts have the capability to include thousands more characters than Type1 and TrueType fonts; this often includes more robust foreign language support. Check carefully to see what your font includes before creating your own.

´ ¨ ` ˆ ˜ ¯ ˘ ˙ ˚ ¸ ˛ ˝ ˇ

áàâäãå ÁÀÂÄÃÅ çÇ

éèêë ÉÈÊË íìîï ÍÌÎÏ

ñÑ óòôöõ ÓÒÔÖÕ

úùûü ÚÙÛÜ ÿŸ

These are standard floating accents and accented characters available in many fonts.

TYPETIP

Creating Accented Characters

Need an accented or foreign character? You might already have it. First, check the Glyph Palette to see if the character you need is available in the font. If not, you can easily create an accented character if both the character and the floating accent are available.

How to create an accented character:

- Place the accent after the character.
- Use baseline shift to raise (or lower) the accent to the desired position
- Use extreme kerning to center the accent over the character.

Accented characters are easily created from floating accents.

EURO

Since 2002, the euro has been the exclusive currency of 12 European countries, including Austria, Belgium, Finland, France (except Pacific territories using the CFP franc), Germany, Greece, Ireland, Italy, Luxembourg, The Netherlands, Portugal, and Spain. The euro symbol looks like a capital C with a double crossbar.

Both Apple and Microsoft have included euro symbols in fonts distributed with their operating systems and applications since 1998, and most fonts released since then contain the euro symbol (it replaces the little-used international currency symbol). The euro symbol can be accessed on a Mac by pressing shift / option / 2, but is most easily located and inserted using the glyph palette.

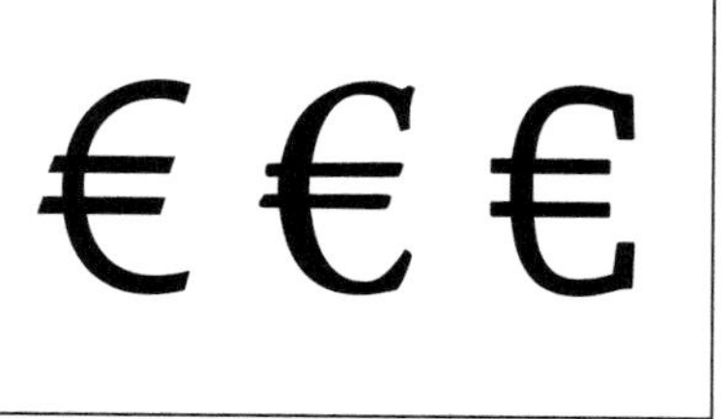

Three examples of the Euro.

Many foundries have remanufactured their font libraries to include the euro mark, and include the symbol in new releases. Others have offered freely available fonts that contain euro glyphs in various weights and styles, designed to blend in with a wide range of typestyles. It's a good idea to download several of these for when you need Euros and are using an older, "pre-euro" font.

FRACTIONS

Fractions are a fairly common element in typeset copy. Considering their frequent occurrence, one would think they would be commonly available or easily created. Unfortunately this is not always the case. On a Mac using Type1 or TrueType fonts, they don't exist, unless there is a separate fraction font or expert set containing them. A few fractions are sometimes available on a PC (1/4, 1/2, 3/4), but they are hidden away. If you do use them, you can't combine the supplied fractions with other ones you create yourself, as they will undoubtedly look very different.

Some design software has the ability to create fractions on the fly; others have plug-ins, extensions, or scripts that do the same thing. OpenType fonts have the capability of containing many fractions, but these extra characters are only accessible via applications that support their extended character compliment. Most OpenType fonts have the ability to make diagonal fractions on-the-fly, but this is another advanced feature that has to be supported by your application. If your applica-

TECHTIP

Fractions in QuarkXPress

Need fractions but your font doesn't have them? QuarkXPress 7.0 has a script that can automatically convert ugly linear fractions to diagonal ones. Try this:

- Type in the numerator, slash and denominator (do NOT use the fraction bar)
- Select the fraction and in the top menu go to Script (under the little icon on the far right) > Typography > Make Fractions

Although the weights of the numerator and denominator are usually too light, it is better-looking than a linear fraction.

NOTE: While you must use the slash and not the fraction bar for this script to run, you can occasionally get a better result of you replace with the fraction bar in the converted fraction, but you might have to kern as necessary for good spacing.

tion does, just turn on the Fractions option in the OpenType menu, type in the numerator, slash or fraction bar, and denominator, and it will automatically convert to a diagonal fraction. This function has to be built into the font (remember, OpenType fonts have a brain), so you'll probably have to try it out to make sure it works.

TYPETIP

Build Your Own Fractions

You can build fractions manually with the options available within your application. It is a bit time-consuming, but the result is a fairly professional-looking fraction. **NOTE:** These instructions are for lining figures, so adjust accordingly for oldstyle figures.

1/2 1/2

1. Begin by typing in the numerator and denominator separated with a slash or a fraction bar (option / shift / 1, or just use the glyph palette). The fraction bar is weighted, spaced, and angled differently than the slash (usually lighter and steeper in angle); but depending on their individual design and which method you use to create fractions, one might look better than the other. The slash bar usually works better for this method, but try them both.

1⁄2 1⁄2

2. Reduce the point size of the numerator and the denominator by about 60 percent.

1⁄2 1⁄2

3. Raise the numerator using baseline shift until it top-aligns with the fraction bar.

1⁄2 1⁄2

4. Adjusting the spacing between these three elements with the kern feature as necessary.

One problem with this method is that the weight of the fraction bar might be too heavy next to the reduced numerals, but it needs to remain cap height to look appropriate. Dependent upon the font used, this method can either look great or shoddy. But if you do make fractions this way, be sure to be consistent throughout your text.

ITC ZAPF DINGBATS

ITC Zapf Dingbats is a wonderful nontypographic font consisting of many useful elements not available in other fonts. It is resident in many printers, meaning it was already in the brain of your printer when you bought it and is automatically available for use.

You will find many uses for Zapf Dingbats. Some of the most commonly used elements are solid circles, squares (and other geometric shapes), arrows, check boxes, hearts, and leaf flourishes. Dingbats can be used for many things, such as calling attention to items in a list, separating paragraphs, and indicating the end of an article as end marks. It is worth the time to become familiar with this font.

ITC Zapf Dingbats

❀❁❂❃❄❅❆❇❈❉❊❋

●❍■❏❐❑❒▲▼◆◗❘❙❚

✢✣✤✥❖✦✧★✩✪✫✬✭

✮✯✰✱✲✳✴✵✶✷✸✹✺✻✼✽✾✿❀

✎✏✐✑✒✈✉✓✔✕✖✗✘

✁✂✃✄☛☞✍✌☎✆❡✙✚✛✜✝✞✟✠✡

❛❜❝❞❢❣❥❦❧♣♦♥❤❥♠

➔→➙⟶➛➜➝➞➟➠➡➢➣➤➥➦➧

➨➩➪➫➬➭➮➯➱➲➳➴➵➶➷➸

➹➺➻➼➽➾

➋➌➍➎➏➐➑➒➓①②③④⑤⑥⑦⑧⑨⑩

①②③④⑤⑥⑦⑧⑨⑩➊➋➌➍➎➏➐➑➒➓

❨❩❮❯❰❱❲❳❴❵❪❫

EXERCISE

Typographic Principles Card Set *(Class Project)*
Regina Rowland, Professor, City College of San Francisco, San Francisco, California

Objectives

- Apply typographic theory by exploring issues of legibility.
- Use type for function and form, syntactically and semantically.
- Demonstrate fully refined design process.
- Refine capacity to collaborate as a team.

Assignment

- Each student chooses one particular typographic rule (or principle) from chapters 4 through 10, designing front and back of cards that belong to a set.
- Each student to follow the layout specifics: 1/1 with bleeds, document size of 3 ½ x 5 ½ inches. Front of card to be used as needed, back of card to follow established grid and structure for listing name of designer, stating the rule, and describing selected typographic rule or principle.
- For each chosen rule, demonstrate the rule itself woven into a concept that refers to an issue of interest in a major city (the city closest to the location of the class is suggested).
- Design and produce, deliver as (1) a comp on bristol board and (2) a final design converted to an electronic file, then printed, and trimmed on a heavy or thick stock.

The success of this set as a whole depends on the quality and consistency each card demonstrates in design and content.

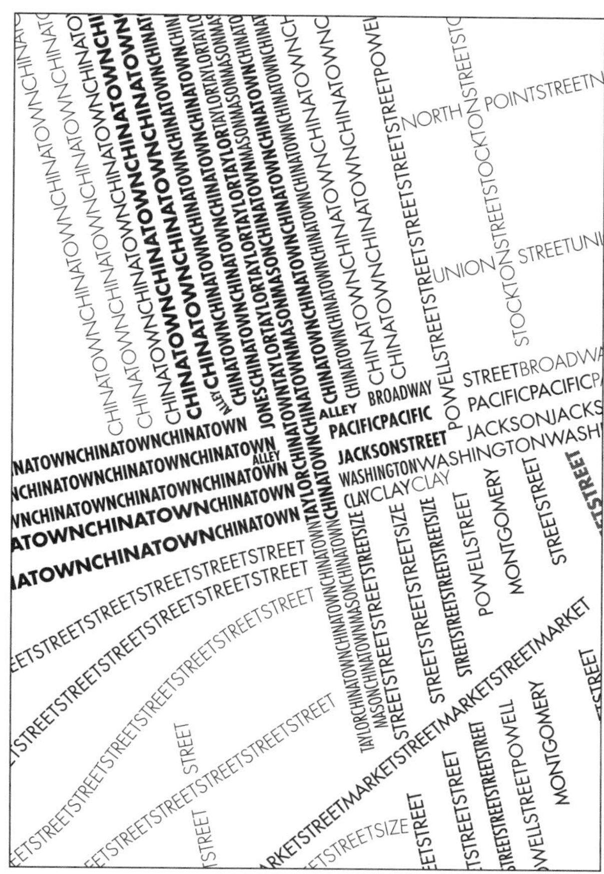

The principle of proportion is creatively expressed by May Gee by using type of different widths and weights to represent the streets and neighborhoods of San Francisco. The denser, blacker type represents the busier areas. Courtesy of May Gee and Églantine Granier-Gwinner.

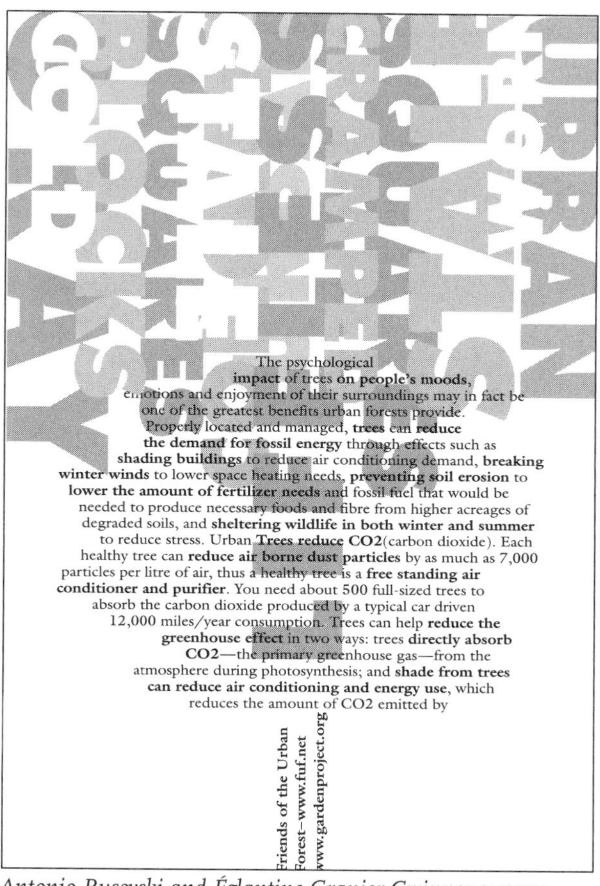

Antonio Rusevski and Églantine Granier-Gwinner express typographic texture by cleverly overlapping different text and display type in varying tints and alignments. The result is an illustration created completely with type. Courtesy of Antonio Rusevski and Églantine Granier-Gwinner.

The typographic theory of proximity, or type grouping, is effectively expressed using the word "WEALTH" in all caps stretched to drop out of the entire background, while the lowercase word "poverty" is set multiple times in a distressed face, crowding the feet of the word WEALTH. Designed by Thomas Jason Carpio. Courtesy of Thomas Jason Carpio.

EXERCISE

Spa Brochure

Ilene Strizver, Faculty, School of Visual Arts, New York, New York

Objective

Design projects with lots of text containing numerous hierarchies of information as well as price lists can be intimidating to any designer. This assignment focuses on confronting, analyzing, and solving this kind of text-intensive design problem. It also requires a mastery of text composition in the chosen software.

Instructor Preparation

Select a spa name, address, and tag line. Research spa brochures and web sites to harvest content. Text should include numerous categories of service, detailed descriptions, and several pricing tiers for each with decimal points. Supplement content with text for new treatments, special services, price breaks, and a 20 percent off coupon. Supply the assignment content in print form as well as a text file for download.

Assignment

Design an 8 ½ x 11 inch, tri-fold (three-panel) brochure for a day spa, as indicated by instructor. Use color, image, illustration, and photographs as desired, as well as colored stock.

Process

Step 1: Read the text carefully and use your imagination to identify a client base. Then imagine the look and architecture of this imaginary spa. The design and layout of the brochure should reflect your audience as well as the personality of the spa. You are encouraged to research other spa brochures to see what works, and what doesn't, in terms of organizing complex text content.

Step 2: The brochure consists of two separate elements: the spa logo or logotype and the body text. Each should be well thought-out. Solve each of them individually, but design them to blend together. Pay acute attention to all type and design details, including appropriate type style, size and leading, folds and margins, accurate informational hierarchy, clear and organized price lists, proper price alignment, and overall consistency. HINT: Start off with an accurate template tri-fold to avoid major changes and adjustments later.

Deliverable

Completed assignment shall consist of one folded dummy of the brochure (front and back), as well as a separate proof of both the front and back, with folds indicated in ½ point perforated or dotted lines.

DESIGNING
TYPEFACE
IS NOT FOR
THE FAINT-
HEARTED IN
MOST CASES
DESIGNING
ULL-BLOWN

CHAPTER ELEVEN

DESIGNING YOUR OWN TYPEFACE

Designing a typeface is not for the faint of heart. In most cases, designing a full-blown, professional-quality typeface should be left to those type designers, letterers, and calligraphers who have a foundation in letterforms and a strong interest in typeface design, as well as the time, patience, and perseverance to pursue it. But if your heart is hardy, read on!

Your design concept might be one that is for your own personal use, a custom job for a client, or a more serious typographic venture that you might want to make available to others. In any case, be realistic and allow your first exploration to be a learning experience more than anything else. No matter how terrific your first creation might seem to your own eyes, a type designer (and a high-quality typeface) is not made in a day. Learning how to draw with bezier curves takes a lot of practice and can be very frustrating until you get to the point where it begins to feel natural and instinctive. In addition, understanding the concepts of spacing, kerning, and hinting are not the same as applying them to an actual typeface, just as appreciating music or fine art is not the same as creating it. So be patient when honing your new skills; your next type venture will most certainly improve from an aesthetic as well as a technical standpoint. Keeping this in mind, it is best to start simple; save your more complicated ideas for later.

HANDWRITING FONTS: A GOOD PLACE TO BEGIN

A relatively simple and fun way to get your typographic feet wet is by making a font out of your or someone else's handwriting. These days, many of us use our computer for much of the writing we do, including invitations, journals, personal notes, and letters. Most typefaces are too formal for these projects, but a handwriting-style font will do nicely and maintain that personal, low-tech look. In fact, sometimes it is hard to tell the difference between an actual handwritten piece and a font, unless you know what to look for.

ITC Grimshaw Hand

A relatively simple and fun way to get your typographic feet wet is by making a font out of your (or anyone else's) handwriting. A handwriting-style font is very unique and individualistic, and can maintain that personal, low tech look and feel in a very high tech world.

ITC Johann Sparkling

A fun and relatively simple way to get your typographic feet wet is by making a font out of your (or anyone else's) handwriting. A handwriting-style font can maintain that personal, low tech look and feel in a very high tech world.

ITC Dartagnon

A relatively simple and fun way to get your typographic feet wet is by making a font out of your (or anyone else's) handwriting. A handwriting-style font is very unique and individualistic, and can maintain that personal, low tech look and feel in a very high tech world.

These handwriting fonts show the extreme diversity of this style of typeface. International Typeface Corporation's (ITC) program to nurture and develop these kinds of designs has provided a wealth of new and interesting typography.

ITC Grimshaw Hand, designed by the late Phil Grimshaw. Based on his own handwriting, this typeface is one of many distinctive typefaces designed during the notable career of this designer of letterforms. He believed that "If you enjoy what you do, and you're lucky enough to be good at it, just do it for that reason."

ITC Johann Sparkling, designed by Viktor Solt. "ITC Johann Sparkling is intended to close the gap between highly formal copperplate scripts and the scribbled look of 'true' handwriting," says Vienna designer Viktor Solt.

ITC Dartagnon, designed by Nick Cooke. "It's a long shot, but it might just work as a font." That's what this English type designer thought after he'd doodled a few free-flowing letters with a chunky pencil one day in London.

The handwriting you select should be an unconnected, noncursive print, not a loopy, connecting script, which can create problems when letters are combined. Once you decide on a handwriting to use, the next step is to have each character written several times so you can pick the best one. Don't forget to include numbers, punctuation, and all the signs and symbols included in most fonts. It is best to gang up these characters on one or several 8 ½ x 11 inch sheets of paper or vellum to make them easier to scan later. Make sure you indicate a baseline, or you will have a lot of trouble later lining them all up in your font-manipulation software.

You might want to try different pens and markers as well as different smooth-textured surfaces, and do a test before drawing the complete character set. Your artwork will then need to be scanned, converted into digital data with a program such as Adobe Illustrator, and imported into a font production program such as Fontlab or Fontographer.

Once the entire process is completed, a font is created and you can see your handwriting coming off your printer. You will be amazed at the final product. Just keep in mind that it is the nature of a handwriting font to be very quirky, individual, and informal–it is a very forgiving place to start, and it is not supposed to be perfect!

ITC Deelirious

A relatively simple and fun way to get your typographic feet wet is by making a font out of your (or anyone else's) handwriting. A handwriting-style font is very unique and individualistic, and can maintain that personal, low tech look and feel in a very high tech world.

ITC Zemke Hand

A relatively simple and fun way to get your typographic feet wet is by making a font out of your (or anyone else's) handwriting. A handwriting-style font is very unique and individualistic, and can maintain that personal, low tech look and feel in a very high tech world.

ITC Deelirious, designed by Dee Densmore D'Amico. The name grows out of the Ds in her name–Dee Densmore D'Amico–and the typeface itself grows out of her distinctive, energetic handwriting (or hand printing).

ITC Zemke Hand, designed by and based on the handwriting of illustrator Deborah Zemke. Deborah jokes that seeing a font of her handwriting "gives me a bit of an identity crisis."

THREE APPROACHES TO DESIGNING A TYPEFACE

If you have decided to do something other than a handwriting font, there are some decisions to be made on how to begin, as well as a different approach to the entire design process. But before you begin, it is a good idea to check foundries and resellers to make sure your idea hasn't already been done before. Why spend hours, days, and possibly weeks and months reinventing a wheel? Be sure to start with something that is not available from other sources.

There are several different approaches to designing a typeface using a computer. They are all used successfully by different designers, and all have their pros and cons.

The most traditional way is to develop a finished drawing of your alphabet before scanning and importing it into Fontographer or Fontlab, after which you can clean it up, add spacing and kerning, run text tests, and fine-tune. This approach requires that you know how to draw pretty well, which is not necessarily a skill that today's neophyte type designers have. Not too long ago, hand-drawing the final artwork was the only way to design a typeface, which was then given to a manufacturer. There was no testing at large and small sizes, no letterform templates, no creating and interpolating other weights on the fly, etc. Many typefaces took months and sometimes years to complete, but every shape, every curve was intentional and well thought-out.

"I don't sit down to design a font. The design for my fonts mostly originates from lettering. All of my typefaces are drawn by hand with a brush or a pen to retain a handwritten feel. I'll do some touching up, and then digitize and touch up some more. Often I'll have to go back and chose different versions of some characters or create entirely new ones if they don't work well when placed with other characters."

—Jill Bell

A more commonly used method is to begin with a drawing or rough sketch of your concept, then complete and fine-tune your typeface after scanning. It is a good idea to begin with as tight a drawing as possible to get you to think about and make deliberate decisions regarding the shapes, curves, and other characteristics of your design. The computer imparts a personality of its own to any work created with it, so to have as much control over the final product as possible, make as many decisions as you can before scanning.

"I rarely draw sketches of complete alphabets. I always draw sketches on paper; usually ten to twenty characters are drawn by hand and the rest are designed on screen. The drawings are sometimes scanned and traced by hand; sometimes they are not scanned and in that case I design directly on screen, putting the sketches alongside."

— Akira Kobayashi

These days, more and more designers are designing an entire typeface on the computer screen; that is, they do no actual hand-drawing at all. This takes a high degree of skill in PostScript drawing tools, as well as a highly developed ability to conceptualize and actualize a concept on screen. This approach might work well for some very geometric designs, but in general, it is not recommended for neophytes. The danger here is that you will leave all the design decisions and fine-tuning of shapes up to the quirks and personality of the drawing tools of your software combined with the limitations of your own skills. Unless you are highly skilled at fine-tuning them, most computer-generated typefaces will have a certain look that identifies the designer as a novice.

"I used to do sketches and scan them... but now I just draw directly on screen. The scanned sketches evolved so quickly, they were instant rubbish. A waste of time."

— Jim Parkinson

PROFESSIONAL GUIDELINES

Once you've decided on a beginning approach, the following guidelines will help you to proceed in a smooth, logical way toward developing your seed of an idea into a full-blown, well thought-out typeface.

1. Begin with a strong, well-developed concept and follow it throughout the design.

2. Have a clear idea what you intend your design to be used for, whether it be text, display, or midrange sizes.

3. Begin by drawing a test word, such as "hamburgefonts," in lowercase, scan it, and then import it into your font-manipulation software. This test word contains most of the character shapes that are used in the rest of the alphabet.

Hamburgefonts
HAMBURGEFONTS

4. Next, typeset copy with these characters and look it over carefully at various sizes. Check characters for consistent width, stroke thickness, and overall color. At the same time, adjust the side bearings (space on the right and left of the character) to allow for optimum even color.

5. When these look good, work on the caps, figures, and the rest of the character complement. Go through the same testing procedure.

6. A good way to work is to create a test document that shows all lowercase combinations, important cap-to-lowercase combinations, and as well a text block. The idea is to adjust both the actual characters and the side bearings to create good overall color and spacing.

7. *Do not kern* the typeface until you have done all of the above. Kerning should be the icing on the cake, and it should not be used as a Band-Aid to fix poor spacing. More kern pairs does not necessarily mean a better-looking font if the original fit is poor.

8. Get away from your project when you can't see it objectively anymore, and take a fresh look in the morning. Our eyes and capacity to observe detail have a daily peak and ebb. Know what your peak is and do your most intensive work then.

9. And, finally, know when to let go: You can't carry your "typechild" forever.

Typographic excellence is result of nothing more than attitude. Its appeal comes from the understanding used in its planning; designer's must care. Contemporary advertising, perfect integration elements often demands unorthodox may require's use compact whatever tooth quiver jellyfish practically expectorated by mad hawk; victors flank gyp who mix ITC QUARTZ HELP BOLTING TENT CONTRAINDICATEDLY SUPERB (247) 371-0639. (800) 754-4732.
AbAcAdAeAfAgAhAiAkAlAmAnApAqArAsAtAuAvAwAxAyAz
BaBeBiBlBoBrBuBy CaCeChCiCoCrCuCyCz DaDeDiDlDoDrDuDy
EaEbEcEdEfEgEhEiEjEkElEmEnEoEpEqErEtEuEvEwExEyEz
FaFeFiFlFoFrFu GaGeGiGoGrGuGy HaHeHiHoHuHy
IcIdIfIgIlImInIoIpIrIsI tJaJeJiJoJu KaKeKiKlKnKrKu
LaLeLiLoLu MaMeMiMoMuMy NaNeNiNoNuNy
OaObOcOdOfOhOiOlOmOnOpOrOsOtOuOvOwOx
UdUnUpUs PaPePiPoPrPsPtPuPy Qu RaReRiRoRu
SaScSeShSiSkSlSmSnSoSpSqStSuSwSy TaTeThTiToTrTsTuTwTy
VaVeViVo WaWeWhWiWoWrWuWy YaYeYiYoYu ZaZeZiZo
aabacadaeafagahaiajakalaamanaoapaqarasatauavawaxayaza
bbcbdbebfbgbhbibbkblbmbnbobpbqbrbsbtbubvbbwbxbybzbc
cdcecfcgchcicjckclcmcncocpcqccrcsctcucvcwcxcyczc
ddedfdgdhdidjdkdldmdndodpdqdrdsdtdudvdwdxdydzd
eefegeheiejekelemeneoepeqereseeteuevewexeyeze
ffgfhfifjfkflfmfnfofpfqfrfsftfufvfwfxfyfzf
gghgigjgkglgmgngogpgqgrgsgtgugvgwgxgygzg
hhihjhkhlhmhnhohphqhrhshthuhvhwhxhyhzh
iijikiliminioipiqirisitiuiviwixiyizjkjljmjnjojpjqjrjsjtjujvjwjxjyjzj
kklkmknkokpkqkrksktkukvkwkxkykzk llmlnlolplqlrlsltlulvlwlxlylzlm
mnmompmqmrmsmtmumvmwmxmymzm nnonpnqnrnsntnunvnwnxnynzn
oopoqorosotouovowoxoyozo ppqprpsptpupvpwpxpypzp
qqrqsqtquqvqwqxqyqzq rrsrtrurvrwrxryrzr sstsusvswsxsyszs ttutvtwtxtytzt
uuvuwuxuyuzu vvwvxvyvzv wwxwywz wxxyxzx yyzy zz
a. b. c. d. e. f. g. h. i. j. k. l. m. n. o. p. q. r. s. t. u. v. w. x. y. z.
a, b, c, d, e, f, g, h, i, j, k, l, m, n, o, p, q, r, s, t, u, v, w, x, y, z,
a'b'c'd'e'f'g'h'i'j'k'l'm'n'o'p'q'r's't'u'v'w'x'y'z'
'a' 'b' 'c' 'd' 'e' 'f' 'g' 'h' 'i' 'j' 'k' 'l' 'm''n'
'o' 'p' 'q' 'r' 's' 't' 'u' 'v' 'w' 'x' 'y' 'z' ." ,"
"a" "b" "c" "d" "e" "f" "g" "h" "i" "j" "k" "l" "m"
"n" "o" "p" "q" "r" "s" "t" "u" "v" "w" "x" "y" "z"
a;b;c;d;e;f;g;h;i;j;k;l;m;n;o;p;q;r;s;t;u;v;w;x;y;z;
a:b:c:d:e:f:g:h:i:j:k:l:m:n:o:p:q:r:s:t:u:v:w:x:y:z:
-a-b-c-d-e-f-g-h-i-j-k-l-m-n-o-p-q-r-s-t-u-v-w-x-y-z-
-A-B-C-D-E-F-G-H-I-J-K-L-M-N-O-P-Q-R-S-T-U-V-W-X-Y-Z-
A. B. C. D. E. F. G. H. I. J. K. L. M. N. O.P. Q. R. S. T. U. V. W. X. Y. Z.
A, B, C, D, E, F, G, H, I, J, K, L, M, N, O,P, Q, R, S, T, U, V, W, X, Y, Z,
A'B'C'D'E'F'G'H'I'J'K'L'M'N'O'P'Q'R'S'T'U'V'W'X'Y'Z'
'A' 'B' 'C' 'D' 'E' 'F' 'G' 'H' 'I' 'J' 'K' 'L' 'M''N'
'O' 'P' 'Q' 'R' 'S' 'T' 'U' 'V' 'W' 'X' 'Y' 'Z'
"A""B""C""D""E""F""G""H""I""J""K""L""M"
"N""O""P""Q""R""S""T""U""V""W""X""Y""Z"
A;B;C;D;E;F;G;H;I;J;K;L;M;N;O;P;Q;R;S;T;U;V;W;X;Y;Z;
A:B:C:D:E:F:G:H:I:J:K:L:M:N:O:P:Q:R:S:T:U:V:W:X:Y:Z:
AABACADAEAFAGAHAIAJAKALAMANAOPAQARASATAUAVAWAXAYAZA
BBCBDBEBFBGBHBIBJBKBLBMBNBOBPBRBSBTBUBVBWBY
CCECFCHCICKCLCMCNCOCRCSCTCUCVCWCXCYCZC
DDEFDGDHDIDJDKDLDMDNDODPDRDSDTDUDVDWDXDYD
EEFEGEHEIEJEKELEMENEOEPEQERESETEUEVEWEXEYEZE
FFGFHFIFJFKFLFMFNFOFPFQFRFSFTFUFVFWFXFYFZF
GGHGIGJGKGLGMGNGOGPGQGRGSGTGUGVGWGXGY

This test document shows lowercase combinations, important cap-to-lowercase combos, and as well a text block. The idea is to adjust both the actual characters and the side bearings to create good overall color and spacing.

EXERCISE

This assignment is part of the Concert Poster Design exercise by Frank Armstrong in chapter 7.

INTRODUCTION TO TYPE DESIGN: SYMPHONY

James Montalbano, Faculty, Parsons School of Design, New York, New York

Objectives

Understanding the fundamentals of type design.

Assignment

Design seven glyphs for a typeface that would be used for the word "Symphony" in the Concert Poster Design exercise from chapter 7 (or select the word or words of your choice). Using Adobe Illustrator and FontLab or Macromedia Fontographer, create a prototype for a digital font. Although the primary objective of your typeface design is consistency of form and space, legibility is also an important factor.

Process

By Hand

• With a pencil and tracing paper or vellum, create several thumbnail designs of the word "Symphony" (using cap and lowercase lettering as shown). When you have decided upon the final design, create a new draft sketch of the entire design making sure that the x-height of each lowercase letter is approximately 1 ½ inches tall.

• Using a ruler, draw guidelines on your draft sketch that correspond to the baseline and x-height of your design.

• With your draft sketch as a guide, render the lowercase o and n as accurately as you can on a new sheet of tracing paper or vellum. Place new sheets of tracing paper over your drawing and redraw and refine the two letters until they are as true to your design ideas as you can make them.

• Once the lowercase n and o are finalized, use the features of the n to help you render the m, the h, and the left part (the stem and the beginning of the bowl) of the p. Use the o to help you render the right side of the p. Render the y and S in proportion to the other glyphs.

• Make sure each drawing of every glyph contains a guideline for the baseline, x-height, cap height, ascender, and descender. Your final character renderings may be end up on several different sheets of paper. This is okay as the digital versions of the characters will be combined later.

• Scan your drawings at 300 dpi and scale them so the distance between the cap height or the ascender guideline (whichever is taller) and the descender guideline is equal to 1000 points. Save each character file as a separate grayscale TIFF (Tagged Image File Format) file.

In Adobe Illustrator

• Open Illustrator Preferences (Illustrator Menu > Preferences or Edit Menu > Preferences). In the Units Preferences (usually found in the "Units & Undo" or "Units & Display Performance" preferences pane), change all units to points (1 point in Illustrator is equal to 1 unit in FontLab).

• In the Clipboard Preferences (usually found in the "Files & Clipboard" or "File Handling & Clipboard" preferences pane), disable the "Copy as PDF" function and enable the "Copy as AICB" function with the Preserve Paths option selected.

• Create a new document that is 1000 points wide by 1000 points high.

• Place one of the TIFF files you saved earlier into your document (File Menu > Place or Edit Menu > Place). Once your TIFF file is placed, make sure it is square and all the guidelines are visible. Adjust your TIFF file in Illustrator so that the cap height or the ascender guideline (whichever is taller) is resting on the document's top edge; the descender guideline is resting on the document's bottom edge; and the left edge of the character is aligned on the document's left edge.

• Make sure your rulers are visible (View Menu > Show Rulers) and drag a horizontal guide off the top ruler for each of the guidelines in your drawing (cap height, ascender, x-height, baseline, descender). Move the crosshairs (located in the top left corner between the horizontal and vertical rulers) so that they align with the left edge of the document and with the Baseline Guide (this will allow your imported drawings to align with the baseline in FontLab).

• In your Layers window (Window Menu > Layers) click twice on the layer with your TIFF file on it, and in the Layer Options window that appears select the "Template" option. Your drawing will dim and the layer will lock.

• Back in the Layers window, click the "Add Layer" button at the bottom of the window to create a new layer on which to digitally draw your glyphs.

• Using the pen tool trace your glyph drawing with lines and Bezier curves, making sure you use as few points as possible. Also make sure that points are placed on the extreme parts of the curves. Horizontal handles of Bezier curves should be truly horizontal (use the shift key to constrain their movement). Vertical handles of Bezier curves should be truly vertical.

• Make sure all shapes and lines in each glyph are filled with black only and contain no strokes. If your glyph does contain strokes use the Object Menu > Expand to outline them.

• Copy your character (Select > All and then Edit / Copy) and, with the character still in your clipboard, open FontLab.

In FontLab

• Find your FontLab Preferences. In the General Preference tab check the "Do not rescale EPS files (on import and export)" option.

• Create a new font document.

• Click twice on the appropriate character in your Font window to open its Glyph window. Paste (Edit Menu > Paste) the character you copied from Illustrator into the Glyph window. Make sure that your glyph is properly positioned on the baseline of your font and close the Glyph window.

• Along with the Illustrator instructions above, repeat the previous steps for each character until you've transferred the entire word Symphony into FontLab.

• Open a new Metrics window (Window Menu > New Metrics Window) and type the word Symphony into the open field at the top of it.

• Making sure the blue M (in the upper left corner) is highlighted, select each character and adjust its left- and right-side bearings so that the spacing is balanced and even between each letter. Zoom in (View Menu > Zoom In) if you need a closer look at any of the letters. Selecting the red K will allow you to adjust the kerning between two individual glyphs.

• Once you're happy with the Metrics and Kerning for your font, open the Font Info window (File Menu > Font Info).

• Click the "Names and Copyright" option to view the "Basic Set of Font Names" pane. Type in a font name into the Family Names field and select Normal as the font weight. Press the build style Button and then press the Build Names Button.

• Click open the "Metrics and Dimensions" preferences and click on "Key Dimensions" to view the "Most Important Font Dimensions" pane. Fill in the Cap height, x-height, and Ascent and Descent values to match the values of your original drawing. Please note that Ascent and Descent values should add up to 1000 when taken as positive integers (i.e., Ascent 800, Descent –200).

• Close the Font Info window.

• Generate your font.

• Mac users choose File Menu > Generate Mac Suitcase to create TrueType or Type1 fonts; or select File Menu > Generate Font to create OpenType CFF fonts. If you're using the "Generate Mac Suitcase" option, make sure that your new font is listed under "Plain" in the Mac Suitcase export window, select Okay and FontLab will generate the final font files.

• Install and use.

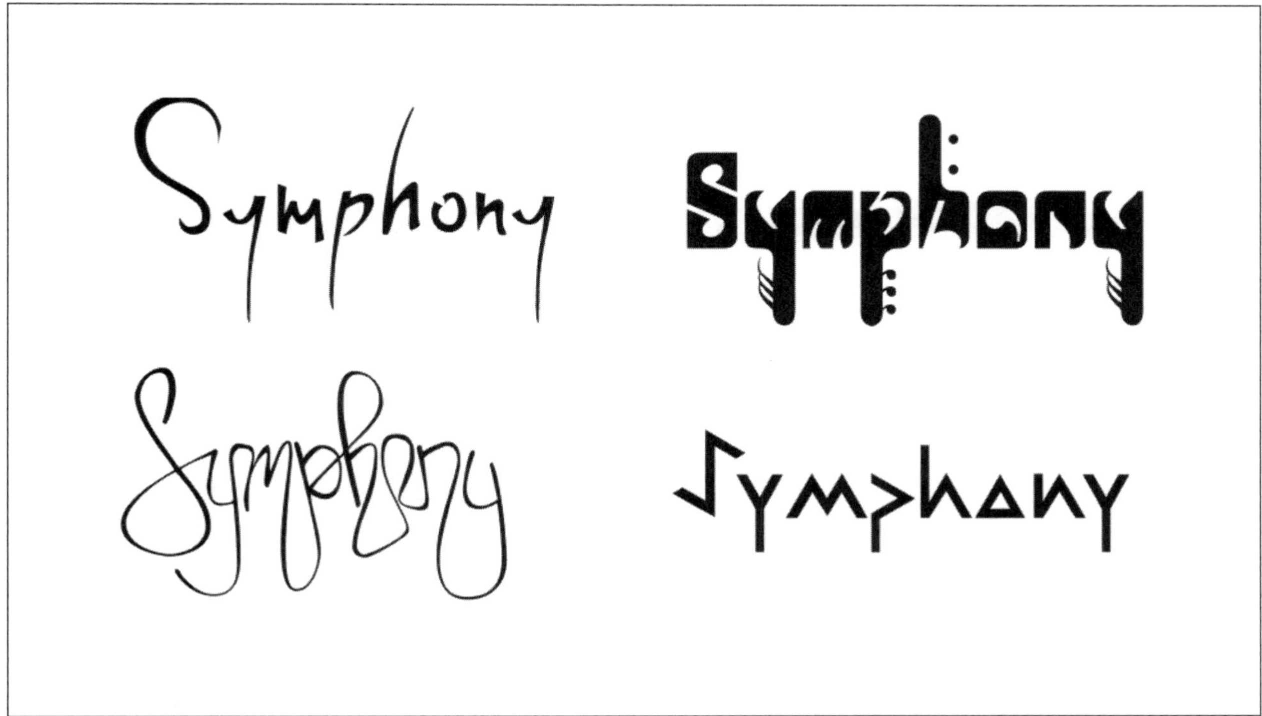

Solutions to the Symphony type design assignment by Holly McGarr, Shawna Kirby, Jennifer Betz, and Matt MacPherson. Courtesy of Holly McGarr, Shawna Kirby, Jennifer Betz, and Matt MacPherson.

EXERCISE

Digitize Your Signature

James Montalbano, Faculty, Parsons School of Design, New York, New York

Objective

To create a digital version of your signature. This come in very handy for personalized uses, email signatures, as well as forms, documents, and PDFs that are completed electronically.

Instructions

The auto-trace method is suggested for this assignment, as it is easier and faster than hand digitization and adequate for most signatures. If you prefer to hand-digitize, refer to the previous assignment, Introduction to Type Design: Symphony, for technical guidance.

Preparation

• Using a black pen or thin marker on paper or vellum, write your signature in a largish but comfortable size. Write it as many times as possible until you get one you like and that will reproduce well at a range of sizes. It can be a connected script or unconnected letters, just make each word of your name is separate.

• Scan your drawings at 600 dpi. Save as a BITMAP TIFF file–bitmap NOT grayscale.

In Adobe Illustrator

• In Illustrator, open the file that contains the bitmap image you want to trace.

• Select the Auto Trace tool. The Auto Trace tool can be found by clicking and holding the Blend Tool in the tool bar; the Auto Trace tool will appear in the pop-up menu.

• Place the cross hair on the section of the bitmap that you want to trace. The cross hair must be positioned within six pixels of the bitmap shape.

• To trace the entire object, click the object. The path starts where you clicked, following the shape and keeping it on the right. The path may be drawn clockwise or counterclockwise, depending on where you click and on the shape of the path.

• To trace part of the object, drag the pointer from where you want the path to start to where you want it to end, keeping to within two pixels of the edge of the shape.

• To connect a new auto-trace path to an existing auto-trace path, drag at the anchor point where you want the paths to connect.

• Make sure all shapes and lines in each glyph are filled with black only and contain no strokes. If your glyph does contain strokes use Object Menu > Expand to outline them.

• Copy your character (Select All > and then Edit / Copy) and, with the character still in your clipboard, open FontLab.

In FontLab

• Find your FontLab Preferences. In the General Preference tab, check the "Do Not Rescale EPS Files (on import and export)" option.

• Create a new font document.

• Click twice on the appropriate character in your Font window to open its Glyph window. Ideally, you should use the glyphs that correspond to the first and last letters of your name. (and middle initial if you use that in your signature) Paste (Edit Menu > Paste) the character you copied from Illustrator into the Glyph window. Make sure that your glyph is properly positioned on the baseline of your font and close the Glyph window.

• Along with the Illustrator instructions above, repeat the previous steps for each word of your signature

• Open a new Metrics window (Window Menu > New Metrics Window), and type the two (or three) words of your signature

• Making sure the blue M (in the upper left corner) is highlighted, select each character and adjust its left and right side bearings so that the spacing is balanced and even between each letter. Zoom in (View Menu > Zoom In) if you need a closer look at any of the letters. Selecting the red K will allow you to adjust the kerning between two individual glyphs.

• Once you are happy with the Metrics and Kerning for your font, open the Font Info window (File Menu > Font Info).

• Click the "Names and Copyright" option to view the "Basic set of font names" pane. Type in a font name (you first and last, or just last name is good) into the Family Names field and select Normal as the font weight. Press the build style Button and then press the Build Names Button.

• Click open the "Metrics and Dimensions" preferences and click on "Key Dimensions" to view the "Most Important Font Dimensions" pane. Fill in the Cap height, x-height, and Ascent and Descent values to match the values of your original drawing. Please note that Ascent and Descent values should add up to 1000 when taken as positive integers (i.e., Ascent 800, Descent –200).

• Close the Font Info window.

GLOSSARY

alignment: The positioning of lines of text: usually flush left, flush right, justified, centered, or contoured.

alternate character: A separate and distinct version of the character in the regular position.

ampersand: Symbol for the word *and* (&).

arm: The upper (horizontal or diagonal) stroke that is attached on one end and free on the other (K).

ascender: The part of a lowercase character (b, d, f, h, k, l, t) that extends above the height of the lowercase x.

asterisk: Starlike symbol indicating a footnote or other additional information (*).

bar: The horizontal stroke in characters such as A, H, R, e, f.

baseline: The invisible line on which most characters sit.

boldface: A bold version of a lighter weight (not necessarily labeled *bold*).

bowl: A curved stroke that creates an enclosed space within a character (which is then called a *counter*).

braces (also called *curly brackets*): A more decorative form of bracket, traditionally used for certain mathematical expressions.

brackets: Punctuation symbols, usually rectangular in design, used to enclose copy within a parenthetical phrase (or copy already enclosed within parentheses).

bullet: A large dot placed to the left of each item in a list for emphasis.

cap height: The height of capital letters measured from the baseline to the top of caps, most accurately measured on a character with a flat bottom (E, H, I, etc.).

capitals: The uppercase letters of an alphabet, usually all the same height.

character: An individual letter or symbol.

condensed: A narrow version of a typeface or character.

counter: The partially or fully enclosed space within a character.

descender: The part of a character (g, j, p, q, y, and sometimes J) that descends below the baseline.

dingbat: A decorative or graphic utility character used in setting type. Dingbats can be included within a type font or be part of an entire dingbat font.

dpi: Dots per inch.

drop cap: An enlarged character that begins at (or aligns with) and drops below the first line of text.

ear: The small stroke that projects from the top of the lowercase g.

ellipsis: A single character consisting of a series of three evenly spaced dots, used to indicate missing type or a continuation of type.

em dash: Punctuation used to indicate a break in thought or to separate a thought within a sentence. It is the longest of the dashes. (See en dash.)

en dash: Punctuation used to indicate a continuation of time, years, and dates; it is wider than a hyphen and narrower than an em dash.

EULA (End User License Agreement): A software license defining the terms, conditions, and restrictions of how a font (or other software) can be used.

euro: The exclusive currency of many European countries since 2002. The euro symbol looks like a capital C with a double crossbar.

expanded: A wide version of a typeface or character.

expert set: A separate font containing characters that don't fit in the main font, often including fractions, ligatures, alternates, and additional accented characters.

extreme indent: First line (or lines) of a paragraph indented to a deeper depth, sometimes to a depth of half the column width.

FFIL: Font suitcase containing bitmap (or screen font) and font metrics, as abbreviated in Mac OS 10 font icons.

font family: A collection of typefaces designed with the same basic skeletal structure but with different finishing details, enabling them to work well together.

font: A complete character set of a particular weight and style of a typeface.

glyph: Any character in a font, including characters, numerals, punctuation, signs, symbols, accents, ding-bats, etc.

hairline: A very thin stroke most common to serif typefaces.

Hamburgefonts: Test word used for designing a typeface; it contains most of the character shapes that are used in the rest of the alphabet.

hanging indent: First line (or lines) of a paragraph extending into the margin to the left of the paragraph.

hints: Instructions that have been incorporated into a font to make type look good on the screen as well as when printed.

hung punctuation: Type that is set with characters, such as quotations, apostrophes, commas, periods, and hyphens, extending beyond the margin for better alignment (also called *optical alignment*).

hyphen: Punctuation used to hyphenate words that break at the end of a line or to connect elements of a compound word.

indent: Space inserted before the first word of a new paragraph.

initial cap: An enlarged character, usually the beginning letter of the first sentence of a paragraph, which is set in a decorative or graphic way.

italics: An angled typeface most commonly designed as a companion to a roman design; usually a unique and separate design, somewhat calligraphic in nature (see *obliques*).

justification: Text set so that all lines have the same line length, aligning on the left and the right. Unjustified text is often called "ragged text."

kerning: The addition or reduction of space between two specific characters to make more even spacing and typographic color.

leg: The lower (horizontal or diagonal) stroke that is attached on one end and free on the other (K).

legibility: The ease with which a typeface design can be read related to the actual design, including its x-height, character shapes, size of its counters, stroke contrast, serifs or lack thereof, and weight.

ligature: A character made from connecting or combining two characters into one (fi, fl).

line spacing (also referred to as *leading*): The vertical space between lines of type from baseline to baseline, usually measured in points.

lining figures: Same-sized numerals that align on the baseline and the cap height.

link: The stroke that connects the top and bottom part (bowl and link) of a two-storey lowercase g.

loop: The lower portion of the lowercase g.

lowercase: The shorter letters of an alphabet containing ascenders and descenders.

LWFN: Outline (or printer font) as abbreviated in Mac OS 10 font icons.

monospacing: Spacing where each character has the same, fixed width, as in typewriter type as well as tabular figures.

obliques: A slanted versions of its roman companion with few or no design changes (see *italics*).

oldstyle figure: A style of numeral that approximates lowercase letterforms by having an x-height as well as ascenders and descenders.

OpenType: Font format jointly developed by Adobe Systems and Microsoft; a superset of Type 1 and TrueType font formats with added enhancements, including multiplatform support, expanded character sets, and glyph substitution.

orphan: A single word or very short line appearing at the beginning of a column or a page.

OTF: OpenType font as abbreviated in Mac OS 10 icons and fonts.

parentheses: Punctuation symbols, usually curved, primarily used to enclose interjected, explanatory, or qualifying remarks.

point: A unit of measure in typography. There are approximately 72 points to the inch, and 12 points to the pica.

PostScript: A computer language developed by Adobe Systems that describes type and graphics in a way that allows for precise, sharp printing at any size.

primes: Symbol used to indicate inches, feet, hours, and minutes. Often incorrectly used in typesetting instead of apostrophes and quotation marks.

printer font (also called *outline font*): The part of a digital font that stores each glyph as an outline in the form of a mathematical description; this outline is scalable, allowing for high-quality printing at any size.

proportional spacing: Spacing used in most typefaces where each character has a unique width (as opposed to *monospacing*).

rag: The in-and-out shape, or contour, that lines of copy make when they are not flush-aligned, or justified.

raised cap: An enlarged character that base-aligns with the first line of type and rises above the body copy.

readability: The ease with which a type setting can be read related to how the type is arranged, including size, leading, line length, alignment, letter spacing, and word spacing.

resolution: The number of dots per inch (dpi), often referred to as high or low resolution.

river: Zagged columns of white space running down justified text; an undesirable result of some justification.

roman: Common term referring to the upright version of a typeface as compared to the italic version.

screen font (also called *bitmapped font*): The part of a Type 1 font that represents the font on the screen.

serifs: The projections extending off the main strokes of the characters of serif typefaces.

shoulder: The curved stroke of the h, m, or n.

small caps: Capital letterforms that are smaller than cap height, often the height of the lowercase letters.

smart quotes (also called *curly quotes*): Typographically correct quotation marks which are design sensitive have an open and a closed version.

spine: The main curved stroke of the S.

spur: A small projection off a main stroke found on many capital Gs.

stem: A straight vertical stroke or main straight diagonal stroke in a letter that has no verticals.

stress: The direction of thickening in a curved stroke.

stroke: A straight or curved line.

style-linked font: A font family engineered so that its true-drawn bold, italic, and bold italic weights can be accessed via an application's style-button or keyboard command.

swash: A fancy flourish replacing a terminal or serif.

tabular spacing (also called *monospacing*): Spacing used for numerals where each has the same total character width (fixed width), allowing them to align vertically in tables, financial statements, and other columns of figures.

tail: The descender of a Q or short diagonal stroke of an R.

terminal: The end of a stroke not terminated with a serif.

titling fonts: Typestyles that have been specifically designed for headline or display setting. Titling fonts differ from their text counterparts in that their scale, proportion, and design details have been altered to look best at larger sizes.

tracking: The addition or reduction of the overall letter spacing in a selected block of text.

TrueType font: Font format developed by Apple Computer and Microsoft known for its expanded hinting capability; primarily used by PC users, it consists of a single file that contains both screen- and printer-font data.

Type 1 font (also called *PostScript font*): Font format developed by Adobe Systems that consists of a screen and a printer font and that is based on a computer language called PostScript, most commonly used by Mac users.

U&lc: Upper and lower case.

widow: A very short line at the end of a paragraph, usually composed of one or two words or a hyphenated word.

word spacing: The amount of space between words. Predetermined from within the font, but adjustable in most design software.

x-height: The height of lowercase letters usually based on the lowercase x, not including ascenders and descenders.

BIBLIOGRAPHY

A Chronology of Printing, by Colin Clair, 1969, Frederick A. Praeger, Publishers.

The Complete Manual of Typography, by James Felici, 2003, Peachpit Press, Inc.

Fontographer: Type by Design, by Stephen Moye, 1995, MIS Press.

Herb Lubalin, Art Director, Graphic Designer and Typographer, by Gertrude Snyder and Alan Peckolick, 1985, American Showcase, Inc.

How to Boss Your Fonts Around, by Robin Williams, 1994, Peachpit Press, Inc.

Jargon, An Informal Dictionary of Computer Terms, by Robin Williams with Steve Cummings, 1993, Peachpit Press, Inc.

The Mac Is Not A Typewriter, by Robin Williams, 1990, Peachpit Press, Inc.

The Macintosh Font Book, by Erfert Fenton, 1989, Peachpit Press, Inc.

The Story of Writing, by Andrew Robinson, 1995, Thames & Hudson, Ltd.

Type and Typography: The Designer's Book of Type, by Ben Rosen, 1976, Van Nostrand Reinhold Company, Inc.

Type From the Desktop, by Clifford Burke, 1990, Ventana Press.

Type in Use: Effective Typography for Electronic Publishing, by Alex White, 1992, Design Press, Tab Books, a division of McGraw-Hill, Inc.

Typographic Communications Today, by Edward M. Gottschall, 1989, MIT Press.

Typographic Design: Form and Communication, by Rob Carter, Ben Day, Philip Meggs, 1985, Van Nostrand Reinhold Company, Inc.

PICTURE CREDITS

P. 16 © Axel Poignant Archive.
P. 17 © 1997 William P. Thayer.
P. 20 © 1999 Sumner Stone. All rights reserved.
P. 23 © International Typeface Corporation.
P. 24 © Rhoda S. Lubalin (Estate of Herb Lubalin).
P. 27 © 2005 Nancy Sharon Collins.
p. 58 (top) © 1991–99 Jim Spiece, Spiece Graphics, Ft. Wayne, Indiana; (bottom) © Courtesy Mysterious Press/Warner Books.
P. 59 © Robert Greenhood.
P. 64 Artwork © 2000 Scorsone/Drueding.
P. 66 (top right) © 2000 The Yupo Corporation; (bottom right) © 1997 Paul Elledge Photgraphy, Inc.
P. 67 (top left) © 1994 Sony Music Entertainment, Inc.; (top right) © 1994 Skillsbank Corporation. This advertisement is a copy of a previous advertising campaign and is not representative of any current promotions offered by Skillsbank Corporation; (right bottom) © 1990 Jill Bell.
P. 68 (both) ©Henderson Bromstead Art.
P. 69 (top left) © Tom Connor, Jim Downey; (top upper right) © David DeRosa; (top lower right) © Leslie Singer; (bottom left) © Global-Dining, Inc.; (bottom right) © 2000 Juvenile Diabetes Foundation.
P. 71 (lower right) © Mohawk Paper Mills, Inc.
P. 77 (right) © The Letterbox.
P. 78 (top right) © 2000 The Yupo Corporation; (center) © International Typeface Corporation; (bottom right) © Andrew M. Newman.
P. 79 (top left) © Houghton Mifflin Company; (top right) © Courtesy of Alfred A. Knopf Publishers, Inc.; (bottom left) © Andrew M. Newman.
P. 90 © The Yupo Corporation.
P. 91 (top) © Fortune Brands, Inc.; (bottom) © Citizens Utilities.
P. 93 ©2005 Polite Design Incorporated.
P. 94 (left) © Doyle Partners; (upper right) © Design firm: Hornall Anderson Design Works, Inc./Client: Mohawk Paper Mills.
P. 95 © Vanderbyl Design.
P. 98 (bottom) © 2001 Studio Blue.
P. 106 © International Typeface Corporation.
P. 107 © Doyle Partners.
P. 110 (top) © Design firm: Hornall Anderson Design Works, Inc./Client: Tree Top; (bottom) © Doyle Partners.
P. 113 (top) © NLP IP Company;
P. 117 © Courtesy of Mohawk Paper Mills, Inc.
P. 133 (top right) © Citizens Utilities.
P. 138 © International Typeface Corporation.
P. 139 (top) © Design firm: Hornall Anderson Design Works, Inc./Client: Mohawk Paper Mills; (bottom) © 1995 NCLR (Eva Roberts, art director and designer; Stanton Blakeslee, designer; Alex Albright, editor).
P. 144 © Design firm: VSA Partners, Inc./Client: C. Stilp, Fox River Paper Co.
P. 159 © International Typeface Corporation.
P. 162 © Design firm: VSA Partners, Inc./Client: C. Stilp, Fox River Paper Co.
P. 169 (top) © The Letterbox.
P. 191 (top right) © Courtesy of Mohawk Paper Mills, Inc.: (left) © Rigsby Design; (bottom right) © Vanderbyl Design.

DIGITAL FONT FOUNDRIES

Adobe Type Library
http://store.adobe.com/type/

International Typeface Corporation
http://www.itcfonts.com/

Monotype Imaging
http://www.fonts.com

The Linotype Library
http://www.linotype.com/

Font Shop
http://www.fontshop.com/

Font Bureau
http://www.fontbureau.com/

Emigre
http://www.emigre.com/

Galápagos Design Group
http://www.galapagosdesign.com/

House Industries
http://houseind.com/

Hoefler & Frere-Jones
http://www.typography.com/

Terminal Design
http://www.terminaldesign.com/

Type Culture
http://www.typeculture.com/

Stone Type Foundry
http://www.stonetypefoundry.com/

Parkinson Type Design
http://www.typedesign.com/

Astigmatic One Eye
http://www.astigmatic.com/

P22
http://www.p22.com/

INDEX

COLOPHON

The cover and title page are typeset in Balboa, ITC Blair, ITC Golden Cockerel Ornaments, Adobe Jenson Pro, Scala, and Shelley Andante Script. The interior pages are typeset in Scala and ITC Blair.